PROTECTING SUB-SAHARAN AFRICA:

THE MILITARY CHALLENGE

PROTECTING SUB-SAHARAN AFRICA:

THE MILITARY CHALLENGE

EDITORS
L du Plessis,
Director: Centre for Military Studies,
University of Stellenbosch

M Hough,
Director: Institute for Strategic Studies,
University of Pretoria

© 1999 by Human Sciences Research Council/CEMIS & ISSUP

All rights reserved. No part of this publication may be reproduced or transmitted in any form or by any means, electronic or mechanical, including photocopy, recording or any information storage and retrieval system, without permission in writing from the publisher.

Protecting Sub-Saharan Africa : the military challenge /
   editors: L. du Plessis, M. Hough. — 1998.
         p.   cm.
   Bibliographical references.
   ISBN 0-7969-1900-3
     1. Africa, Sub-Saharan — Military policy. 2. Africa, Sub-Saharan — Armed Forces. 3. Africa, Sub-Saharan — Defenses. 4. Africa, Sub-Saharan — Strategic aspects I. Du Plessis, L. II. Hough, M.
     1998
     355.033067—DC21

Cover design: Enalja Louw and Jeannie Mentz
                of the College for Educational Technology
Layout and
design: Mari Nel

Published by:
HSRC Publishers
Private Bag X41
Pretoria

Printed by:
Insto Print
Pretoria

"In an unpredictable world African states must be able to protect the people, resources, and the sovereignty of the countries on the continent. This security has to be ensured by the capacity of Africa's own defence forces, which need to be developed and strengthened."

Joe Modise,
South African Minister of Defence,
1998

Contributors

Doctor (Colonel) Louis du Plessis is Director of the Centre for Military Studies of the University of Stellenbosch. He specialises in trends in security thinking and military training.

Professor (Doctor) Michael Hough is Director of the Institute for Strategic Studies of the University of Pretoria. He is Professor of Political Science and specialises in African politics.

Major General Deon Mortimer (retired) served in the South African National Defence Force. He lectures on land warfare at command and staff colleges.

Doctor Theo Neethling is a senior researcher at the Centre for Military Studies of the University of Stellenbosch. He specialises in peace support operations.

ADDRESS

Centre for Military Studies (Cemis)
South Africa 012 674 4820
louis@cemis.co.za

Institute for Strategic Studies (Issup)
South Africa 012 420 2034
pulles@libarts.up.ac.za

Preface

The idea of a publication on sub-Saharan Africa's military potential developed from the need to understand the nature of sub-Saharan armed forces. It also responds to the observation that articles in this field are often based mainly on quantitative analysis with the main emphasis on battle orders and related technical detail on the one hand, and largely focusing on the role of the military in politics, on the other hand. While each of these approaches fulfils a certain purpose, the aim of this book is to incorporate aspects of both, but also to cover the middle ground between them, which seems to receive insufficient attention in the African context. This includes the determinants of military power and potential; military security in the sub-Saharan African context; the historical roles and capabilities of the security forces; and the challenges of effective ground forces, air forces and maritime defence. Inter-African defence co-operation (especially on the regional level) and participation in sub-Saharan peace support operations represent two of the relatively recent roles that are *inter alia* assigned to military establishments.

Except in South Africa, literature on the primary roles and capabilities of armed forces in sub-Saharan Africa tends to have been more prolific in the Cold War period than in the post-Cold War environment. The marginalisation of Africa; the increasing prevalence of internal rather than inter-state conflict (although the distinction is often blurred); the emphasis on arms control, demobilisation and reduction in the size of armed forces; increasing attention to civil military relations and to the secondary roles of armed forces; new initiatives to establish security and defence co-operation, and a re-definition of the concept of security and threat perception, have contributed to this shift in emphasis.

This book therefore seeks to include some of the more recent approaches to the study and analysis of sub-Saharan African military establishments, but also to focus on their primary roles (and corresponding equipment) and to place it all in both a contemporary and historical perspective. The focus is on developments in the armed forces (and their position in society) during the period from the middle of the 1960s to the middle of the 1990s, that is on the first three decades after the independence of most sub-Saharan states. Flowing from this, the last chapter explores some probabilities for future developments.

The research includes theoretical perspectives as well as practical examples and brief case studies. It was obviously not possible to include extensive detail on the nature and functioning of the military establishments in every country in sub-Saharan Africa, and a *capita selecta* approach was therefore followed. Furthermore, the emphasis is on official military establishments, although it should be borne in mind that dissident movements have in certain instances succeeded in obtaining some conventional military capability.

The Editors
Pretoria
January 1999

Contents

1. The determinants of military power and potential ... 1
   Deon Mortimer

2. The historical development of sub-Saharan military capabilities ... 21
   Louis du Plessis

3. The changing historical roles of sub-Saharan armed forces ... 57
   Louis du Plessis

4. The challenge of effective sub-Saharan ground forces ... 93
   Deon Mortimer

5. The challenge of effective air power in sub-Saharan Africa ... 115
   Michael Hough

6. The challenge of effective sub-Saharan maritime defence ... 143
   Louis du Plessis

7. Participation in sub-Saharan peace support operations ... 183
   Theo Neethling

8. Armed conflict and defence co-operation in sub-Saharan Africa ... 221
   Michael Hough

9. Prospects for sub-Saharan armed forces in the twenty-first century ... 257
   Louis du Plessis

Chapter 1

THE DETERMINANTS OF MILITARY POWER AND POTENTIAL

Deon Mortimer

1 INTRODUCTION

Measuring the strength of nations is, and will be, a difficult task since much of the equation depends on intangibles. Obviously not everything is intangible but the influence of what is can be overriding.

Similarly, measuring military power and potential, a sub-set of the strength of nations, is also governed by intangibles, equally difficult to take into account.

A number of writers have focused attention on the subject; for example, Cline,[1] Knorr[2] and Jones[3]. It is clearly not possible to cover the field fully in a single chapter; this one will approach the problem from three perspectives: Cline's analysis of conventional military capability, Knorr's study of military potential, and the idea of an "adult" or "mature" defence capability.

2 MEASURING THE POWER OF NATIONS

Cline approaches the problem by means of a formula which attempts to measure national power.[4] His formula is:

$Pp = (C + E + M) \times (S + W)$ where

Pp = perceived power
C = critical mass: population plus territory
E = economic capability
M = military capability
S = strategic purpose
W = will to pursue national strategy

Cline emphasises that his formula deals with measurement in macrometrics and explains patterns and trends. The formula is probably not suitable for precise measurement. Nevertheless, it can be used as a guide.

2.1 Critical mass

In element C, critical mass, population and territory are relevant. With respect to population,[5] population size is a clearly perceived element of power, and larger populations thus imply greater power. Interestingly though, in the case of the two most populous nations, India and China, it is argued that their very large populations are a hindrance rather than an advantage. In respect of territory,[6] size is also deemed to be important. This is, however, qualified by the strategic location of a country. A combination of a large population and territory constitutes a critical mass of importance.

2.2 Economic capability

The next element in Cline's formula is E for economic capability. A number of variables are relevant here; for example, in advanced industrial societies self-sufficiency in raw materials can, in peacetime, be a liability as trade is an important contributor to the economic health of a nation. During hostilities, however, dependence can be a definite drawback. This underlines the intangible nature of much of the problem. Gross national product (GNP) as a measurement of economic capability is an important criterion for national capability. The higher its GNP, the more powerful is a nation. Special economic strengths and weaknesses, however, qualify this. The first aspect is the availability of an energy source (petroleum, coal, natural gas, nuclear). Of these, petroleum is by far the most important. As for critical non-fuel minerals, such as iron ore, copper, bauxite, chromite and uranium, possession of one or more of them lends special economic strength. Regarding industry, the production of crude steel, aluminium and building material (cement) is an important consideration. Food is the next important special economic strength (or weakness). Self-sufficiency in food is highly desirable, and here the emphasis is on the export and import of three major commodities: wheat, course grains (e.g. maize) and rice. Import of any of the three is regarded as a minus, export as a plus. International trade[7] is the last of the qualifiers, as trade is a good indication of leverage in international economic relations.

2.3 Military capability

M represents military capability in Cline's equation.[8] However it can be used "only in gross macrometric terms", although proposals which reduce the "gross" element are made. While there is no doubt about the overwhelming importance of nuclear weapons, only conventional weapons are at present a factor in sub-Saharan Africa.

Conventional forces continue to influence perceptions of military capability, and are more likely to be involved in operations. One of the most important points here is that estimates of military power based on manpower figures, equipment and other quantitative figures are "notoriously unreliable". Instead, it is the intangibles such as troop skill, morale, leadership, strategies, flexibility, mobility and reach which, while they cannot be quantified and thus tend to be ignored, can be decisive. The majority of the armed forces of the world are in reality police forces, capable only of defensive operations for the protection of national territory. Their real role is domestic: to control own population and as a factor in domestic political contests.[9]

A number of factors can be used to modify raw statistics of manpower and weapons into units of estimated military power, i.e. combat capability. Four elements are considered in arriving at a conversion factor: first, manpower quality. This is not a consideration of the inherent quality of the men and women who enlist but of troop training, unit morale and officer leadership. This last, very important factor, takes the better part of a lifetime to develop. Second, weapons effectiveness. Both quantity and quality of weapons are important but must be considered in the context of the armed forces concerned — namely, can they be used effectively? Third, infrastructure and logistic support. Having obtained weapons, can they be kept in service? Can they be maintained? Is there a flow of consumables (spares, ammunition, fuel, clothing, food)? Is the source of equipment and consumables local or imported? Are there ports, air bases, workshops, communications systems? Shortcomings in a significant number of these will seriously diminish combat capability. And last, organisational quality. This element considers armed forces as an organisation: the ability to manage; to maintain readiness; to formulate plans for carrying out assigned missions; to command and control, and to adapt to circumstances as they develop. Relevant combat experience is also important, as armed forces are inclined to drift away from reality during peacetime.[10]

A further factor to be considered in determining military capability is strategic reach.[11] This is defined as a "function of geographic position and the capacity for long-range projection of manpower and firepower".[12] Geographic position can give reach because of the number of neighbouring countries; for example, the former Soviet Union had strategic reach owing to the very many countries it shared borders with, stretching from Western

Europe to the Pacific. Strategic reach as a result of long-range projection of manpower and firepower depends on sea- and airlift. It is greatly enhanced by having the capability to force entry into the target country; that is, having an amphibious and/or airborne assault force.

Nations that spend exceptional amounts of their GNP (above eight per cent) on defence are perceived to be in a special class.[13] This, however, applies only to countries with significant military forces.

2.4 National strategy and national will

The final two items in Cline's equation are national strategy (S) and national will (W). They are the most intangible of the factors discussed and it is therefore difficult to allocate values to them. But Cline rates them so highly that he multiplies the sum of the concrete element by the sum of the values for national strategy and will. This approach emphasises the importance of the human element in national power, and must be taken into consideration in any attempt to determine military power and potential. It is further worth noting that Cline considers those who control political decisions at the highest level the most important strategists. A clear national strategy is considered to be essential to the exercising of power. Small powers are often forced to follow the lead of the major (super) powers, but they can themselves operate locally or regionally.[14]

National will is the essential quality for carrying out a national strategy. It is not a constant and fluctuates over time and according to the particular strategy. It is greatly affected by the authority of the national leadership, irrespective of how that leadership has come to power. National will is much strengthened if the national strategy is skilfully explained to the nation and wisely formulated. Three elements are important in national will: the degree of cultural integration of the people, effective national leadership, and the relevance of the national strategy to national interest as perceived by the population.[15]

2.5 Perceived power

It remains to point out that Cline's equation refers to "perceived power". He does not advance it as a means for intelligence analysis of a prospective or actual enemy. However, for the purposes of a book of this nature his formula does serve: this book is "perceiving" the military power and potential of sub-Saharan Africa. Furthermore, power is "perceived" until it is employed, when the judgment of reality enters into the equation and actual power emerges. The lesson to be drawn from Cline is that military power depends to a large extent on non-military elements: population, territory, economic capability, strategic purpose and national will. Military power itself is not all concrete — there are several intangibles, all of which either enhance or decrease the raw figures of troop strength and weapons. If these are not considered, an incorrect view of the military power of an armed force will be obtained.

3 MILITARY POTENTIAL

Cline's approach discussed above looks principally at the situation as is. To understand potential, further analysis is needed. Klaus Knorr, in his book *Military Power and Potential*, addresses this aspect in detail. He feels that there are two "types" of potential which he calls military potential and war potential.

He defines war potential as the economic resources available for mobilisation in time of war. This is a more restricted term than military potential, especially important during the wars of attrition conducted in the period from 1880 to the 1940s. Then, the coalition (or country) with inferior manpower and industrial capacity was the loser. War potential has lost some of its importance because of nuclear weapons: they can lead to short wars in which war potential will not have time to become effective. However, for the non-nuclear powers this is still a factor, as it is in contests between nuclear and non-nuclear powers. For war potential to be important, wars have to go on for a "longer" period (not defined), which is unusual in the post-World War II period.[16]

Military potential is, according to Knorr, one of the bases of military power and is equal to the national resources available for producing and maintaining forces.[17]

It applies equally during peace and war, and determines the ability to export arms and provide military assistance. A nation's military strength is the sum of its ready forces and its ability to augment them. Three broad categories or factors that determine a state's military potential can be identified; namely, economic and technological capacity, administrative skill and the political foundations of military power.[18]

Knorr's detailed discussion of these three factors reveals a similar approach to that of Cline. Like Cline, he emphasises the importance of those elements that are difficult to quantify, such as administrative skill, and the efficiency with which resources diverted to the military sector are transferred to effective military forces. His discussion regarding the political foundations of military power also focuses on intangibles; for instance, motivation to allocate resources to the military; what governs public support for such policy; and how foreign inputs (for example of weapons and finance) can make up for shortcomings in national resources.[19] As stated, Knorr and Cline agree in their general approach, although not in all detail about methodology.

4 MATURE ARMED FORCES

Armed forces are living organisations and develop under the influence of external and internal stimuli. So, for example, the

Union Defence Force (UDF) of 1912 (the year of its establishment) was a vastly simpler organisation than the South African Defence Force (SADF) — which it became in 1957 — of 1994. It was simpler not only because all armed forces were simpler in 1912 than in 1994, but because its role had changed dramatically. The UDF of 1912 was part of an imperial force (the British Empire) and had a localised role. Its doctrine and weapons were those of the Empire, and it had a place in imperial defence. The senior officer of the British Army of that time was designated the Chief of the Imperial General Staff. There was a Committee of Imperial Defence to co-ordinate the armed forces of the Empire (including the dominions). The SADF of 1994 was the armed force of a republic, which was by that time cut off from contact with all but a few countries. It was largely dependent on its own resources: own doctrine, own training, own weapons. An arms industry had developed whose principal function was to supply the SADF with arms designed according to South African doctrine for Southern African conditions. (This is not to say that no assistance and arms were obtained from foreign sources — much was. The principle remains true, however.)

Why the difference? Mainly it had been forced by circumstances. As late as 1966 the doctrine taught in the South African army's staff college was British, with some exercises received directly from Camberley. Then a process started to develop an own doctrine to suit the circumstances of the SADF and South Africa. As the SADF became involved in operations (especially after Operation Savannah in Angola during 1975) this accelerated. It was further expedited as former allies ended training opportunities (for example, the United Kingdom, United States and France) and the arms embargo began to have an effect. Internal factors (such as insight into inappropriate doctrine, operational experience and weapons availability); external factors (such as loss of allies, loss of foreign training opportunities and enemy doctrine); and, very important, a new role — that of the armed force of a particular state with its own national strategy —

converted the SADF into something different from what the UDF had been.

If the UDF could be described as "adolescent" in that it received guidance from a more mature force, then the SADF of 1994 was mature, fully developed. Maturity is important as it is an indication of the capability of a specific armed force to conduct independent operations. Forces that are not mature are subject to control by external factors: weapons and consumables (especially ammunition and spares) can be refused; training facilities can be closed to an armed force in disrepute; and logistic support (information, technical aid and sub-assemblies for upgrades) can be withheld. An adolescent force can maintain only relatively short conventional operations — that is, until it runs out of consumables or until its major equipment breaks down for lack of maintenance. This is not a claim for military autarchy, which is probably not possible (except for superpowers) or desirable. But if an armed force is to fight alone for a prolonged period, a great degree of self-sufficiency is necessary.

What are the characteristics of a mature armed force? First, the state it serves must be capable of formulating a national strategy. It must be capable of developing a foreign policy, be capable of planning ahead, be capable of administering itself efficiently (and not least, be able to collect taxes and otherwise finance itself). The state must have an infrastructure (roads, railways, communications, power supplies, and educational facilities, including tertiary institutions). With this background, the armed force should be able to develop a doctrine and acquire armaments to carry it out. It should be able to train its personnel to execute the doctrine, which means training from private soldier to at least one-star rank. Industry should be developed to provide at the very least the consumables needed and to maintain equipment. Preferably industry should be capable of designing and developing at least some of the equipment required, and particularly electronic equipment. Competent industry, in turn, demands an ability to do research and development; and that calls for an advanced scientific community.[20] For a state to develop a national strategy there should be research institutes and non-governmental agencies that can study, propose and debate alternative policies in the fields of government (for example foreign policy) and defence.

To summarise, if an armed force is to be more than what Cline describes as "in reality a police force" maintained primarily to control its own population,[21] it has to develop beyond "adolescence".

All that has been stated above must be considered in context. Two adolescent forces can fight each other. The problem arises when an adolescent force has to face a mature force, and even then the outcome is not guaranteed. Ultimately, probably the most important aspect is will. By combining superior will power with superior strategy and with sufficient material support from allies, North Vietnam was able to defeat a superpower, albeit at a terrible cost in lives.[22]

5 MODEL FOR NATIONAL ARMED FORCES

Traditionally armed forces are organised to fight on land, at sea and in the air. The question that arises is whether this is simply a matter of tradition or whether there are real reasons for such organisation. The answer is positive; there *are* real reasons for this "separation of powers".

One of them is that the focus of warfare, and thus of the forces, is geographically defined — land, sea or air. "(W)ar is technologically, tactically and operationally different on land, at sea, and in the air".[23] Since this difference exists, men and women of the armed forces must be trained to excel in one of these fields. It is difficult enough to be successful in the details of that one without trying to master another. But this does not alter the fact that war is won jointly; and the greatest contribution that each service can make to successful joint operations is to be proficient in its own geographical sphere. Joint warfare must not only be preached, however; it must also be practised, and doctrine and training have to precede practice.

Having said this, it must be added that land warfare is probably still the first among equals. "The ultimate determinant in war is the man on the scene with the gun".[24] Air and sea forces thus act to enable land forces to conclude wars successfully.

Gray adds a fourth geographical area of warfare, space, to the three mentioned above. In the sub-Saharan African context this can however be ignored, since none of the states has any capability in this area at this stage, nor are they likely to have in the medium term.

The question also arises as to Africa's place in the so-called revolution in military affairs (RMA) which it is contended is at present taking place. The RMA is generally described as being in the field of information (or information-age) warfare. This is defined as the ability to acquire and process, to disseminate and use information at an extremely high rate.[25] In an article discussing the implications for Africa of the changing nature of warfare, Van Vuuren adds the following: increasing destructiveness and accuracy of weapons, the vast distances over which force can be projected and growing capacities to gather intelligence. He predicts an increased focus on information collection, using the full electromagnetic spectrum, remotely piloted sensors and sophisticated analysis of enemy target systems.[26]

It is foreseen that conflict in Africa will be of low intensity, the so-called "grey area" of conflict. Very few manifestations of information warfare are evident, and doubt is expressed that it can be applied in the African context.[27] Broad spectrum communications jamming is however feasible, and commercial electronic expertise can assist in obtaining a capability for information warfare.[28]

In sub-Saharan Africa one will find that most armed forces are divided into land, air and naval branches. There are no known "space" forces, and not all countries have navies; some of them are landlocked. In others, air forces are organised as integral parts of the land forces (i.e. they are not independent). Naval forces are also at times integrated with the land forces. There is little evidence of an information warfare capability in sub-Saharan Africa, although there is an electronic warfare capability in, for example, South Africa.

The preceding analysis focused primarily on national armed forces. However, in the sub-Saharan African context, it needs to be borne in mind firstly, that membership of regional security arrangements or bilateral defence agreements can supplement national military capabilities. Although still a relatively undeveloped concept in the African context, recent military intervention on behalf of Kabila's government in the Democratic Republic of Congo (DRC), *inter alia* by certain members of the Southern African Development Community (SADC), is an example of the augmentation of national military capabilities by an alliance system. However, as discussed in subsequent chapters, the legal base for such intervention; the cost to the contributing countries and the question as to whether this can be recouped from the country receiving assistance; as well as the effect of such assistance on the eventual political and not only the military outcome, especially in instances of internal conflict, are debatable.

In sub-Saharan Africa, governments as well as rebels, in situations of internal conflict, have attempted to augment their capabilities through the employment of private military companies and mercenaries. It has been alleged that unlike mercenaries, military companies advertise their services and are legally registered, often in an offshore tax haven.[29]

The services rendered by private military companies include operational support, military advice, logistical support, security services and crime-prevention services. In Sierra Leone and Angola, Executive Outcomes (EO) is, for instance, said to have played an instrumental role in altering the course of the war and enabling a peace agreement to be signed. However, the ability of private military companies to influence long-term conditions in the countries in which they have operated is limited. In the case of Sierra Leone, EO's contract was terminated in January 1997, and in May 1997, six months after the peace agreement had been signed, the elected government was overthrown in a *coup*. Similarly, in Angola the 1994 Lusaka Accords have still not yet been fully implemented.[30]

In addition, assistance from private military companies may entail significant cost to the government making use of these services.[31]

Despite condemnation of mercenary activities and steps taken by, for example, the South African government to ban such activities by its citizens and by foreigners operating within its borders, it has been stated that "outlawing mercenarism will be difficult to achieve in Africa. The OAU Convention on the Elimination of Mercenaries does not apply to states employing them. Its drafters could only conceive of the use of mercenaries by insurgents and liberation movements".[32]

Finally, although the analysis, also in later chapters, will focus largely on formal armed forces, the role of para-military forces (presidential guards, gendarmerie and militia forces) also has to be taken into account. These forces are currently generally smaller than the regular forces, or form part of the regular forces,[33] but they are sometimes better equipped and at times better trained. In some cases they have been regarded as an alternative source of armed support for the head of state should the regular armed forces become disloyal. In other cases they have been seen as a threat to incumbent regimes. The use of para-military forces can lead to shortages of skilled regular personnel, affect morale among regular officers and generally have a deleterious effect on a country's military capabilities.[34] In some cases militias are not part of the official para-military forces, but rather part of private armies loyal to a particular factional leader, clan or ethnic group.[35]

6 ROLES OF ARMED FORCES

Historically, the external functions of military force were emphasised, specifically in the conduct of war. Although this is predominantly still the primary role of military force, its functions have been broadened to include: defence against external aggression; deterrence against various types of threat; coercion as a means of supporting diplomacy; and a protective structure for the operation of other instruments of foreign policy.[36]

Domestic functions of armed forces imply protection of the existing social order and support of the governing elite. In this regard, it has been stated that in African states, for example, "the primary military focus is on internal order and security, as well as an overriding concern for status and interests in competition with other social institutions".[37]

Specific missions of the armed forces in peacetime, often referred to as "secondary roles", include assistance (also to other countries) in cases of natural disaster; participation in peace support operations; support to police forces in upholding law and order; and a role in socio-economic development. The latter two functions are specifically characteristic of developing countries.

The *South African Constitution* of 1993, for instance, provides that the SANDF may be employed in the following functions:

- for service in the defence of the Republic, for the protection of its sovereignty and territorial integrity

- for service in compliance with the international obligations of the Republic with regard to international bodies and other states
- for service in the preservation of life, health or property
- for service in the provision or maintenance of essential services
- for service in the upholding of law and order in the Republic in co-operation with the South African Police Service under circumstances set out in law where the said Police Service is unable to maintain law and order on its own
- for service in support of any department of state for the purpose of socio-economic upliftment[38]

The *South African White Paper on Defence* of 1996 qualifies the above functions, by stating:

> It is the policy of government that the above functions do not carry equal weight. The primary function of the SANDF is to defend South Africa against external military aggression. The other functions are secondary.
>
> The size, design, structure and budget of the SANDF will therefore be determined mainly by its primary function. However, provision will have to be made for the special requirements of internal deployment and international peace support operations.[39]

In addition to any formal roles assigned to armed forces, military intervention in politics — in the form of *coups d'état* or of indirect military rule where the armed forces indirectly dictate government policy or influence it to a considerable extent while state power remains formally in civilian hands — has become a regular occurrence especially in sub-Saharan Africa.[40]

In the following analysis, the emphasis will be on military power in sub-Saharan Africa with specific reference to conventional combat and counter-insurgency capability, in both interstate conflict and internal conflict. But other roles of the armed forces, including peacetime roles, will also be referred to. With increasing emphasis being placed on regional security regimes and peace support operations, the role of the military in this regard also requires some analysis.

7 CONCLUSION

In studying the armed forces of the sub-Saharan region with the object of determining military power and potential, one should look beyond the obvious of a mere tabulation of personnel and equipment. Not only do non-military elements (for example Cline's concepts) have to be considered, but also the sociological development of both the nation and its armed forces — a difficult task requiring extensive data and expert opinion from many disciplines. Military power forms part of the broader concept of national power; it contributes to national power while it in turn is affected by the other elements of national power, such as population and territory, economic capability and national strategy.

The military capability of a country includes elements such as human resources (active and ready reserves, and quality personnel in terms of doctrine, training, morale and leadership); weapons effectiveness; military infrastructure; logistic capability; organisational quality; strategic reach; and the defence budget as a percentage of the GNP as well as the *per capita* expenditure per soldier. An item of particular importance is a national arms industry. Alliances, allies and foreign suppliers can also have a bearing on capabilities.

It needs to be emphasised that military power should be assessed relatively. This means considering the military strength of a nation in relation to that of an actual opponent; taking into account the concrete aims of a war, and a concrete situation, time and geographical setting.[41] Different requirements may apply regarding the ability to wage static or highly mobile operations; defensive or offensive operations; and to deter or defend. The importance of the issue at stake for each adversary, and the freedom of action that each party has, are also obvious factors.[42]

Lider summarises the different concepts relating to military power by stating that it may be interpreted as the actual military capability of a country in relation to opponents (or hypothetical opponents); as potential or latent military power which can be mobilised in an emergency; and as putative military power as it is perceived by other states.[43] To this, as set out above, Knorr adds the concept of war potential. The concepts *military power* and *military strength* are sometimes used interchangeably, although the latter has been interpreted as referring to that which is possessed rather than a relation between two or more quantums of such strength.

REFERENCES

1. Cline, R S, *World power trends and US foreign policy for the 1980s*, Westview Press, Boulder, Colorado, 1980.
2. Knorr, K, *Military power and potential*, D C Heath, Lexington, 1970.
3. Rosen, S J and W S Jones, *The logic of international relations*, Third Edition, Winthrop Publishers Inc, Cambridge, 1980.
4. Cline, R S, *op cit*, pp 16-23.
5. *Ibid*, pp 35-40.
6. *Ibid*, pp 40-45.
7. *Ibid*, pp 53-82.
8. *Ibid*, p 94.
9. *Ibid*, pp 119-121.
10. *Ibid*, pp 121-123.
11. *Ibid*, pp 132-134.

12. *Ibid*, p 132.
13. *Ibid*, pp 134-135.
14. *Ibid*, pp 146-148 and p 178.
15. *Ibid*, pp 166-178.
16. Knorr, K, *op cit*, pp 16-20.
17. *Ibid*, p 15.
18. *Ibid*, pp 21 and 25.
19. *Ibid*, pp 26-30.
20. See for instance Cilliers, J, "Defence research and development in South Africa – The role of the CSIR", *African Security Review*, Vol 5, No 5, 1996.
21. Cline, R S, *op cit*, p 121.
22. Rosen, S J and W S Jones, *op cit*, pp 204 and 215-216.
23. Gray, Colin S, "The changing nature of warfare?", *Naval War College Review*, Spring 1996, Vol XLIX, No 2, p 18.
24. *Ibid*, p 15, quoting R Adm J C Wylie, *Military Strategy*, Naval Institute Press, Annapolis, 1989.
25. *Ibid*, p 18.
26. Van Vuuren, I, "The changing nature of warfare: Implications for Africa", *African Security Review*, Vol 7, No 1, 1998, p 57.
27. *Ibid*, pp 58-59.
28. Gray, C S, *op cit*, p 14.
29. Shearer, D, "Private Armies and Military Intervention", *Adelphi Paper 316*, IISS, February 1998, p 21.
30. *Ibid*, pp 25-26 and 67.
31. *Ibid*, p 51.
32. Olonisakin, F, "Mercenaries fill the vacuum", *The World Today*, Vol 54, No 6, 1998, p 148.
33. International Institute for Strategic Studies, *The Military Balance 1997/98*, Oxford University Press, 1997, pp 236-263.

34. Barrows, W L, "Changing Military Capabilities in Black Africa", in Foltz, W J and H S Bienen (eds), *Arms and the African: Military Influences on Africa's International Relations*, Yale University Press, London, 1985, p 106.

35. Hills, A, "Warlords, Militia and Conflict in Contemporary Africa: A Re-examination of Terms", *Small Wars and Insurgencies*, Vol 8, No 1, Spring 1997, p 40.

36. Lider, J, *Military theory: Concept, structure, problems*, Gower Publishing Co, England, 1983, pp 24-25.

37. *Ibid*, p 28.

38. RSA, *Constitution of the Republic of South Africa* (Act 200 of 1993), Section 227.

39. RSA, *White Paper on Defence*, May 1996, p 34.

40. Lider, J, *op cit*, pp 30-35.

41. *Ibid*, p 40.

42. Beaufré, A, *An introduction to strategy*, Faber and Faber, London, 1965, p 26.

43. Lider, J, *op cit*, p 41.

Chapter 2

THE HISTORICAL DEVELOPMENT OF SUB-SAHARAN MILITARY CAPABILITIES

Louis du Plessis

1 INTRODUCTION

During the 1990s the role of armed units and gangs in the ongoing crisis in virtually all of Central Africa, stretching from Northern Angola and Congo Brazzaville through the new Democratic Republic of the Congo, Burundi, Rwanda and Uganda to Somalia, Ethiopia, Sudan and Eritrea, have elicited grave questions on the historical nature, capabilities and roles of armed forces in sub-Saharan Africa.

The aim of this chapter is to set up a framework that plots the historical development of the military capabilities of the armed forces in sub-Saharan societies during the first decades after independence in the 1960s. The internal and external roles of these forces are not a subject of this chapter (but will, in fact, be discussed in a following chapter). Moreover, speculation about possible future trends will be limited, since the focus will not be on present force developments, but on historical abilities.

Like so many contemporary perspectives on sub-Saharan Africa, the conclusions are tentative and not definitive or prescriptive.

Often individual cases can be cited that run counter to the trends described here.

Two introductory remarks should be made: First, the present focus of news reports on the political roles of the sub-Saharan armed forces, especially their involvement in *coups* and authoritarian domestic action, may have distorted the military nature of such forces. It may therefore be prudent to investigate military capabilities separately.

Moreover, applying well-known concepts to sub-Saharan societies in general, or to their military forces in particular, may easily lead to reasoning errors common among those unfamiliar with the underdeveloped nature of great parts of the unique African continent. When Western social, political or military scientific concepts are taken at face value, the naive assumption may be made that what is described as "the armed forces" of sub-Saharan societies are similar and comparable to the forces in more developed areas. This is not always the case, as will become evident in the discussion.

The analysis will begin with a description of the political, social and economic circumstances under which sub-Saharan armed forces were established. The focus will be on domestic peace and progress as indispensable preconditions for the development of a national defence capability.

To determine the degree to which sub-Saharan armed forces have developed despite the disadvantages of societal problems, a model will be presented to identify the fundamental processes linked to military proficiency. The essential elements are those of financing defence; recruiting adequate human resources; utilising competent human resources; providing armament and logistics; and ensuring operational mobility.

After sketching the insignificant position of most of these forces at independence, the model on the determinants of military capability is applied to investigate the historical trends in sub-

Saharan armed forces. Finally, the main arguments are summarised and conclusions drawn.

2 FROM COLONIAL TO INDEPENDENT SOCIETIES

Towards the end of the previous century almost the entire African continent was colonised by European powers – particularly Britain, France, Germany and Portugal – while during the second half of the twentieth century Africa experienced a liberation from European political domination.

During pre-colonial and colonial rule the political identity of Africans was defined within the boundaries laid down during the scramble for Africa and primarily by their allegiance to a leader or by positions within administrative demarcations.

In the period following World War II, most of the Arab-speaking northern African countries became free, joining the ranks of the few countries that had had independent status prior to the war. Ghana (in 1957) was the first of the black colonial sub-Saharan nations to achieve independence. The next decade (the 1960s) saw 32 colonies, protectorates and trust territories achieving independence – see Table 1. No fewer than 17 of them – mainly francophone territories – achieved independence in the single year of 1960.[1]

It is often maintained that the independence of Eritrea from Ethiopia in 1993 and the election of the black nationalist Nelson Mandela as president of South Africa in 1994 marked the culmination of the African struggle for national independence.[2]

During the 1960s, in the first years of sub-Saharan independence, black nationalists sought state power as a means of transferring the control of political authority and economic resources from foreigners to Africans. While sub-Saharan states became vehicles for achieving the goals of political sovereignty and economic development they also had to face a series of grave problems as regards survival and growth.

Since peace and progress within societies constitute important prerequisites for the development of any credible degree of military efficiency or deterrence, the problems of internal strife and economic underdevelopment necessarily undermine the creation of a military capability. Consequently, before investigating the features of military efficiency, some serious challenges to peace and progress in sub-Saharan societies should be considered.

2.1 Challenge of peace

Since many of the independent "states" were often largely fictitious entities that were sustained as diplomatic or judicial units,[3] sub-Saharan societies were faced with a string of insurgencies, separatist movements and full-blown civil wars during the three decades after independence in Africa.[4] These problems had a negative effect on most long-term planning for development.

Armed campaigns to take control of the state contributed to the overthrow of repressive regimes, but often also to political violence and even to civil war and a collapse of state authority.

The reasons for the internal and cross-border wars were often linked to ethnic divisions. Despite political leaders' ideological emphasis on nation building, tribal tensions from the colonial period became more articulated, and ethnic cleavages and clashes became a major disruptive factor.[5]

Several African governments were confronted by wars of secession, such as those in southern Sudan, in eastern Nigeria (Biafra) and in Katanga (now Shaba in the Congo). Some of the wars that have been fought to liberate countries from repressive regimes, such as in Uganda (1971) and more recently in Liberia, Rwanda and Congo Brazzaville, have resulted in intensified violent conflicts and the massacre of civilians.[6]

TABLE 1:
FROM COLONIAL TO INDEPENDENT SUB-SAHARAN SOCIETIES
POST-WAR INDEPENDENCE PROCESS: IN CHRONOLOGICAL ORDER

Country	Date	Country	Date
Sudan	01-01-1956	Burundi	01-07-1962
Ghana	06-03-1957	Uganda	09-10-1962
Guinea	02-10-1958	Zanzibar (now part of Tanzania)	10-12-1963
Cameroon	01-01-1960	Kenya	12-12-1963
Togo	27-04-1960	Malawi	06-07-1964
Mali	20-06-1960	Zambia	24-10-1964
Senegal	20-06-1960	The Gambia	18-02-1965
Madagascar	26-06-1960	Botswana	30-09-1966
Congo (Kinshasa)	30-06-1960	Lesotho	04-10-1966
Somalia	01-07-1960	Mauritius	12-03-1968
Benin (as Dahomey)	01-08-1960	Swaziland	06-09-1968
Niger	03-08-1960	Equatorial Guinea	12-10-1968
Burkina Faso (as Upper Volta)	05-08-1960	Guinea-Bissau	10-09-1974
Côte d'Ivoire	07-08-1960	Mozambique	25-06-1975
Chad	11-08-1960	Cape Verde	05-07-1975
Central African Republic	13-08-1960	The Comoros	06-07-1975
Congo (Brazzaville)	15-08-1960	Sao Tomé and Príncipe	12-07-1975
Gabon	17-08-1960	Angola	11-11-1975
Nigeria	01-10-1960	Seychelles	29-06-1976
Mauritania	28-11-1960	Djibouti	27-06-1977
Sierra Leone	27-04-1961	Zimbabwe	18-04-1980
Tanzania (as Tanganyika)	09-12-1961	Namibia	21-03-1990
Rwanda	01-07-1962	Eritrea	24-05-1993

Source: *Africa South of the Sahara 1997*, Europa Publications, London, 1997, p 22. Northern African (Arab) countries are excluded from the original table.

During the first decades internal and cross-border conflicts erupted in every region — see Table 2.

West Africa was characterised by internal conflict in countries such as Togo and Liberia. In Togo the "ethnic cleansing" of non-Kabye personnel from the army caused soldiers to flee to Ghana, and Liberia became the home of a fierce civil war, despite the presence of a foreign peace-keeping force and a United Nations monitoring team.[7]

Even in the more prosperous Nigeria, the First Republic collapsed largely as the result of ethnic tension in the army's officer corps. Heavy-handed attempts to correct the overrepresented Ibo people by promoting less well-educated northerners helped spur a *coup* in 1966. Since the civil war, successive regimes have striven to avoid the impression that one group is being favoured over another in the officer corps.[8]

In southern Sudan in East Africa the Sudanese government became involved in a war against the Sudanese People's Liberation Army, while Somalia experienced what can best be described as a worst-case scenario, with five major factions contesting power.[9]

While the predominantly white Southern African governments in South West Africa (later Namibia), Rhodesia (later Zimbabwe) and South Africa resisted the onslaught of the black nationalist political and guerrilla forces for a while, they eventually accepted multi-racial and multi-ethnic power sharing within a democratic political structure. The demographic composition and level of cultural development of the populations promoted this development. Angola and Mozambique were less fortunate, having suffered long-term civil wars. Only in the 1990s were these two countries able to start on the road to recovery.[10]

Over the past decades internal and cross-border clashes tore the Central African states on both sides of the Congo river apart, and since the 1970s the struggles between the Tutsi and Hutu

TABLE 2:
CHALLENGE OF PEACE

SUB-SAHARAN ARMED CONFLICT AND FATALITIES – 1945-1994			
Country	Event	Date	Fatalities
Angola	Independence	1961-76	55 000
Burundi	Hutu/government	1972	110 000
Chad	Rebels/government	1980-87	7 000
Congo Kinshasa	Katanga	1960-65	100 000
Ethiopia	Eritrean revolt	1974-92	75 000
Ghana	Konkomba/Nanumba	1981	1 000
Guinea-Bissau	Independence	1962-74	15 000
Kenya	Mau Mau revolt	1954-56	15 000
Liberia	Reprisals for putsch	1985-88	5 000
Madagascar	Independence	1947-48	15 000
Mozambique	Independence	1965-75	30 000
Nigeria	Biafrans/government	1967-70	1 000 000
Nigeria	Islam/government	1980-81	5 000
Nigeria	Islam/government	1984	1 000
Rwanda	Tutsi/government	1956-65	105 000
South Africa	Political/ethnic violence	1976	1 000
South Africa	Political/ethnic violence	1983-94	16 000
Sudan	Civil war	1963-72	500 000
Uganda	Buganda/government	1966	1 000
Uganda	Idi Amin massacres	1971-78	300 000
Uganda	Tanzania/Idi Amin	1978-79	3 000
Uganda	Army/people	1981-87	308 000
Zambia	Civil strife	1964	1 000
Zimbabwe	Patriotic Front/Rhodesia	1972-79	12 000
Zimbabwe	Ethnic and political violence	1983-84	4 000
TOTAL			2 685 000

Source: International Institute for Strategic Studies, *Strategic Survey 1996/97*, Oxford University Press, London, 1997, map: Status of armed conflict 1994-1997 - Sub-Saharan Africa.

peoples gave rise to successive military regimes, *coups* and massacres in Rwanda and Burundi.

United Nations peace keeping and peace enforcement failed not only in Somalia and Angola, but also in traumatised Central

Africa. In Rwanda, for example, a three-year UN peace-keeping operation failed to halt the ethnic genocide that resulted in between 500 000 and one million deaths. Between April and July 1994 Hutu extremists systematically hacked down, shot and blew up tens of thousands of Tutsis and Hutu moderates. About 70 000 people have been jailed for the massacres, but no functioning legal system exists to deal with them. More than 250 000 women were raped and an estimated 47 000 children orphaned.[11]

The problem with military violence is that it hinders the building of infrastructures, the establishment of stable security structures and the development of civil societies. At the same time it creates a cycle of increased conflict. Once the boundaries of peaceful political opposition have been crossed, the possibility of resorting to further violence is enormously increased.[12]

The lack of political stability and the cycles of sub-Saharan strife had serious effects on human and animal life and on the standard of living.[13] In addition to the loss of life as a direct result of military action, the mentioned and other examples of sub-Saharan wars in the first decades of independence often destroyed food supplies and livestock. Since veterinary services proved impossible to maintain, animal disease spread rapidly and resulted in massive stock losses. Physical infrastructure — such as village wells, roads and bridges — was wrecked, and the fragile sub-Saharan social welfare and security services disrupted. Schools and clinics were closed, ransacked or destroyed, immunisation programmes were discontinued and hospitals placed under immense strain.

The internal and cross-border battles caused massive disturbances in the settlement of whole communities, often displacing them into vast squatter settlements on the edges of towns, and giving rise to international refugee problems. The wars also wrecked religious and other normative or value systems, undermined all faith in family, social or organisational codes and sometimes caused whole societies to succumb to fatalism.

Such circumstances are necessarily detrimental to the development of well-organised and self-disciplined military forces.

2.2 Challenge of progress

In addition to a degree of peace and national unity, the establishment of military capability is promoted by a stable, if possible representative, government and by constant economic and financial improvement. The question is whether and to what extent sub-Saharan societies meet these demands.

The fact is that after independence most of the new sub-Saharan rulers sought to monopolise, rather than to share, state power. Only in a very few countries have political parties been able to contend consistently in national elections by universal suffrage. In a number of others, such as the Sudan, Congo, Benin, Nigeria and Uganda, party competition soon gave way to military governments.[14]

In this connection Malan maintains that conflict and insecurity in sub-Saharan Africa are primarily products of poor governance and the politics of exclusion – typically of ethnic or religious minorities.[15]

In most sub-Saharan countries, ruling parties formed one-party states. They argued that ethnic divisions must be overcome and that the people must be united in pursuit of development. In many cases one-party states were replaced by military rule. When elections were held, the outcome often depended on the alignment of the military.[16] Furthermore, the military rulers typically claimed to act in the interests of the whole nation against the corruption and sectionalism of politicians. Although they denied their own political ambitions, the military commanders usually acted in the interests of all or a part of the armed forces.

The army officers were just as susceptible as the politicians to the temptations of office and were even more likely to resort to authoritarian measures to deal with opposition. Moreover, the flow of arms to strengthen their own position and that of their ethnic group, continued. *Coups* by rivals set precedents for further counter-*coups*, whether against military regimes or their civilian successors, as happened for example in Benin, Ghana and Nigeria.

Although political leaders have been elected in several societies, many ruling parties of the mid-1990s have not accepted the legitimacy of the opposition. For gangs and many young men, the use of weapons has become a source of livelihood and a way of life. In countries such as Nigeria and Rwanda, and more recently Burundi, Kenya and Congo Kinshasa, political leaders have been able to incite violence when particular groups have feared that their own security and access to local resources were being threatened.[17]

During the first three decades of independence it gradually became clear throughout Africa that the hopes invested in national independence and economic development had not been realised. African rulers, whether drawn from civilian politicians or military officers, had lost moral credibility as a result of unsolved basic problems: arbitrary and corrupt government; the exclusion of significant class, regional and ethnic groups from sharing in political decisions; and increasing economic and personal insecurity.[18]

By the mid-1990s sub-Sahara was experiencing constant transition and unrest, in which armed forces often played a role. The changes directly influenced military capability. In Southern Africa, states such as Angola, Lesotho, Malawi, Mozambique, Swaziland and Zambia were experiencing political and socio-economic instability.

Moreover, the economic, humanitarian and security problems of mass refugee emigrations have focused attention on Burundi,

Rwanda and Zaire, as well as on Liberia and Sierra Leone. By 1993, after three decades of independence, sub-Saharan Africa was host to more refugees and displaced persons than any other region of the world: 20 million, of which 80 per cent were women and children.[19]

While Angola and Nigeria both experienced a further period of political uncertainty, displacement of the population together with persistent civil unrest continued through 1995 and 1996 in the two Congos, Somalia and Sudan. In fact, no sub-Saharan country has surmounted economic hardship.[20]

Seen in an international context, African governments also lost some of the aid funds as the attention of the Western industrialised countries turned to the reconstruction of Eastern and Central Europe.

From a developmental point of view the tragic fact is: Through the 1970s and 1980s much of sub-Saharan Africa experienced a steady decline in living standards and by the beginning of the 1990s most African states were bankrupt.[21]

It is essential to comprehend this general lack of internal peace and unity, of political stability and accountability, and of a civilised standard of living and economic growth, in order to assess the obstacles to the development of sub-Saharan military capabilities.

3 CHALLENGE OF MILITARY CAPABILITY

By way of introduction a few comments will be made on how military proficiency may be evaluated and on the situation at the time of independence. The main determinants will then be analysed.

3.1 Evaluating military proficiency

The societal processes that determine the development of efficient armed forces (as was pointed out in a previous chapter) may be classified in various ways. The most crucial processes are financing defence; recruiting military manpower; utilising competent human resources; providing armament and logistics; and ensuring operational mobility. All of these factors are, to a greater or lesser degree, intimately related to trends in broader civilian society.[22]

These five factors are interrelated. The military budget is the most obvious requirement of military planners; if it is not met, not one rifle can be bought. The first human resource determinant stresses manpower quantity; the second, the even more decisive educational and technical quality of available resources. Armament and logistics are the two indispensable physical prerequisites for armed forces, while the ability to be mobile and operational makes it possible to measure and assess military efficiency.

After introductory remarks on the situation during sub-Saharan independence, the main features that constitute military capability will be applied to the region, followed by a summary of the arguments and the main conclusions.

3.2 Position at independence

At the time of independence, African states lacked the parliamentary, administrative and military tools that nations traditionally possessed to shape or alter their external environment. Sub-Saharan military units had played the role of maintaining internal security in a few colonies. Only a few military units in some French and British colonies had any kind of tradition. Otherwise, these structures, often called "armies", had insignificant roles and outdated equipment. Moreover, with very few exceptions, African armies played no part in achieving independence and therefore had little status.[23]

It has been maintained that in retrospect (from 1966) the events in the first years after independence serve to illustrate "the essential military weakness of the independent African states in the starkest possible way."[24]

A military report written a decade later (in 1977) is even more critical: "The level of training and determination of African troops is exceedingly low by almost any standard. Intelligent and resolute leadership is almost entirely lacking. African military capability is far removed from the standard displayed by the Viet Cong and the North Vietnamese Army."[25]

Also in the first decade after independence, it is argued that, comparing African armies with their counterparts in developed states may be dismissed as futile, as even the most significant sub-Saharan armed forces, according to Ray Cline, were assumed to be so small, poorly equipped and poorly trained as to appear inconsequential.[26]

However, as will be pointed out, several far-reaching changes have taken place since the 1960s and 1970s, especially in certain fields and regions. Furthermore, as Arlinghaus correctly maintained, some previous perceptions may have been true on a global scale only because, in regional terms, even a relatively small but effective force can be potent.[27]

The exploration of the determinants of sub-Saharan military capability will start with one of its vital roots: the need for funds.

4 FINANCING DEFENCE: FROM EXPANSION TO CONSTRAINT

The ability of a state to provide budgetary resources for national defence is directly linked to the level of wealth in a society.

In the first years after independence most sub-Saharan governments were eager to expand their military forces. By the 1970s and 1980s many ambitious political leaders were depleting material resources, exceeding financial limits and increasing foreign debt in attempts to expand the personnel, equipment and capabilities of their armed forces, often to defend the immediate safety of their regimes. This problem was also exacerbated in the 1990s by the realities of internal strife. See Table 3 for expenditure on defence in selected countries in 1994.

The countries that were embroiled in conflict in the early 1990s, such as Angola, Chad, Mozambique and Somalia, have spent between 15 and 40 per cent of their national budgets and between 5 and 10 per cent of their gross national product (GNP) on the military. Judged from the perspective of rational economic management, the irony is that, at the same time, these countries as well as others such as Ethiopia and Sudan, all ranked in the lower 15 per cent of the human development index of the United Nations Development Programme and were spending only between 0,6 and 6 per cent of their GNP on priority development sectors.[28]

Many sub-Saharan governments also spent disproportionate amounts of their GNP on military hardware and activities because of the creation of several paramilitary forces. Sometimes the paramilitary units were better equipped than the regular forces. Examples are the *gendarmerie* in francophone Africa. In Gabon the Presidential Guard was always considered more capable than the army. The main reason was the insecurity of regimes, and the utility of paramilitary forces in providing a potential counterweight, should the regular armed forces come under the sway of ambitious leaders. This was demonstrated in 1982 for example, when Kenya's General Services Unit, an element of the police, helped to put down a *coup* attempt by junior officers and enlisted men of the Kenya Air Force.[29]

It is a normal fact of budgeting that the high cost of equipment and skilled military manpower may have a debilitating effect on any economy, as the thoroughly analysed ordeals of many communist and right-wing totalitarian states illustrate. The ironic fact is that the cost of arming a threatened state to defend its economic interests may be greater than the benefits that such

TABLE 3:
FINANCING DEFENCE IN SUB-SAHARAN STATES

EXPENDITURE ON DEFENCE IN SELECTED COUNTRIES: 1994					
Country	% of GDP	US $ million	Country	% of GDP	US $ million
Angola	8,7	501	Mozambique	8,0	102
Botswana	4,6	131	Namibia	2,2	49
Cameroon	1,4	115	Nigeria	1,0	1 139
Congo Brazzaville	1,7	47	Senegal	2,0	88
Côte d'Ivoire	0,8	68	South Africa	2,5	3 893
Ethiopia	2,6	106	Sudan	2,2	298
Ghana	0,9	80	Tanzania	3,5	103
Kenya	2,2	180	Uganda	2,4	87
Lesotho	13,0	18	Zaire (now Congo, Dem Rep)	1,9	114
Madagascar	2,2	28	Zambia	1,0	37
Malawi	1,6	20	Zimbabwe	3,5	191

Sources: Africa Institute of South Africa, *Africa at a Glance: Facts and Figures 1996/7*, Pretoria, 1996; and International Institute for Strategic Studies, *The Military Balance 1995/96*, Oxford University Press, London, 1996.

a defence practice may provide. This was also true of the growing expenditure on sophisticated arms for many sub-Saharan states after independence.[30]

The problem of military expenditure is exacerbated by the above mentioned financial marginalisation of sub-Sahara. The end of the Cold War has caused a major loss of international interest in sub-Saharan Africa, which is widely regarded as a financial black hole and of little economic or security relevance to the rest of the world. Black Africa is barely on the periphery of world consciousness and is noted mainly when yet another disaster makes the headlines. The rest of the world is concentrating on its own security problems and on re-organising itself.[31]

The result of societal underdevelopment and poverty is that since the mid-1990s financial constraints rather than perceived threats have been dictating the size and structure of sub-Saharan defence forces. In general, the development of balanced conventional military capabilities and the procurement of conventional military equipment received limited attention.

During the 1990s defence was becoming a lower priority even in the budgets of most Southern African states compared to the increasing priority of social spending. In fact, the financial constraints created pressure to demobilise. In some societies a conscious effort was made and policies formulated to reduce the role of the military through a demobilisation programme. Demobilisation may be defined as the process by which armed forces – either government or opposition or guerrilla forces – downsize and sometimes even disband. In many countries a demobilisation programme formed part of a much broader transformation from a wartime to a peacetime economy, in which resources are transferred to non-military sectors and used for the reconstruction of an infrastructure.[32]

The problem is that elements within the military community and civilian society normally resist manpower reductions. Reasons are often the fear of unemployment and of the threat that ex-soldiers may constitute. It took Nigeria a decade to complete its demobilisation effort after the 1967-1970 civil war. The same is true of Zimbabwe in the 1980s, where the integrated forces of the previous government and two guerrilla armies were larger and more expensive than that required by the new regime. Furthermore, cuts in military budgets are often merely transferred to other state departments. For example, while defence expenditure in Zimbabwe as a percentage of GNP declined from 8,8 in 1980 to 6,7 in 1989, many former combatants found employment in the civil service. In South Africa a concerted effort is being made in the 1990s to restructure and demobilise the newly integrated national defence force. The outcome of this process is yet to be perceived.

The point is this: Although there was a strong tendency to expand military personnel in the first decades of independence, many sub-Saharan states, even Zambia and Zimbabwe in the more stable and prosperous Southern Africa, were forced by financial considerations to cut back on military personnel and defence expenditure from the middle of the 1980s. Moreover, budget constraints over virtually the entire sub-Sahara have directly influenced the level of equipment. Consequently the states have started either to buy second-hand equipment, or to upgrade existing equipment.

It may be generally concluded that the ambitious exploitation of scarce resources in the first two decades of independence, when up to 40 per cent of the national budget was spent on military purposes, has been replaced by a more cautious, conservative approach to military expansion. In fact, during the 1990s several countries were decreasing their military expenditure, often under international pressure.

5 RECRUITING HUMAN RESOURCES: QUANTITY

The development of a defence and operational capability furthermore depends on the availability of personnel for military roles. Available manpower makes it possible to create a balanced and flexible force. This is far more than a force composed simply of riflemen. Such a force enables policy-makers to develop a capability in fields such as artillery, armour, air support and naval power.

A basic fact is that, unlike the relative stability in, for example most European societies, the size of the indigenous armed forces in most sub-Saharan countries continued to grow, not only directly after decolonisation but also in the decades following the early years of independence — as represented by the figures for

1966, for 1981 (after 15 years) and for 1996 (after 30 years) — as shown in Table 4. This growth is valid not only for most smaller states, such as Togo (2 000 to 7 000 members) or Malawi (1 000 to 10 000) but also for stronger states, such as Kenya (5 000 to 24 000), Zimbabwe (4 000 to 43 000), Congo Kinshasa (32 000 to 49 000) and Nigeria (12 000 to 77 000).

Furthermore, the demographic composition of societies necessarily played a key role in recruiting members for armed forces and in the growth potential and actual size of these forces and their weaponry. The link between population and military manpower is evidenced in the size of the armed forces of the demographically dominant sub-Saharan countries — those who currently have more than 25 million members — Congo Kinshasa (46 million), Ethiopia (53 million), Kenya (29 million), Nigeria (107 million), South Africa (44 million), Sudan (30 million) and Tanzania (30 million).

In addition, as elsewhere, the perception of threat was an important stimulus for increasing military organisations; and a significant relationship existed between threat and size. The greater the perceived threat to a regime — externally and also internally — the more likely it was to expand its armed forces.[33]

The larger armies have tended to develop not only among larger populations but also in societies where racial, ethnic and regional cleavages threatened integration. Examples are: Angola, Ethiopia, Nigeria, Somalia, South Africa, Sudan, Zimbabwe and Zambia and in virtually all the Central African states, such as Congo Kinshasa, Uganda, Rwanda, and Burundi.

Major secessionist movements, as represented by the Nigerian civil war or Ethiopia's Eritrean rebellions, have provoked dramatic increases in size and armament. So, too, have threats from neighbours, as when Tanzania armed heavily in response to Uganda's menaces under Idi Amin. In 1979 Tanzania's forces pushed across the border and overthrew Uganda's mercurial dictator.[34]

Based on the fact that even in smaller countries that have been relatively free from conflict, armies have tended to increase, it can be concluded that gradual military growth seems to be a long-term trend.[35]

However, it should be realised, that military manpower figures, as substantiated by the figures for countries elsewhere (such as Iraq), may provide only a rough, often misleading, indicator of military proficiency.[36]

- For instance, the dramatic increases registered by Ethiopia were not matched by proportionate increases in capabilities. Although military effectiveness did increase as new units equipped with modern weapons were integrated into the Ethiopian ground forces, the growth in capability has not been commensurate with the growth in numbers.

- Likewise, the reduction of the size of the Nigerian army has not made the military less effective. In fact, it has possibly become more effective, because it has created a more manageable organisation able to allocate a greater portion of its resources to training.

The quantity of citizens available for recruitment is not the only criterion for a defence or war-fighting organisation to fulfil its functions adequately; the quality of human resources is an essential dimension.

6 UTILISING HUMAN RESOURCES: QUALITY

The competence of human resources pertains first to the availability of citizens with characteristics such as developed skills and the ability to command units, and second to the existence of military training programmes to achieve this.

Compared to highly civilised societies, the challenge of competence was especially acute in the poor sub-Saharan countries between the 1960s and 1990s because of the generally low level of development of the intellectual, scientific and technological skills that were available to military organisations. This became especially obvious in the shortages of personnel skilled in operating purchased foreign weapons systems and in managing the complex logistical organisations associated with them.

Military forces require specialists — from riflemen, to repairmen, to planners. To recruit and train such specialists may become a difficult problem in societies that have limited educational and technological resources, especially when many skilled professionals have fled Africa for employment elsewhere. Furthermore, and ironically, when specialised resources are focused upon and absorbed by military skills, this inevitably results in further economic stagnation, as occurred in Somalia in the 1980s.[37]

A few military establishments have developed the competence of the soldiers, often with considerable outside assistance, while relaxing the emphasis on ideological or ethnic factors or on loyalty to a specific political leader or movement. Examples are Kenya, Zimbabwe and Ethiopia, because of a perceived necessity; Malawi, Senegal and Tanzania, because of a sense of domestic security; and Nigeria and Botswana, because of a need for greater professionalism. However, the underdeveloped nature of society as a whole limited what could be done to improve combat capability.[38]

Also, armed forces can hardly be deployed without effective commanders. As a result of a permanent sense of insecurity, few African regimes have encouraged the promotion of intelligent and self-confident commanding officers. On the contrary, the fear of a *coup d'etat* caused many political leaders to take measures to deprive potential rivals within the armed forces of a power base. Loyalty often took precedence over competence. Officers tagged as too bright or too popular were often relegated to obscure administrative posts with no troops to command.

Moreover, such officers were often physically eliminated in the first decades of independence, for example in Ethiopia under Mengistu and in Uganda under Idi Amin.[39]

In favour of quality manpower, it may be pointed out that formal and effective military training was increasingly emphasised not only in South Africa but also in other prominent sub-Saharan powers, such as Ethiopia and Nigeria, where military colleges or military academies have been established.[40] In addition, many African countries organised national youth movements or national service organisations whose members were given some form of paramilitary training. In times of national emergency these movements form a pool of manpower trained for typical military duties.

Since indigenous programmes only occasionally provided more than basic training, foreign expertise, in the form of foreign advisers and especially foreign military schools, became essential for advanced training. This inevitably increased their dependence on external powers and promoted their political influence. In fact, gaining influence is often an important reason for extending military assistance to a recipient state.

Since becoming independent, sub-Saharan armed forces have sent officers for military training to a variety of foreign states, including former colonial powers such as Britain and France; states playing a leading role in the Third World such as India or Yugoslavia; a variety of Arab countries in the Middle East and North Africa; and even to other African states. In the 1970s and 1980s, until the collapse of the communist systems, training by the superpowers – the United States and the Soviet Union – played a crucial role in their quest to advance their own position.[41]

Despite limitations, foreign training programmes for African officers often effectively served both donor and recipient. For instance, the strong ties and goodwill that had developed during

TABLE 4:
RECRUITING AND UTILISING HUMAN RESOURCES

SUB-SAHARAN ARMED FORCES 1966-1996: HUMAN RESOURCES (IN THOUSANDS)									
Country	1966	1981	1996	Population 1998	Country	1966	1981	1996	Population 1998
Angola	-	33	97	11 346	Lesotho	-	-	2	2 083
Benin	2	3	5	5 800	Liberia	3	5	3	3 201
Botswana	-	2	8	1 527	Madagascar	4	20	21	14 291
Burkina Faso	2	4	10	11 124	Malawi	1	5	10	10 273
Burundi	1	6	22	6 673	Mali	4	5	7	10 517
Cameroon	4	7	22	14 240	Mauritius	-	-	2	1 157
Cape Verde	-	-	1	438	Mozambique	-	27	11	18 755
Central Afr Rep	1	2	5	3 589	Namibia	-	-	8	1 741
Chad	1	3	30	6 810	Niger	1	2	5	9 687
Congo Brazzaville	2	10	10	2 859	Nigeria	12	156	77	107 000
Congo Kinshasa	32	22	49	46 307	Rwanda	2	5	33	8 137
Côte d'Ivoire	4	7	14	15 425	Senegal	6	10	13	8 955
Djibouti	-	2	10	683	Seychelles	-	-	1	72
Equatorial Guinea	-	-	1	490	Sierra Leone	1	3	14	4 972
Eritrea (former part of Ethiopia)	-	-	55	3 784	Somalia / Somali Republic	10	63	undecided	6 000
Ethiopia (lost Eritrea)	35	230	120	53 000	South Africa	22	93	100	44 411
Gabon	1	2	5	1 390	Sudan	19	71	89	30 485
The Gambia	-	-	1	1 135	Tanzania	2	45	35	30 220
Ghana	17	15	7	18 345	Togo	2	4	7	4 560
Guinea	5	10	10	7 022	Uganda	6	8	50	20 398
Guinea-Bissau	-	6	9	1 129	Zambia	3	16	22	9 574
Kenya	5	15	24	29 214	Zimbabwe	4	35	43	11 577

Notes: Some countries became independent *after the 1960s*, while even for several independent countries *no figures* existed before the mid-1970s. A few countries include *semi-military forces* (such as the gendarmerie) in the armed forces, others not. Moreover, recent military figures for countries in *volatile sub-regions* change rather quickly.

Sources: International Institute for Strategic Studies, *Adelphi Paper 27*, London, 1966; International Institute for Strategic Studies, *The Military Balance 1981/82*, Oxford University Press, London, 1981; Arlinghaus, B E and Baker, P H, *African Armies : Evolution and Capabilities*, London, Westview Press, 1986; International Institute for Strategic Studies, *The Military Balance 1996/97*, Oxford University Press, London, 1996, and *The Military Balance 1997/98*, Oxford University Press, London, 1997.

United States training assistance to Liberia, helped to provide continuity in US-Liberian relations following the *coup* by enlisted men in 1980 that overthrew President William Tolbert. The United States was able to develop a working relationship with the new leadership who sought radical change, while at the same time continuing the training programme and supporting the new regime in instilling discipline and professionalism among troops.[42]

It may be concluded that although military expertise was, in general, negatively influenced by low levels of intellectual, scientific and technological development in the broader post-independent sub-Saharan societies; by the emigration of skilled professionals; and by the promotion of loyal rather than competent officers, a degree of military professionalism was promoted through comprehensive internal and foreign training programmes.

7 PROVIDING ARMAMENT AND LOGISTICS

A material capability is crucial in modern war. Without effective weapons systems with a reasonable firepower and the logistical ability to supply and move own forces and their armament, it is impossible to employ even a numerically strong military organisation. This poses a huge problem for sub-Sahara. The (previously discussed) relatively low level of economic development and progress in most sub-Saharan states inevitably implies a limited capacity for arming and supplying military forces.

The determinant of arming forces is intimately linked to the provision of firepower, defined as the ability to direct projectiles with explosive power accurately over great distances. Firepower, in turn, depends on logistics, that is on supply and maintenance. Feeding, clothing, housing, paying and nursing large numbers of military personnel, as well as supplying, fuelling, repairing, calibrating and replacing their equipment is a complex task. As no military organisation can be sustained without a well-developed logistics system, this criterion creates a clear distinction between more and less efficient sub-Saharan states.[43]

At the time of independence African states were among the most lightly armed in the world by almost any criterion. In the mid-1960s few sub-Saharan states possessed heavy weapons systems, such as tanks and field artillery, or more sophisticated arms, such as surface-to-air missiles, guided-missile attack boats, or jet combat aircraft.

However, from the mid-1960s to the mid-1970s there was a significant expansion in the acquisition of more powerful weapons systems, such as armoured vehicles and combat aircraft. The aim was to improve the firepower of the immature military forces as quickly as possible.[44] Certain types of equipment have proved useful in the operational environment of sub-Saharan Africa, such as light, wheeled, armoured

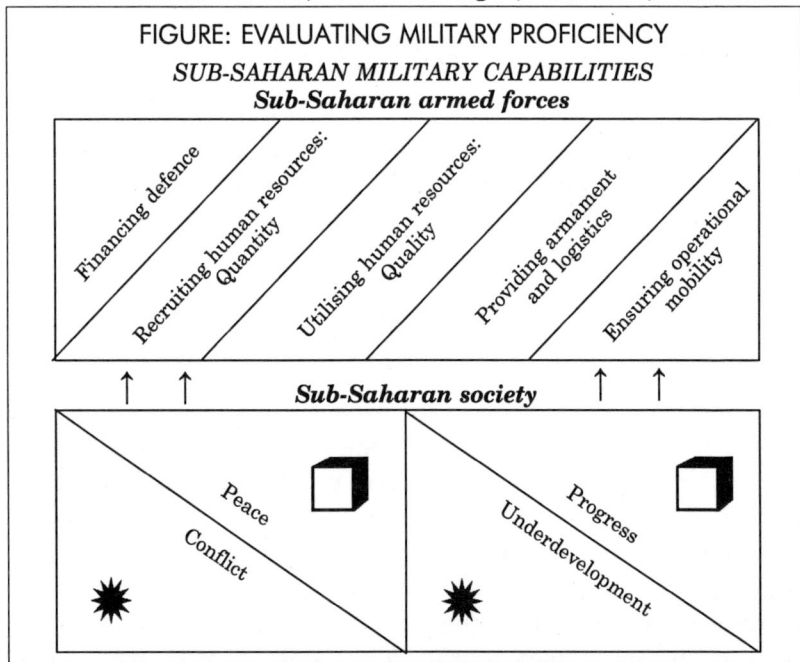

vehicles; helicopters; light stol (short take-off and landing) aircraft; armed jet trainers and naval patrol craft.[45]

Sub-Sahara indeed presents its own challenges for armament and logistics. General wear and tear on armoured fighting vehicles increases drastically in African conditions, requiring maintenance at more regular intervals. The lifespan of tank tracks, for example, is also considerably shorter. Air filters and air intakes also need special attention, as they are easily clogged by leaves.[46]

Moving logistical and combat support vehicles over rough terrain is even more difficult than moving armoured fighting vehicles. Logistical vehicles struggle to keep up with the fighting force, and furthermore the vehicles and their cargoes are severely damaged by the vegetation.[47]

Especially in war, a logistical advantage in sub-Saharan conditions may ensure success.

- Where the Ethiopian army had lost control of vast stretches of territory during 1977 in the northern and southern parts of the country, it made dramatic gains against Somalia in the Ogaden and against insurgents in Eritrea once the Soviets and Cubans assisted it to improve significantly its own logistical system.[48]

- Tanzania's advance into Uganda between January and April 1979 was indicative, not necessarily of fighting ability since organised resistance was minimal, but of the basic accomplishment of setting up a logistical system that extended as far as over 1 500 kilometres from its tail in Dar-es-Salaam into the Ugandan hinterland.[49]

Moreover, a high level of logistical ability depends on the establishment of efficient and flexible military industries. Such industries did and do support the defence forces operating in some countries, such as Nigeria, Namibia and Zimbabwe.

However, only South Africa maintains heavy military industries. A significant problem flows from the fact that to date very little research and development activities have taken place in sub-Saharan states, with the result that, with minor exceptions, they did not adapt their equipment to African conditions.

The development of small, indigenous defence industries in a handful of countries reduced dependence on foreign sources to some extent and provided a degree of self-sufficiency in smaller items, such as quartermaster-type stores and landmines. However, during three decades of independence, most states have accumulated a mix of Western and former Soviet equipment in their inventories. This has complicated training, maintenance and combined operations.

With the exception of South Africa, sub-Saharan states have imported almost all matériel. Although a few have produced small arms ammunition, the weapons using the ammunition, the military vehicles, spare parts and other items were and are obtained almost entirely from technologically more advanced countries abroad. From this standpoint, all sub-Saharan states are, with the exception of South Africa, on roughly an equal footing.[50]

Although sub-Saharan states have thus expanded their arsenal of weapons systems over a period of three decades — normally by importing them from abroad (often to the disadvantage of the needs of civilian society, however) — limitations in firepower, in logistical ability and in defence production capacity have continuously influenced the crucial factor of operational mobility.

8 ENSURING OPERATIONAL MOBILITY

The environment of sub-Saharan Africa can be described as a vast landscape, requiring strategic and long tactical moves. The terrain is often rugged, densely vegetated and flat, the soil mostly sandy and studded with tree trunks or rocks, and the weather extremely hot, with cold winters. The dense African bush favours infantry.[51]

With this in mind, operational mobility may be defined as the ability to quickly move troops, equipment and supplies on a large scale, and to deploy them for combat. Although the emphasis here is on military operations rather than on international peace-keeping, or on the type of domestic political adventures sub-Saharan forces often become involved in, a first aspect is simply delivering troops and equipment to a new location.

During the 1980s most states developed the ability to airlift very small units over short distances. A few can airlift battalion-size units over relatively great distances. Very few have sealift capabilities. It is true that a country that lacks adequate military transport may commandeer civilian trucks and aircraft to move troops. Moreover the acquisition of a few C-130-type aircraft, and the maintenance skills and training required, can transform an army (as it has Nigeria's) from a largely homebound establishment to one capable of projecting at least limited force somewhere on the continent.[52]

A second, far more complex, aspect is utilising weapons systems for mobile warfare. Such systems may include armoured vehicles, self-propelled artillery, combat aircraft and naval patrol craft. This ability requires a sound economic base to afford such complex systems a high level of maintenance, effective command-and-control structures and intensive training.

Mobility in combat is among the most difficult capacities to acquire, and only a few sub-Saharan countries are really capable of conducting highly mobile combat operations. According to Barrows, "the white-led Rhodesian forces" (in the 1970s), which relied heavily upon air strikes and mobile raids against guerrilla bases in neighbouring countries, were unmatched in this respect.[53]

In the three decades after independence the most frequent type of warfare witnessed in sub-Sahara was based on guerrilla and counter-guerrilla operations. However the availability of sophisticated weapons and training has tended to accelerate a tendency towards conventional dimensions. In many situations it was a normal progression from the hit-and-run-tactics of the early stages of an armed insurgency to the more set-piece clashes of the later stages.[54]

The late 1970s and 1980s showed no shortage of African armies in combat or potential combat situations, and the successful execution of basic strategic manoeuvres indicated a capability that previously did not exist. Several sub-Saharan countries improved the combat effectiveness of their armed forces in the 1970s and 1980s. Examples are: Ethiopia, Kenya and Tanzania in East Africa, Senegal and Nigeria in West Africa, and Malawi and Botswana in Southern Africa.[55]

By the 1970s, sub-Saharan Africa also provided examples of improved tactical flexibility, such as the successful advance of the Somali National Army into the Ogaden region of Ethiopia which reportedly proceeded with considerable efficiency, especially in the co-ordination of supplies, and Tanzania's invasion of Uganda.[56]

Examples suggest that many African countries can mobilise significant manpower for the military when hostilities threaten. During the 1970s three wars illustrated a mobilisation capability that was previously unknown − the Angolan civil war, the Ogaden war and the Tanzania-Uganda war. They showed how a national army or guerrilla army can be expanded rapidly to meet a fast-developing conflict situation.[57]

Although there are signs of stagnation and even regression in individual countries, the trend of gradually improving operational mobility will probably continue as some states acquire additional weapons and especially technical skills.[58]

9 CONCLUSION

To make valid generalisations and draw conclusions on the historical characteristics of sub-Saharan armed forces is easier said than done owing to the many differences found between regions and between states within the same region. The security forces are almost as diverse as sub-Saharan geography, politics and languages. They range in size from the light infantry battalions of Togo and Benin to the substantial military establishments of Nigeria and South Africa equipped with modern weapons systems. They vary in effectiveness from the disciplined Malawi army to the rather chaotic gangs of Uganda, Rwanda and Burundi in the strife-torn lake area. Their responses to civilian control contrast sharply from the headstrong forces of Congo Kinshasa (the new Democratic Republic of the Congo) to the obedient army of Zimbabwe.

The perspectives in this chapter focused on the main features of the armed forces of sub-Saharan societies over the first decades of independence, and are based on three challenges faced by these societies. The challenges of peace and progress constitute the background, as well as the conditions for any kind of military capability.

Peace often eluded the new societies as a result of numerous insurgencies, separatist movements and civil wars, aggravated by *coups* and armed campaigns to gain control of the state. Owing to the internal divisions in many countries and the role of dissident forces, more sub-Saharan armies existed in the mid-1990s than sub-Saharan states! In addition to the problem of peace, political and economic progress also evaded the new societies who were afflicted by one-party or military rule, mass refugee emigrations and a steady decline in living standards throughout the 1970s and 1980s. It is often justly asserted that political stability has proved, and is likely to prove, a more important precondition for an effective army than military capability is for political stability.[59]

To ascertain to what degree sub-Saharan states could develop military capabilities despite the disadvantages of the mentioned societal problems, fundamental processes linked to military proficiency were identified — those of financing defence; recruiting adequate human resources; utilising competent human resources; providing armament and logistics, and ensuring operational mobility. (See the explanatory figure.)

This model was explained by pointing out that a sound military budget may be judged the most obvious need of military planners, without which nothing can be purchased and not one soldier employed. Following from this, the first human resources determinant stressed the quantity of manpower; the next, the even more decisive educational and technical quality of available resources. Armament and logistics were defined as the two indispensable physical prerequisites for armed forces, while it was argued that operational mobility provides a method of measuring and assessing military efficiency.

During the independence celebrations of the 1960s the challenge to establish a credible military capability could have seemed overwhelming to most states, because their so-called "armies" had insignificant roles, outdated equipment and little status. Nevertheless, despite the mentioned societal problems, several categories of military proficiency gradually developed.

In the first decades of independence disproportionate amounts of GNPs were spent to recruit and arm military forces, and sometimes up to 40 per cent of national budgets was used for military purposes. Since then a more cautious, conservative approach to military expansion has been adopted. In fact, during the 1990s several countries were reducing their military expenditure, often under international pressure.

As can be seen (in Table 4), the quantitative size of armed forces has continued to grow during the past three decades, determined by factors such as the demographic composition of the different societies, their threat perceptions and the nature of the cleavages that endangered integration. The numerically strongest forces developed in states such as Congo Kinshasa, Ethiopia, Kenya, Nigeria, South Africa, Sudan, Tanzania and Zimbabwe. It was concluded that incremental military growth, even in smaller countries, seemed to be a long-term trend.

The generally low-level intellectual, scientific and technological development in most societies made it difficult to recruit high quality human resources, especially specialists, for military organisations. This state of affairs was aggravated by the emigration of skilled professionals; a lack of commitment to standards of military professionalism; and the promotion of loyal, rather than competent, staff officers and commanders. However, effective military training received increasing attention in the more prominent sub-Saharan powers, where military colleges or military academies have been established. In addition, foreign advisers and training at foreign military institutions contributed to the advancement of the officer corps.

The problems of economic progress had a direct impact on arming and supplying sub-Saharan forces — processes that are indispensable for ensuring the necessary firepower and mobility. In general, most states in the region lacked modern equipment and weapons systems. This pertains not only to the inoperability of navies, which has always been a weak point, but also to air forces and armies. Many states nevertheless purchased relatively powerful weapons systems such as armoured cars and combat aircraft, but often to the disadvantage of the needs of relatively poor civilian societies. Where armament and logistical capability could be improved with foreign support, armed forces such as those of Ethiopia and Tanzania increased their mobility dramatically. Although, with the exception of South Africa, sub-

Saharan states import most *matériel*, light military industries were developed in countries such as Nigeria, Namibia and Zimbabwe.

During the first decades of independence, limitations in fire power, logistical capability and defence production have restricted the ability to move troops, equipment and supplies quickly and to deploy them for combat. Most states have acquired the ability to airlift very small units over short distances, but only a few can airlift battalion-size units over relatively great distances. Very few have sealifting capabilities.

Although the most frequent type of warfare in sub-Sahara was based on unconventional guerrilla and counter-guerrilla operations, the availability of sophisticated weapons and training has tended to accelerate the progression from the hit-and-run tactics of irregular operations to the fire-and-movement tactics of mobile operations.

However, mobility in combat is among the most difficult capabilities to acquire, and only a few sub-Saharan countries are really capable of conducting mobile combat operations, deploying armoured vehicles, self-propelled artillery and combat aircraft. One reason is that this capability requires not only an effective command-and-control system, but also a sound economic base and a high level of maintenance.

Ongoing change is common to the majority of sub-Saharan military organisations.[60] While most have grown at least moderately during the first decades of independence, some have undergone extraordinary expansion. What were small constabulary forces before independence — most often employed as extensions of the police in colonial empires — have become, by African standards, relatively large professional forces, sometimes armed with sophisticated equipment. Some sub-Saharan military organisations have reached a watershed as they have moved towards becoming national armed forces and at times even international actors.

REFERENCES

1. Africa Institute of South Africa, *Africa at a Glance: Facts and Figures 1996/7*, Pretoria, 1996, p 87.

2. Williams, G, "Africa in retrospect and prospect", *Africa South of the Sahara 1997*, Europa Publications, London, 1997, p 3.

3. Cornwall, R, "Democratisation and security in Africa", *African Security Review*, Vol 6(5), 1997, p 16.

4. Heitman, H, "Security and Africa's armed forces at the end of the 1990s", *ISSUP Bulletin*, 4/95, Pretoria, p 5.

5. Thom, W G, "Sub-Saharan Africa's Changing Military Capabilities", in: Arlinghaus, B E and P H Baker, *African Armies: Evolution and Capabilities*, London, Westview Press, 1986, p 104.

6. Williams, G, *op cit*, p 4.

7. Heitman, H, *op cit*, pp 6, 8.

8. Barrows, W L, "Changing military capabilities in Black Africa", in Foltz, W J, and H S Bienen (eds), *Arms and the African — Military Influences on Africa's International Relations*, Yale University Press, New Haven, 1985, p 105.

9. Heitman, H, *op cit*, p 9.

10. *Ibid*, p 9.

11. Malan, M, "Treading firmly on the layered response ladder: From peace enforcement to conflict termination operations in Africa?", *African Security Review*, Vol 6, No 5, 1997, p 47.

12. Cornwall, R, *op cit*, p 18. Compare C Clapham, *The African State*, presentation to the conference of the Royal African Society on Sub-Saharan Africa: The Record and the Outlook, St John's College, Cambridge, 14-16 April 1991. For an enlightening discussion, see International Institute for Strategic Studies, *Strategic Survey 1996/97*, Oxford University Press, London, 1997, pp 212-224.

13. Cornwall R, *op cit*, p 17.

14. Williams, G, *op cit*, p 4.
15. Malan, M, *op cit*, p 46.
16. See the discussion by Williams, G, *op cit*, pp 4-5.
17. Williams, G, *op cit*, p 10.
18. *Ibid*, p 3.
19. See the executive summary of a research programme conducted by the World Bank, "Demobilisation and reintegration of military personnel in Africa: The evidence from seven country case studies", in: Cilliers, J (ed), *Dismissed*, Institute for Defence Policy, Halfway House, 1995, p 12.
20. *Africa South of the Sahara 1997*, Europa Publications, London, 1997, p v.
21. Cornwall, R, *op cit*, p 15; Williams, G, *op cit*, p 3.
22. Compare the model in Barrows W L, *op cit*, pp 102-120.
23. Thom, W G, *op cit*, p 104.
24. Wood, D, "The Armed Forces of African States", *Adelphi Paper 27*, IISS, London, April 1966, p 4.
25. Watson, T, "The Angolan Affair 1974-76", *US Air War College Research Reports*, No 257, April 1977, p 75.
26. Compare Cline, R S, *World Power Assessment: A Calculus of Strategic Drift*, Westview Press, Boulder, Colorado, 1975.
27. Arlinghaus, B E, "African Armies – An Analytical Approach", in: Arlinghaus, B E and P H Baker, *African Armies: Evolution and Capabilities*, London, Westview Press, 1986, p 1.
28. World Bank, *op cit*, p 12.
29. Barrows, W L, *op cit*, p 106.
30. For an elaboration of these costs and benefits, compare Arlinghaus, B E, *Military Development in Africa: The Political and Economic Risks of Arms Transfers*, Westview Press, Boulder, Colorado, 1984. See also Arkhurst, F A (ed), *Arms and African Development*, Praeger Publishers, New York, 1970, pp 23-30.
31. Heitman, H, *op cit*, pp 2, 12.

32. World Bank, *op cit*, pp 13, 24. See this report for a study of six sub-Saharan countries. By the time of the report, Zimbabwe and Namibia had completed a demobilisation programme while Angola, Mozambique, Uganda and Chad had a programme under way.

33. Barrows, W L, *op cit*, p 115.

34. *Ibid*, p 101.

35. Thom, W G, *op cit*, pp 98-99. Compare International Institute for Strategic Studies, *The Military Balance 1997/98*, Oxford University Press, London, 1997: Sub-Saharan Africa, pp 230-263.

36. Barrows, W L, *op cit*, p 101.

37. Cornwall, R, *op cit*, p 16; Barrows, W L, *op cit*, pp 102-103.

38. Barrows, W L, *op cit*, p 108.

39. For an analysis of the harmful effects upon military capabilities of the survival techniques of African politicians, see Barrows, W L, "*Dynamics of military rule in Black Africa*", paper presented to the conference on How to Look at Africa in the 1980s, Washington DC, September 1982.

40. Thom, W G, *op cit*, p 104.

41. For a table of the number of Soviet and Eastern European military personnel in sub-Saharan Africa and the United States involvement in military training programmes in sub-Saharan Africa at the beginning of the 1980s, see Barrows W L, *op cit*, pp 109-110.

42. Barrows, W L, *op cit*, p 111.

43. *Ibid*, p 111.

44. Thom, W G, *op cit*, pp 101-102.

45. *Ibid*, p 103.

46. Dippenaar, J M, "Armour in the African environment", *Mailed Fist*, IDP Monograph Series, March 1996, p 46.

47. *Ibid*, p 46.

48. Barrows, W L, *op cit*, p 112.

49. *Ibid*, p 112; *Africa South of the Sahara 1997, op cit*, pp 975-976.

50. Barrows, W L, *op cit*, p 101.
51. Dippenaar, J M, *op cit*, pp 44-46.
52. Barrows, W L, *op cit*, pp 112-113.
53. *Ibid*, p 113.
54. Thom, W G, *op cit*, pp 108-109.
55. *Ibid*, p 103; Barrows, W L, *op cit*, pp 115-116.
56. Thom, W G, *op cit*, p 103.
57. *Ibid*, p 99.
58. Barrows, W L, *op cit*, p 116.
59. *Ibid*, p 118.
60. Compare evaluations by Barrows, W L, *op cit*, p 99; Arlinghaus, B E, *op cit*, p 2; Thom, W G, *op cit*, p 110.

Chapter 3

THE CHANGING HISTORICAL ROLES OF SUB-SAHARAN ARMED FORCES

Louis du Plessis

1 INTRODUCTION

The aim of this chapter is to provide a framework that will outline the basic internal and external roles played by the armed forces in sub-Saharan societies during the first decades after independence in the 1960s. Speculation about future possibilities is limited, since the focus is not even on present developments but on historical trends.

The inherent weakness of any such macroanalysis is that all general statements are, at best, precarious and tentative. Many individual cases can be cited that run counter to the trends described here. This chapter contains only a cursory investigation, and the conclusions are not dogmatic, but tentative, ideas.

Nonetheless, theory should not be confused with practice. The "roles" referred to in this chapter are the actual activities the military forces were or are involved in. These roles are not the functions listed for armed forces in constitutional documents with vague moral intentions, but the roles they have fulfilled or are fulfilling within the realities of the sub-Saharan societal and regional landscapes. This machiavellian distinction is crucial.

The analysis commences with two frameworks that illustrate the historical roles of sub-Saharan armed forces. The first interprets the role of the military within the context of the fundamental needs of states; the second defines the nature of the civil-military relationship. Owing to the historical inclination of sub-Saharan armed forces to intervene in domestic politics, this theoretical distinction is likewise crucial.

After describing the rule of colonial powers, the main activities of the sub-Saharan forces after independence in the 1960s are analysed. Next a record of military intervention is given, and then an attempt is made to clarify this role. In the following section the mechanisms utilised by the civilian leadership to maintain authority and to ensure a professional role for the armed forces are investigated.

After identifying a series of internal functions of the armed forces to provide policing, technological, medical and educational services to civilian society, the focus turns to the external dimension. The growing foreign involvement of sub-Saharan armed forces is discussed before the main conclusions are made.

A few introductory comments should be made here on the nature of armed forces:

Napoleon Bonaparte may have been correct in stating that without armed forces there is neither independence nor civil liberty. However Edmund Burke's warning is equally valid — that armed forces may pose a great threat to liberty. The reasons lie in their nature.

Although it is sometimes maintained that African "armed forces" often behave in a similar and uniquely "African" manner, they necessarily have many conceptual identities and characteristics in common with other armed forces, because of their function as the organised military institutions of sovereign states.[1]

Unlike members of most civilian organisations, members of armed forces function in strictly disciplined structures that focus not simply on doing a job but also embrace a way of life. This happens within a rigid hierarchy of ranks, often with a high level of self-sufficiency in communications and transport, and linked to training in the use of weapons systems. Moreover, soldiers normally see themselves as different from civilians. When this organisational ability and emotional cohesion are combined with a virtual monopoly of arms, armed forces may indeed become a self-serving sector — and a danger to other citizens — if society cannot control them.[2]

2 ARMED FORCES AND THE NATURE OF STATES

When attempting to provide an analytical framework for understanding the evolving role of sub-Saharan armies, some of the fundamental needs of states must be taken into consideration, such as ensuring survival, territorial integrity and economic well-being.[3]

Even in the 1980s, the term "states" was used far more often than "nations" to refer to the political, social and economic structure of many African countries, because the survival of a particular tribal or ethnolinguistic group was viewed as paramount. This phenomenon was linked to forms of protracted social conflict and also to instances in which governments became unable to function effectively beyond the confines of their capitals.

Because military organisations usually reflect the divisions in their societies, it is logical that the African military has often been directly involved in domestic African politics. In fact, the loyalty of the military has tended to be not to the state as a whole, but to the segment of society that the military represents or to a specific party in power or to a particular leader.

Military leaders were often drawn into the competition for leadership, as a result of their need for self-aggrandisement or for the sake of nationalism — the latter being fuelled by public perceptions of the man on horseback as the national saviour. The military was normally vastly stronger than civilian political parties, and thus able to impose its will without accountability. Sub-Saharan armies were capable of suppressing internal discord and competitive political activity.

The military have thus often been protectors of regimes rather than protectors of states or nations. As such they did contribute to stability and to the survival of the state, but only in the narrower sense by ensuring that someone or some group was in power for a reasonable period of time. Representativeness or effectiveness was not their first concern.[4]

Although the armed forces were seldom called upon to defend the independence of the state, they nevertheless symbolised the sovereignty that was extended by former colonial powers, and were accepted by international organisations and respected by the world community.

Before examining the motives, attitudes and actions of sub-Saharan forces, a few distinctions should be made regarding the relation between society in general and the military in particular. Of special significance is the relationship between members of the security forces and the political leadership.

3 CIVIL-MILITARY RELATIONSHIP

To a greater or lesser extent all armed forces intervene in politics. At the one end of the continuum of intervention there is what may be seen as the typical influence of a compartment of society, such as legitimate inputs into the defence budget decision-making process. The further one moves away from civilian control in the direction of the opposite pole, there is first what may be called "blackmail", or the intimidation of civilian authorities, and then "displacement" of one set of civilian politicians by another. The final position is pure militarism, which may be labelled "supplantment", where the military seize power and install themselves in office.[5]

Although civilian control over military institutions can be classified in many ways, the following distinctions may be helpful:

In the traditional model, exemplified by seventeenth century European monarchies, civilian supremacy is maintained because there is very little difference between the civilian and military elites. They may for example have the same roots in the aristocracy. With the introduction of standing armies in the 1800s, this system gradually disappeared.[6]

In modern societies, the alternatives defined by Huntington in a classic study are: objective and subjective control.[7] In the model of objective control, as applied in Western parliamentary democracies and also referred to as the liberal model, the officers' corps consists of self-disciplined individuals maintaining a high level of institutional discipline and military professionalism. The armed forces have internalised respect for civilian authority.

In the model of subjective control as practised in totalitarian regimes, such as Nazi Germany or the former Soviet Union — also referred to as the penetration model — the armed forces become an integral, though subordinate, part of the political authority. Inculcated with societal values, they often have a high level of membership in the governing party. A parallel political chain of command also exists.

If civilian institutions are effective over an extended period, it is more likely that self-restraining military professionalism will develop, as in the objective model of control. The lower the effectiveness of civilian institutions, the more likely it is that control will fall within the subjective model.[8]

FIGURE 1: CONTROL OF ARMED FORCES

MILITARISATION → CIVILIANISATION

Ruler-type Model	Penetration Model	Liberal Model
Lack of control	*Subjective control*	*Objective control*
Maximisation of military rule	Integration into political elites	Institutional self-control
Military intervention	Military politicisation	Military professionalism

A distinction is thus made between two poles of civilian control, namely between politically impartial, professional armed forces, such as those normally found in developed democracies, and politically involved armed forces that are inclined to govern society.[9] (See Figure 1.)

- The politically neutral defence force regards the existing social and political processes as legitimate, does not seek to create an independent kind of pro-military political party and strives to enhance professionalism, since involvement in sectional and partisan politics may distract it from its field of expertise and destroy its cohesion and unity of purpose.

- Somewhere in the middle may be found the force comprising politically active officers. The officers' corps is often highly politicised and is organisationally linked to governing elites, regulated by civilian norms and directed by the civilian leadership.

- In contrast, the ruler-type armed force at the other end of the scale evades military self-discipline, as well as civilian discipline; rejects the existing social and political processes; tends to maximise rule through its own political organisation; does not fear civilian retribution, and believes that military rule is the only solution to political disorder.

Ruler-type armed forces often find disengagement from politics for longer than a few years virtually impossible.

When sub-Saharan forces are placed within the context of these relationships, it will be argued that, despite their protestations of political neutrality, many African officers preferred the ruler-type model and had such a strong appetite for political power that, in a sense, *coups d'état* have become institutionalised in Africa.[10]

4 INTERNAL INTERVENTION BY SUB-SAHARAN ARMED FORCES

In order to attempt to explain the inclination to become involved in domestic power struggles and the nature of such intervention by sub-Saharan forces, it is necessary to make a few remarks about the colonial background of sub-Saharan states before examining the subsequent unconstitutional changes of government since independence and some main features of, and reasons for, this behaviour. Only then will it be possible to identify the main mechanisms of control in those states where civilian authority has been maintained.

4.1 From colonialism to independence

Throughout Africa the rule of colonial powers, as well as the rule of tribal leaders, was established through force. Whether European governments or the Zulu king, Chaka, were in power, resistance to authority was quelled by military means. African troops were used to maintain an indigenous version of *pax Britannica* or *pax Gallica*.

According to Welch[11] the colonial period was marked by "armies of Africans" rather than "African armies". In World War 1 about 845 000 "natives" fought in French armies, and in World War 2 approximately 166 000 men from British-ruled Africa and 141 000 from French-ruled Africa served in the colonial powers' armed forces outside their home territories. Military planners emphasised the acceptance of the military goals of the colonial powers, expected obedience and paid scant attention to building national armies. Until the eve of independence, with the exception of a few military units in British and French colonies, black Africans were rare in the ranks of non-commissioned officers and practically non-existent among commissioned officers.

In the early days of independence, at the beginning of the 1960s, few African heads of state found it necessary to utilise military strength to quell internal dissent. However, as African presidents recognised the importance of coercion and decided to protect their position by directly ensuring the loyalty of the armed forces, the veneer of non-involvement disappeared entirely.

The disintegration of the federations of French West Africa and French Equatorial Africa, and the repatriation of African enlistees to their countries of origin from French forces, started in francophone states what had occurred earlier in British-ruled colonies. With the departure of the Europeans and the virtual elimination of white people from command positions, what were described as "armies of Africans" were incrementally transformed into "African armies".[12]

4.2 Unconstitutional changes of government

The record of unconstitutional changes of government in sub-Saharan Africa is significant in several respects.

- Military *coups* escalated over time as the process of decolonisation created ever more sovereign states. After three decades, by the end of the 1980s, armed interventions had become the principal method by which sub-Saharan governments were changed, with Southern Africa as the major exception.

- Following the great wave of sub-Saharan independence between 1960 and 1963, military *coups* swept through the continent. In 1965 there were four *coups*; in 1966 there were six.

- On average, there have been three successful *coups per annum* during the past quarter-century. It may be added that for every successful *coup*, there have been at least two unsuccessful ones.[13]

- Another meaningful fact is that most of the *coups* have been directed against civilian administrations, often for a second or third time. But since the second decade of independence (the 1970s), an increasing proportion have been staged by a military unit against a military government, as in Nigeria, Ghana and Sudan.[14]

- Between the establishment of the first independent states in sub-Sahara at the end of the 1950s and 1996, 28 countries experienced violent changes of government — 21 of them more than once. In total there have been 79 such changes. In all but two cases, the governments were overthrown by military officers, and military rule occurred in both single-party and multi-party states.[15]

- The extent of this behaviour pattern of the armed forces is evident from the fact that, since becoming independent, more than half the members of the Organisation of African Unity have been subject to successful *coups*.

Furthermore, all types of African states have experienced military intervention.[16]

- This is true of African states of all colonial backgrounds — British and French, Belgian, Italian and Portuguese.

- Military intervention has been experienced by those who are ethnically relatively homogeneous such as Somalia, and by those of marked ethnic pluralism, such as Uganda.

- The military staged *coups* in states characterised by no-party systems, such as Ethiopia; one-party systems, such as Ghana; and multi-party systems, such as Benin.

- Drastic military intervention in government took place in very poor states such as Mali and Burkina Faso, and in more prosperous ones such as Nigeria.

- Military intervention occurred in relatively populous societies such as Zaire and Nigeria, and in the least populous, such as Benin and Togo.

- It occurred in states small in size, such as Burundi and Rwanda, and in large ones, such as Sudan and Chad.

Moreover, African armed forces have been involved in staging *coups* irrespective of their military capabilities. Unprofessional and ill-equipped armies, such as those of Niger and Sierra Leone, seem to be no different in this respect from more effective military organisations, such as those of Nigeria and Somalia.[17]

Where civilian rule eventually replaced military rule, friction between newly established governments and the armed forces often developed over issues such as the defence budget. While civilians did not give the same priority to upgrading military capabilities, military commanders judged budgetary cuts as excessive and provocative, dangerously impairing military functions. Consequently, the return to civilian rule was often not irreversible and permanent.[18]

A next step will be to attempt to interpret this lack of the type of civilian control that prevails, and is often taken for granted, in developed societies.

4.3 Clarifying military intervention

In an impressive volume of literature it is argued that an almost endless list of general circumstances may induce military forces to intervene in politics. These circumstances range from government repression and maladministration to regional and ethnic conflicts, from economic crises to personal ambitions. Although the intention is not to repeat this debate here, it is crucial to draw attention to the predominant circumstances in sub-Sahara.

Two general, but fundamental, factors should be borne in mind here. First, in the absence of genuinely democratic means for changing the government in power, such as elections, *coups d'état* became an attractive option in sub-Saharan Africa over a period of three decades — they were often the only viable option.[19] The second factor pertains to attitude and perception: members of the sub-Saharan armed forces often came to believe that their organisation had a special responsibility to govern. Thus, when grievances against existing policies and leaders developed, they felt obliged to intervene.[20] In fact, military officers were often encouraged by civilians to do so.

Although it was difficult to develop credible theories based upon statistical or qualitative analyses of the causes of these *coups*, several studies have nevertheless identified certain key elements.[21] A primary question is: What may be regarded as fundamental reasons for military intervention in sub-Saharan societies? The underlying assumption is that an accumulation

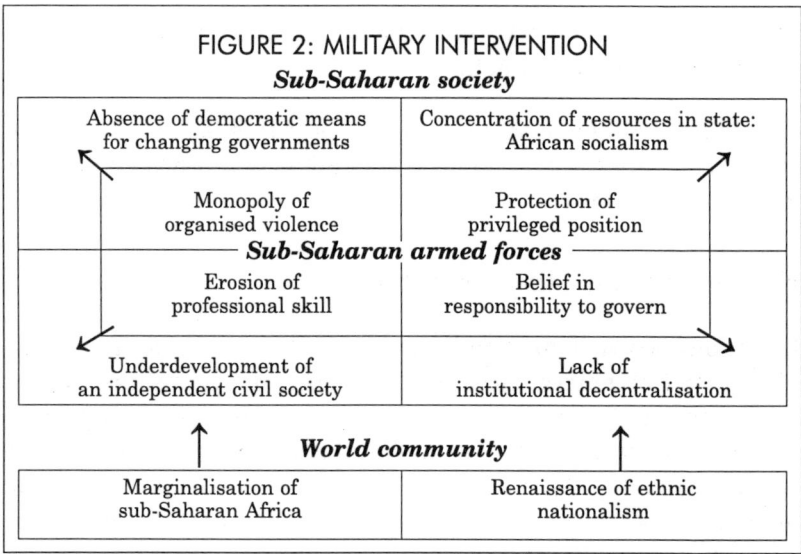

and a convergence of these reasons may make intervention more probable. (See Figure 2.)

The first category of reasons pertains to the characteristics of sub-Saharan military institutions.

When surveying the societies that have been at the mercy of military officers since independence, it becomes clear that the security forces (military and police) have enjoyed a virtual monopoly of organised state violence. Even in the 1990s, civilian institutions in most sub-Saharan societies are weak and the armed forces, no matter how small, represent virtually the only disciplined organisations.[22]

The level of professional qualifications and competence is another key factor. The replacement of European by African officers within a few years after independence resulted in the erosion of professional skills and often in a decline in *esprit de corps* and a breakdown in discipline. This indigenisation of the officers' corps lessened constraints on military adventurism in the political sphere.

For example, in March 1957, when Ghana attained independence, there were 209 Britons and 29 Africans in the army officers' corps. Four years later African officers controlled every facet of the army. In 1958 the Nigerian army had 45 African and six times as many British officers; by 1965 the army was completely Africanised.[23]

A relatively low level of skill, professionalism and self-discipline has often made it easy for local leaders to use the armed forces for the personal purposes of the new leadership. This is reflected in the judgement of the expatriate attorney-general of President Kwame Nkrumah: "The basic error of General H T Alexander and those other British officers who believed in a non-political army was the assumption that it was in fact practical. Everyone who enters an army must still retain, to some degree, the political views which he has before he enlisted ... The rank and file, in the infantry at least ... had very little education ... Such men could be persuaded to do anything under the orders of those immediately superior to them."[24]

The relatively low level of education in the civilian and military communities also made it possible for one well-organised unit, without regard for or fear of civilian authority, to change the people in power. In fact, *coups* have seldom involved more than a few hundred troops, a tiny proportion of the total armed forces.

Another series of reasons relates to the nature of the post-independent state.

The sub-Saharan state is often defined in terms of what is called "African socialism". The state is the largest employer of skilled and educated labour. It monopolises contracts with local and foreign businesses, it is the main source of loans and assistance to businessmen and farmers, and it has almost total control over clinics, schools, sanitation and communication. It often finds itself governing a new nation without a developed civil society.[25]

Furthermore, the lack of institutional differentiation is aggravated by a lack of institutional decentralisation. In many sub-Saharan countries the concentration — of the presidential palace, the residences of ministers, government buildings, airports and radio stations — in the capital city, makes an armed rebellion relatively simple.[26]

The result of this overwhelming concentration of resources has been the tendency of African citizens, including the military, to attempt to extend their economic standing with the government and even to control the central structures of the state.

It may be correctly maintained that a sub-Saharan *coup* is usually not an attempt to mediate between antagonistic groups in society but, on the contrary, a bid by a section of the military, often of one ethnic group, to protect and extend its privileged position in competition with other societal interests. The rhetoric in favour of patriotism or public order is often a smokescreen to conceal the sectional interests and the will to dominate of soldiers.[27]

Over the years sub-Saharan *coups* became more populist. With the old-style *coups*, which started and ended in the capital, regimes were generally toppled in a matter of hours or days, leaving the civilian population untouched and the state machinery intact. With the new style *coups*, which began on the periphery, the rebellions were prolonged and costly in human life and property.[28]

Ethnocentrism became an even more central driving force than before. The Zagawas people triumphed over the southern and the northern peoples in Chad in 1981-1982; the Tigre over the other ethnic groups in their struggle against the government in Ethiopia in 1988-1989, and the Tutsi minority over the Hutu in Rwanda.[29]

This newer type of *coup* displaced (and is still displacing) whole communities and devastated lands and industries. Much as the previous military rulers had to rely on the support of their own ethnic groups, the victorious ethnic group in these more populist struggles became the new privileged class, since their leaders were forced to rely on their support.[30]

In addition to the persistence of these (above-mentioned) trends, two specific global factors may facilitate increased, rather than decreased, military interventionism in the immediate future; namely, international marginalisation and ethnic nationalism. First, the preoccupation of the prosperous Western nations with Eastern Europe, the Middle East and the CIS republics is directly linked to the marginalisation of sub-Saharan Africa in world politics. Instead of being guided out of militarist adventures by development programmes and diplomatic pressure, the subcontinent will probably be increasingly overlooked. Greater than being fought over may be the danger of being politically and economically ignored.[31]

Moreover, the outside world is providing the slowly modernising sub-Saharan societies with many role models for separatist movements, which have resulted in the creation of internationally recognised states such as Armenia and Croatia, Estonia and Latvia, Czechia and Slovakia. A global renaissance of nationalist sentiment and secessionism suggests that the status of sub-Saharan colonial borders will not remain sacred and may be challenged.

The continuing ethnic conflicts, linked to poor socio-economic conditions and the political turmoil related to an unstable process of democratisation in most sub-Saharan states, indicate a high potential for internal instability and thus military intervention. The countries at highest risk are those where the above-mentioned reasons for intervention intersect. Of special significance may be developments in Angola, Rwanda, Burundi and Congo Kinshasa (the new Democratic Republic of the Congo) where the state structure of Zaire has collapsed.

However, it is essential to define not only the nature of military intervention but also that of military non-intervention, and to identify some procedures associated with civilian supremacy.

5 CIVILIAN CONTROL OF SUB-SAHARAN ARMED FORCES

The persistence of law-abiding military forces in several sub-Saharan states during the first decades after independence, and also of governing military forces that in due time succumbed and submitted to civilian authority, focuses the attention on two related issues: first, on the phenomenon of the demilitarisation of politics, when armed bureaucrats are induced to return to barracks; and second, on the mechanisms employed for establishing and maintaining sound civilian rule. After a brief reference to the dilemma of civilianisation, some basic methods of political control exercised during the past decades will be identified.

5.1 Problems of civilianisation

The timing of civilianisation is significant. It was found that the African military often disengaged from politics when the privileged cadre could not fulfil the needs of the citizens and when the cadre itself started to disintegrate — especially when it became clear that there was a growing divergence between their personal interests and those of the ordinary soldiers in the barracks.[32]

However, by allowing the civilianisation of politics, armed forces lose control of the allocation of public resources from which they benefit so lavishly. African military disengagement from politics is therefore often described as conditional, rather than conclusive.

Another important issue in this regard is the governing cycle. Civil-military relations in the majority of sub-Saharan states during the past quarter-century have been characterised by a cyclical pattern of successive *coups*, counter-*coups*, disengagements and weak civilian rule.[33] This may not end suddenly as a result of pressure from the West to introduce multiparty political systems.

In one model in which those African countries that have avoided *coups* in the first decades after independence are analysed, three major explanations for the persistence of civilian control are distinguished. One is understandably the presence of foreign patrons, such as France. Another is the role of a particular political leader who is popular, manages a moderately institutionalised state and allows a degree of political competition. A final factor is military recruitment practices that emphasise *inter alia* that political and military leaders have similar ethnic backgrounds.[34]

In a later model, civilian control in the first decades after independence appeared to be associated not only with strong civilian leadership and some manipulation of ethnic loyalties in the armed forces, but also with officially sanctioned party competition and economic growth.[35]

5.2 Mechanisms of subjective control

Well over a third of the continent's states have remained free of military domination since independence. A number of regimes have maintained civilian authority over their military establishments for periods exceeding 25 years; namely, the Ivory Coast, Cameroon, Senegal, Gabon, Swaziland, the Gambia, Botswana, Tanzania, Mauritius, Kenya, Malawi and Zambia.[36]

When civilian society has established and maintained its authority over the military in sub-Saharan Africa, it owes most of its success to the subjective, rather than the objective model (as defined earlier).

A basic truth is that civilian governments were (and are) inclined to extend their military capability when they could thereby enhance their own authority. In the case of internal resistance by ethnic or regional groups, an increased military capability strengthens the hand of governments by making negotiations a more attractive option for guerrillas, while at the same time increasing government bargaining power. Moreover, minor forms of disorder, such as riots and demonstrations, can be contained all the more readily as police and army effectiveness improves.[37]

It is thus necessary to identify some of the main mechanisms whereby this civilian penetration of sub-Saharan forces takes place. (See Figure 3.)

5.2.1 Maximising material service conditions

Sub-Saharan regimes often maintained stability by maximising the material service conditions of pay and privileges. Normally a very high percentage of the defence budget was, and is, used for benefits for members of the armed forces rather than for military hardware.[38]

Senior officers have, for example, been selected for overseas diplomatic posts that carry special allowances. Such posts often presented the rare opportunity of returning home with a duty-free car. In several countries, such as Zambia and Kenya, the senior officer ranks were admitted into the inner circles of privilege by the allocation of land grants for commercial farming.

Related to this practice is that of political co-option.

5.2.2 Political co-option

Even middle-ranking officers have been temporarily drawn into government circles by appointment to the boards of parastatals or as regional governors.

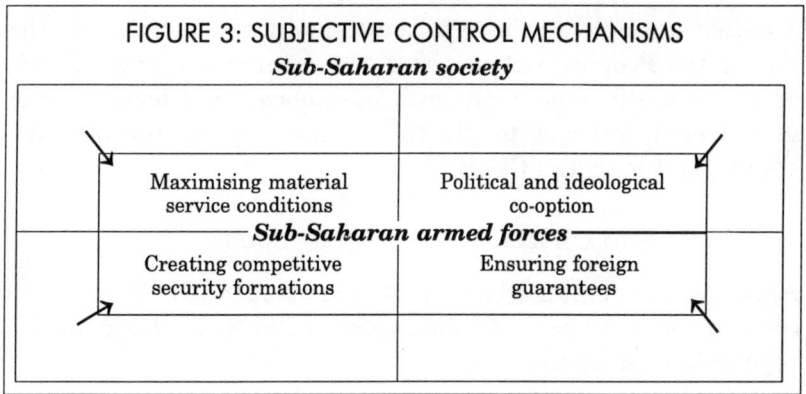

For a long period the Tanzanian armed forces, for example, formed part of the governing elite, with the frequent transfer of officers from the Tanzanian People's Defence Force to ministerial positions, and back again. The same mechanism of co-optation was followed in other states such as Gabon, Zambia and the Ivory Coast.[39]

5.2.3 Ideological socialisation

Another technique is to deliberately indoctrinate the armed forces with the ideological values of the party-state. The neutrality of the armed forces (as followed within the model of objective control) is replaced by an ethos whereby enthusiasm for the existing regime becomes an essential quality in a military officer.

In 1962 the Ghanaian Minister of Defence argued that the armed forces owed loyalty not only to Ghana but to the Convention People's Party and to President Kwame Nkrumah personally. The minister issued a directive that party education would be introduced into the army and that officers were to attend extended courses at the Kwame Nkrumah Institute of Ideological Studies. This became a prevailing model in sub-Sahara.

Another example is the systematic political education in the Tanzanian People's Defence Force. Members were expected not only to identify completely with the policies and leadership of government, but also to join the governing party (initially the TANU, and later the CCM).[40]

5.2.4 Creating competitive security formations

Another prominent mechanism used in independent Africa is the creation of rival security formations to keep a check on the regular armed forces.

In addition to the well-established systems in Kenya and Tanzania, the elaborate National Security Service that developed in Ghana is worth mentioning. It consisted of five units: military intelligence, counter-intelligence, a Cuban-trained bodyguard, special intelligence and the President's own guard regiment.

In Zaire, Mobutu Sese Seko ensured political longevity against resistance through the creation of numerous security agencies. Among these the Civil Guard was Egyptian-trained, the army's special 31 Brigade was French-trained, and the élite Special Presidential Division was Israeli-trained. This practice proved so effective against military intervention that, in the long run, the only way to change the well-entrenched dictatorship was through a bloody civil war which ended in 1997.

5.2.5 Ensuring foreign guarantees

An effective method of civilian control, and indirectly a part of the subjective model, is obtaining guarantees from foreign powers.

Examples are the francophone African states, of which almost all signed defence agreements with Paris after independence. The standing French garrisons in the Central African Republic, Djibouti, Gabon, Ivory Coast, Cameroon and Senegal have been an abiding hallmark of the continued French presence over more than three decades and have ensured stability.

A large number of African states have also provided military assistance to protect endangered neighbours from the political ambitions of their own armies. Guinea has intervened on no less than five separate occasions to support friendly civilian regimes. Tanzania has given military assistance to governments in the Comoros, the Seychelles and Uganda.[41]

Once the subordination of the military has been engineered, subjective control may be effective. Its limitations lie in the fact that it can be implemented only at great risk and that it differs fundamentally from the liberal democratic model.

Objective control, associated with democratic systems, will probably truly take root in sub-Sahara only at the beginning of the 21st century after a period of social change. Such change will have to create important prerequisites for military self-discipline, such as a much higher national level of education, economic competitiveness and an institutionalised civil society.

In addition to the periodical, cyclical or continuous intervention in domestic politics by most sub-Saharan forces, they have often also been defender, supporter and developer of the nation. Before dealing with their external involvement, a few remarks will be made about the internal service functions that these forces render.

6 NATIONAL SERVICE BY SUB-SAHARAN ARMED FORCES

The activities that will be identified are all related to assisting the national community and pertain to promoting internal stability, economic progress and nation-building.

Maintaining internal law and order in support of the police to guarantee some kind of parliamentary leadership and to ensure the rule of law is often regarded as an indispensable contribution of the armed forces to the integration of society. In fact, in the years following independence, most African states expected their forces to do little more than establish a fitful official presence in outlying areas and to control potential unrest in the principal cities.[42] In the more stable, developing societies, such as Botswana, Kenya, Namibia, Nigeria, South Africa and Zimbabwe, the armed forces have often played (and still do) a more prominent role in internal security than in external defence.[43]

Since a culture of continuous fighting and insurgency has become established in sub-Saharan Africa and has frustrated most attempts to construct a viable political order,[44] the role of maintaining internal law and order, rather than concentrating on typical military training objectives and preparing for mobile operations, is often regarded as crucial to the many divided and disjointed societies.

Furthermore, because the military was often the most professional and best organised administrative structure in the decades after independence, it was able to play the role of development agent and to contribute substantially to economic progress. This was especially true when other state departments were still underdeveloped and ineffective.

Sub-Saharan governments sometimes assigned to armed forces the task of erecting large infrastructures still much needed in many societies. The armed forces contributed to combating the devastating effects of drought by constructing dams for the irrigation of land, they built schools and roads, and participated in numerous medical programmes, notably vaccination campaigns. They even participated in the promotion of literacy.[45]

Sub-Saharan armed forces also played a less tangible, but sometimes even more influential, role of nation building through patriotic military training. This normally entailed the preservation of societal cohesion within countries whose borders did not correspond to the natural contours of African nationalities. The defence forces discouraged regional secessionist attempts and became "that cement which was essential for keeping together heterogeneous populations".[46]

According to the Gabonese Minister of Defence, young people in sub-Saharan Africa acquired or strengthened the belief in national unity and other important values during national service. Among these were a strong sense of duty, respect for the public weal, physical and mental endurance, and punctuality.[47]

When the armed forces are used for tasks that are not directly related to protecting the territorial integrity of the state but instead are civilian in nature, politicisation can occur and military professionalism can decline. However, these non-military tasks are nearly always only temporary tasks.

In the past, utilisation of the military for policing, technological, medical and educational services to civilian society was also typical of newly established and fast-modernising non-African states, such as Israel and Indonesia. Only after a governmental system had been solidly established could it afford to concentrate the talents and energies of uniformed personnel on solely military tasks.[48]

Although the agendas of sub-Saharan forces were predominantly domestic, something must be said about their gradually increasing external involvement.

7 EXTERNAL INVOLVEMENT OF SUB-SAHARAN ARMED FORCES

The international community has often found it difficult to come to terms with the role that sub-Saharan armies have played in the internal politics of their countries.[49] After the growth of military capabilities during the first decades of independence, a serious strategic question that is being asked is whether the future external involvement of these forces will be that of inflicting damage on neighbouring states or of self-disciplined national self-defence in co-operation with their neighbours. The aim of this section is to provide a few perspectives on the past external roles of the sub-Saharan forces.

Directly after the period of independence in the 1960s, the African interstate system was characterised by norms such as the stability of borders and non-interference in the internal affairs of other countries.[50] However, the relatively stable relations were eroded by an unbalanced and uneven military growth in Africa that tended to promote opportunities for increased and more severe armed conflict. The gap between military weaker and stronger African nations widened, and a growing disparity in economic and military capability among states increased the chances of seeking military solutions to interstate conflicts.[51]

Two aspects of the external roles will be highlighted: the emergence of regional powers and the occurrence of interstate conflict and co-operation.

7.1 Emergence of regional powers

Despite the fact that there is little indication of any foreign military intervention that may overturn the military balance of power in sub-Saharan states, a feature of the sub-Saharan environment is the development of regional military powers. These powers may be defined as states that have attained sufficient military proficiency to enable them to influence events beyond their borders. A few examples will illustrate this.

- In the 1970s and 1980s South Africa became widely recognised as the strongest state in sub-Sahara, comparable to a medium-sized European power.[52] In this period South African society was characterised by an increased threat perception, a sharp rise in defence spending and military involvement in policy-making.[53] After the transition to a multiracial democracy in 1994, South Africa maintained and even increased its status as the main power in Southern Africa.

- Another case is Ethiopia. After the 1974 *coup*, the Ethiopian army expanded significantly, becoming the so-called vanguard of the revolution, the force to secure Ethiopia against all threats. The previously US-trained military adapted well to the influx of new Soviet equipment and responded positively to intense retraining during the 1977-1978 Ogaden War.

- In West Africa, Nigeria has emerged as a regional power, with an impressive military manpower and an expanding economic ability bolstered by its population and oil wealth.

- During the 1980s it became clear that some other states had also developed military potential in their regions, such as Senegal in West Africa, Zaire (now the Republic of the Congo) in Central Africa, Zimbabwe in Southern Africa, and Tanzania and Kenya in East Africa.[54]

However, it is notable that the countries that achieved some kind of regional influence for a certain period before 1990, all suffered from internal weaknesses. On the one hand, domestic instability contributed to the amassing of military power; on the other, internal strife prevented them from acting as regional leaders. Examples are South Africa's growth in power during the black liberation struggle, Ethiopia's massive buildup in response to internal and external threats, and the expansion of Nigeria's army during the civil war.[55]

The conclusion is that regional military powers were emerging and were becoming significant role players in local conflicts and regional security.

7.2 Interstate conflict and co-operation

While military forces may be drawn into interstate conflicts, they may also become involved in joint interstate ventures.

During the first two decades of independence the first of these tendencies was often followed; namely, of being drawn into conflict and controversy. Violations of boundaries, airspace and maritime territorial limits abounded in Africa. They occurred when military forces pursued insurgents, intimidated or destabilised neighbours, or tried to control access to natural resources.[56] It can be argued that the increase of these incidents, and of the interstate conflicts that they caused, were indications of the growth of African military capabilities.[57]

In the 1980s regional powers succeeded in dominating their neighbours to such an extent that they could reap economic benefits without incorporating these states. On the other hand, weaker states were beset by uncontrollable insurgent groups — some externally supported — who used their territory as a sanctuary for incursions into neighbouring countries, while the host country paid a heavy price. Internal instability became contagious. This was especially true of the Central African subregion, stretching from Northern Angola and Congo Brazzaville through the new Democratic Republic of the Congo, Burundi, Rwanda and Uganda to Somalia, Ethiopia, Sudan and Eritrea.

Internal hostilities in one country often spilled over to its neighbours. Events in Rwanda can hardly be separated from those in Burundi. They, in turn, spilled over to Uganda and the new Republic of the Congo. Similarly, for many years the problems of the Shaba province in the the then Zaire routinely spilled over to Zambia. Kenya has suffered banditry across its borders with Somalia and Sudan, and Kenya's vessels have been seized by Somali pirates.[58]

In the 1990s it became evident that most sub-Saharan armies had yet to develop adequate capabilities to meet the challenges of internal insurrection or to deter incursions by stronger regional powers.

Albeit without the same determination and assertion as some Middle Eastern or Southeast Asian states, several developing sub-Saharan powers became capable, during the 1970s and 1980s, of violating the territorial integrity and threatening the survival of neighbouring regimes. However, this did not entail the destruction, conquest or indefinite occupation of their countries. Invasions were (and are) usually limited to cross-border incursions and retaliatory strikes.[59] In addition, more so than elsewhere, Central and East Africa became the sub-region in which some governments developed the practice of, and ability for, supporting dissident ethnic groups in bordering states.[60]

Although the most frequent type of warfare in sub-Sahara was guerrilla and counter-guerrilla operations, the availability of sophisticated weapons and training has tended to accelerate the progression from the hit-and-run tactics of irregular operations to the fire-and-movement tactics of mobile operations.[61]

However (as was argued in a previous chapter), mobility in combat is among the most difficult capabilities to acquire, and only a few sub-Saharan countries are really able to conduct mobile combat operations and to deploy armoured vehicles, self-propelled artillery and combat aircraft.

With reference to the previous emphasis on the tendency to military intervention, it should be noted that military governments in sub-Saharan Africa have not been more willing than civilian regimes to use force across borders. Civilian-led Tanzania, for example, sent troops against Uganda just as readily as militarist Somalia committed forces to fight in the Odagen, or Amin's Uganda to fight in Tanzania.[62]

In some areas conflict made way for co-operation. During the first decades after independence only a few cautious steps were taken in the direction of joint regional security structures. Slowly

FIGURE 4: BASIC ROLES OF SUB-SAHARAN ARMED FORCES
RELATIONSHIP OF ROLES: 1960-1990

Internal

Unconstitutional military intervention in the governing of society
Involvement in mechanisms for the civilian control of the military
Maintaining law and order and countering ethnic resistance
Providing technological and educational services to the nation

Destabilising or assisting neighbouring societies
Training for or conducting mobile combat operations
Developing interstate security structures
Participating in interstate peace-keeping operations

External

but surely however external military co-operation took root, first in the form of signing defence agreements and then, more tangibly, as military assistance to protect endangered neighbours — mostly against the aspirations of their own military forces. Eventually some of the more confident states became involved in cross-border operations to solve conflicts and to secure peace.

The fiasco of the United Nations' peace-keeping operation in Somalia and its inability to contain the conflict in Rwanda negatively impacted on the willingness of the international community to become involved. There was no eagerness to repeat either experience.[63] However by the 1990s it became apparent that gradually developing multilateral security structures might indeed contribute to the definition of at least one decisive new role — joint interstate peace-keeping operations.

Several sub-Saharan states expanded their conventional military training by including instruction in such operations at military colleges. A number of them, such as Nigeria, Ghana, Ethiopia, Kenya, Zimbabwe and Tanzania, have also contributed troops to peace-keeping operations.

In this way sub-Sahara was taking steps to develop the capacity to manage its own conflicts.

By the end of the third decade of independence, a select group of states — Nigeria, South Africa and Kenya, with Zimbabwe a possible fourth partner — had proved themselves capable of providing manpower and logistics to sustain an extended foreign operation.[64]

It may be concluded that, although their domestic activities dominated sub-Saharan forces for many years, the incremental development of military capabilities, especially in some societies (as discussed in a previous chapter), was related to the emergence of regional powers, which resulted not only in instances of external military intimidation but also in greater multilateral co-operation. This inevitably points to expanded external roles for sub-Saharan armed forces. (See Figure 4.)

8   CONCLUSION

This chapter commenced with two frameworks to contextualise the historical roles of sub-Saharan armed forces. The first interpreted the military within the fundamental needs of African states, such as ensuring survival, territorial integrity and economic well-being. The second defined the nature of the civil-military relationship, outlined the continuum of military intervention and the traditional, objective and subjective models of control, and contrasted the control models with the activities of ruler-type military forces. Owing to the historical tendency of sub-Saharan armed forces to intervene in domestic politics, these introductory definitions were essential.

After describing the rule of colonial powers, it was pointed out how the main activities of post-independence sub-Saharan armed forces were related to the unconstitutional changing of governments. On average, there have been three successful *coups per annum* during the past quarter-century, and for each success there have been at least two failed *coup* attempts. In this account it was shown that every type of sub-Saharan state has experienced military intervention.

When attempting to clarify this phenomenon, it was maintained that such action by armed forces is connected to a series of factors. Some of them pertain to the absence of genuinely democratic means for changing governments; many are related to the characteristics of sub-Saharan military institutions which enjoyed a virtual monopoly of organised state violence and experienced an erosion of professional skills when the colonial officers withdrew. Other factors are the nature of the post-independent state, with its overwhelming concentration of resources in the political leadership, and the non-existence of a viable civil society.

Proceeding from the fact that more than a third of the continent's states have nevertheless remained free of military domination, the nature of the mechanisms of civilian authority in these societies were analysed within the framework of the previously-defined model of subjective control. It was argued that the role of the military was directly influenced by societal processes, such as maximising the material service conditions for officers, ideological socialisation and the creation of competing security formations.

In addition to military intervention in domestic politics, sub-Saharan armies often performed other internal functions related to serving the national societies. Three dimensions of this role were distinguished. First, the military supported the other branch of the security forces, the police, in maintaining law and order and the rule of law. In most states, including the more stable ones such as Botswana, Kenya, Namibia, Nigeria, South Africa and Zimbabwe, this function has been more prominent than external military activity. Second, the armed forces, in the role of developmental agent, constructed parts of the infrastructure, including dams, schools and roads, and participated in programmes to promote health and literacy. Third, the forces utilised military service to inculcate a belief in national unity and other values.

Moving to the external dimension, the trend was underlined that, during their gradual development over three decades, the sub-Saharan forces were also instrumental in the rise of a few regional powers, such as Nigeria, Ethiopia, Kenya, South Africa and Zimbabwe. The armed forces of several states, especially those that were very dependent upon one another, became involved in cross-border excursions and in destabilising their neighbours. Although the most frequent type of warfare was unconventional, some armed forces developed a capacity to conduct mobile combat operations.

Recently several states have started to play the more positive role of multilateral co-operation, such as the development of joint regional security structures, the signing of defence agreements, military assistance to protect endangered neighbours and peacekeeping operations.

Internal intervention and governing their respective societies proved to be an important and time-consuming function for the armed forces during the first decades of independence. However, in many states civilian society was successful in securing authority over the soldiers through the mechanisms of subjective control. In this process the military gradually acquired professionalism. In addition, sub-Saharan forces often played a major part in combating internal disorder and in countering insurgencies of all kinds, thus ensuring the sovereignty of the state. This role was complemented by functions that promoted economic progress and nation building.

When identifying the most important roles played by the sub-Saharan armed forces during the first three decades after independence, it may be argued that, in general, the energies and activities directed at internal matters tended to dwarf external involvement and to overshadow the development of joint structures and the conduct of joint operations. This is typical of the armed forces of young and modernising societies.

REFERENCES

1. Arlinghaus, B E, "African Armies — An Analytical Approach", in: Arlinghaus, B E and Baker, P H, *African Armies: Evolution and Capabilities*, London, Westview Press, 1986, p 2.

2. See the systematic arguments in Finer, S E, *The Man on Horseback: The Role of the Military in Politics*, New York, Praeger, 1962.

3. *Ibid*, p 3.

4. *Ibid*, p 3-4.

5. Finer, S E, *op cit*, Chapter 10.

6. Baynham, S, "Civil-military relations in post-independent Africa", *South African Defence Review*, 3/1992, p 6.

7. Huntington, S P, *The Soldier and the State*, Random House, New York, 1957.

8. Goldsworthy, D, "Civilian control of the military in black Africa", *African Affairs*, Vol 80-318, January 1981, p 56.

9. Compare the more diverse distinctions in Perlmutter, A, *The Military and Politics in Modern Times: On Professionals, Praetorians, and Revolutionary Soldiers*, New Haven, Conn, Yale University Press, 1977, pp 102-114.

10. Welch, C E Jr, "From 'Armies of Africans' to 'African Armies': The Evolution of Military Forces in Africa", in: Arlinghaus, B E and P H Baker, *op cit*, pp 22-23.

11. *Ibid*, pp 16-17.

12. *Ibid*, p 17.

13. Baynham, S, *op cit*, p 3.
14. *Ibid*, p 3.
15. Africa Institute of South Africa, *Africa at a Glance: Facts and Figures 1996/7*, Pretoria, 1996, p 91.
16. Welch, C E, *op cit*, p 18.
17. Barrows, W L, "Changing military capabilities in Black Africa", in Foltz, W J, and H S Bienen (eds), *Arms and the African — Military Influences on Africa's International Relations*, Yale University Press, New Haven, 1985, pp 116.
18. *Ibid*, p 116-117.
19. See the scholarly discussion by Welch, *op cit*, pp 18-19.
20. Compare the concept "disposition to intervene" by Finer, S E, *op cit*, pp 23-71.
21. See Nelkin, D, "The Economic and Social Setting of Military Takeovers in Africa", *Journal of Asian and African Studies* 2 (1967), pp 230-244; Thompson, W R, *The Grievances of Military Coup-Makers*, Beverly Hills, California : Sage, 1973; Wells, A, "The Coup d'Etat in Theory and Practice: Independent Black Africa in the 1960s", *American Journal of Sociology* 79 (1974), pp 871-887; Jackman, R, "The Predictability of Coups d'Etat: An Example with African Data", *American Political Science Review* 72 (1978), pp 1262-1275; and McGowan, P, "The Predictability of African Military Coups d'Etat, 1960-82 : A Replication and Extension", *Paper presented at the annual meeting of the International Studies Association*, Mexico City, 1983.
22. Baynham, S, *op cit*, p 3.
23. *Ibid*, p 4.
24. Bing, G, *Reap the Whirlwind: An Account of Kwame Nkrumah's Ghana from 1950 to 1966*, London: MacGibbon and Kee, 1968, p 418.
25. Cornwall, R, "Democratisation and security in Africa", *African Security Review*, Vol 6(5), 1997, pp 16-17.
26. *Ibid*, pp 16.
27. Baynham, S, *op cit*, p 4-5.

28. See the enlightening study by Gershoni, Y, "The changing pattern of military takeovers in sub-Saharan Africa", *Armed Forces and Society*, 23(2), Winter 1996, pp 235-248.
29. Compare International Institute for Strategic Studies, *Strategic Survey 1996/97*, Oxford University Press, London, 1997, pp 217-218.
30. Gershoni, Y, *op cit*, pp 243-245.
31. Baynham, S, *op cit*, p 12.
32. *Ibid*, p 5.
33. J Adekanye, "The politics of the post-military state in Africa", in Clapham, C, and G Philip (eds), *The Political Dilemmas of Military Regimes*, Croom Helm, London, 1985, pp 76-77.
34. Goldsworthy, D, *op cit*, p 73.
35. Welch, C E, *op cit*, pp 23-24.
36. Baynham, S, *op cit*, p 6.
37. Barrows, W L, *op cit*, p 117.
38. Goldsworthy, D, *op cit*, p 60; and Goldsworthy, D, "Armies and politics in civilian regimes", in Baynham, S (ed), *Military power and politics in black Africa*, Croom Helm, London, 1986, pp 97-128.
39. Baynham, S, *op cit*, p 8-9.
40. *Ibid*, p 9.
41. *Ibid*, p 10.
42. Barrows, W L, *op cit*, p 101.
43. Thom, W G, "Sub-Saharan Africa's Changing Military Capabilities", in Arlinghaus, B E and P H Baker, *op cit*, pp 104-105.
44. Cornwall, R, *op cit*, p 18. Compare J Mayall, *The Hopes and Fears of Independence : Africa and the World, 1960-1990*, presentation to the Conference of the Royal African Society on Sub-Saharan Africa: The Record and the Outlook, St John's College, Cambridge, 14-16 April 1991.
45. Ngari, I, "African military perspectives", *African Armed Forces*, December/January 1995, p 13. Compare Heitman, H, "Security and

Africa's armed forces at the end of the 1990s", *ISSUP Bulletin*, 4/95, Pretoria, p 14.

46. Ngari, I, *op cit*, p 12.
47. *Ibid*, p 14.
48. Barrows, W L, *op cit*, pp 106, 108.
49. *Ibid*, p 120.
50. Bienen, H, "US Foreign Policy in a Changing Africa", *Political Science Quarterly*, Fall 1980, p 444.
51. Thom, W G, *op cit*, pp 105-106.
52. *Ibid*, p 107. Compare Du Plessis, L, "A perspective on perspectives: The expanding focus of South African thinking on security", *Strategic Review for Southern Africa*, Vol XVII, No 2, November 1995, pp 35-37.
53. Jaster, R, "South Africa's Narrowing Security Options", *Adelphi Paper 159*, IISS, London, 1980, p 27.
54. Thom, W G, *op cit*, p 108. Compare the analysis in International Institute for Strategic Studies, *Strategic Survey 1996/97*, Oxford University Press, London, 1997, pp 212-224.
55. Thom, W G, *op cit*, pp 106-107.
56. "Destabilisation in Southern Africa", *Economist*, 16 July 1983, pp 19-28.
57. Arlinghaus, B E, *op cit*, pp 4-5.
58. Heitman, H, *op cit*, p 11.
59. Arlinghaus, B E, *op cit*, p 5.
60. Barrows, W L, *op cit*, pp 118-119.
61. Thom, W G, *op cit*, pp 108-109.
62. Bienen, H S, "Militaries as foreign policy actors", in Foltz, W J, and H S Bienen (eds), *op cit*, pp 169-170.
63. Heitman, H, *op cit*, p 12.
64. *Ibid*, pp 14-15.

Chapter 4

THE CHALLENGE OF EFFECTIVE SUB-SAHARAN GROUND FORCES

Deon Mortimer

1 INTRODUCTION

During the 1980s it was claimed that the majority of armed forces in the world are in reality police forces whose real purpose is domestic; that is, the control of their country's own population through involvement in domestic politics.[1]

This statement is to a large extent substantiated when sub-Saharan African armies are studied to determine their capability and role.

This chapter will classify the land forces of sub-Saharan Africa into forces capable of conducting conventional operations or capable only of internal security duties (also referred to as counter-insurgency or COIN). It will look at a typical model for land forces, compare the sub-Saharan land forces to this model and compare the forces to each other. A number of case studies will examine selected armed forces in various regions of sub-Saharan Africa in some detail. In conclusion, opinions will be expressed as to other roles these forces are capable of.

2 TYPICAL MODEL FOR CONVENTIONAL OPERATIONS

Typically, a force capable of conducting conventional operations should have the following components:[2)]

2.1 Combat forces

These are the elements which actually engage the enemy. They consist of infantry, armour, and reconnaissance elements. By means of fire and manoeuvre they close in on and destroy the enemy or alternatively prevent the enemy attaining his objectives. The three elements must be able to meet a potential enemy in respect of composition, skills, numbers and technology. An imbalance in any one of these requirements would make a successful operation very doubtful.

2.2 Combat support forces

These forces assist combat forces in attaining their objectives. Such support is typically provided by the artillery, signals, engineer and intelligence branches of armies. Artillery provide the bulk of the fire support (guns, rockets and missiles). Without this, infantry and armour will rarely succeed in an attack. Communication, provided by signals, is the nerve system of armies, and co-ordinated command and control is well-nigh impossible without good communications. Engineers breach and create obstacles; provide, maintain or destroy roads and other means of transport (for example railways, airfields, waterways). Intelligence about the enemy is one of the principal needs of commanders to enable them to plan successfully to defeat the enemy.

2.3 Combat service support

No force can operate without food, petroleum, oils, lubricants, ammunition and other supplies. A logistic support is as important as combat forces themselves. It includes supply, repair and medical services. In addition certain personnel services are called for, such as those provided by military police and chaplains.

A major shortcoming in the provision of any of the above elements is usually fatal to the conduct of successful field operations.[3]

2.4 Base support

To back-up the field force, a base organisation is needed to provide training, medical support, accommodation and a logistics system for base echelon maintenance of arms, transportation, fighting vehicles, etc. Shortcomings here will mean that an army has a very limited capacity to operate in terms of time — weeks and perhaps months but certainly not years.

2.5 Air and naval co-operation

Ground forces are very dependent on air support. The minimum expected from an air force is to create a favourable situation, i.e. one in which the enemy air force cannot operate freely. Close air support, interdiction, reconnaissance and transportation are all of immense importance to ground forces. If one party has these facilities and the other does not, chances of success for the latter are very limited — for example, Iraq in the Gulf War. Ground and naval co-operation is more restricted, but transportation and amphibious operations are two ways in which army and navy can co-operate. Naval co-operation is generally less critical but is at times essential to successful land operations.

With regard to the required operational capabilities, Barber states that "(a) determination of the operational tasks to be accomplished is an essential component of a relevant national security policy. A nation needs to develop military force capability to perform those operational tasks that are appropriate to its situation and its perception of threats. The selection of types, scopes and emphases of operational tasks exerts a strong influence on the types, sizes and costs of military forces and combat systems".[4] Where threats are primarily perceived as domestic, military forces have to be structured and equipped to meet them, and co-ordination between military forces and other domestic security agencies such as the police will be required.

Sub-Saharan African ground forces therefore have to be analysed and compared not only in quantitative or qualitative terms, but also in terms of the missions that they are capable of undertaking.

3 ORIGIN OF SUB-SAHARAN ARMIES

The majority of sub-Saharan armies have developed from colonial armed forces. Raised by colonial powers, they had largely a police and internal security function. The historical legacy is thus that it is acceptable for armies to be involved in internal operations. During the two world wars, colonial powers raised forces which were involved in conventional operations. For example, the war in German East Africa was fought mainly between black African troops raised respectively in Germany and Britain.[5] (Indian, British and South African troops were also involved at times.) During the Second World War, Britain again raised African units for conventional warfare — for example, the 81st and 82nd West African Divisions in the Gold Coast (Ghana) and Nigeria, and the 11th East African Division in Somaliland, Kenya, Uganda, Tanganyika (Tanzania), Nyasaland (Malawi) and Northern Rhodesia (Zambia). The three divisions operated successfully in Burma against the Japanese.[6] After the war, these conventional forces were demobilised and the situation returned, by and large, to the pre-war one — i.e. forces raised largely for internal security duties. Colonial forces in the French and Portuguese empires exhibited a similar history.

4 SUB-SAHARAN ARMIES COMPARED TO THE TYPICAL MODEL

Even a relatively superficial study leaves no doubt that the armies of the majority of states have little capacity for offensive operations. Even their defensive capabilities must be considered doubtful. Many of them are small (18 states of 44, i.e. 41 per cent, have a personnel strength of less than 7 000) and they are ill-equipped.[7] Even such equipment as they have is of doubtful utility because of problems of maintenance and supply. A study of national infrastructure reveals little capacity to help the military maintain equipment. For example, an underdeveloped telecommunication system indicates an inability to repair, maintain or install military communication networks and equipment; inadequate roads, railways and waterways indicate that it will be difficult, and slow, to deploy even such forces as exist; and a widespread absence of an arms industry indicates the lack of a sustainable military effort, as foreign military suppliers are notorious for terminating supplies in times of need. The lack of organisational balance is related to a fragmented military ability. A typical example is the existence of parachute forces in the army without a corresponding transport capability in the air force. Add to this obsolete equipment, and a picture of forces capable of very limited conventional operations emerges.

5 COMPARATIVE ANALYSIS OF SELECTED ARMIES

Very little information is available about the logistic capabilities of sub-Saharan forces. It should be noted that no matter how low a force is rated, if its opponent is even weaker it may have a significant capability — it is relative strength that counts.[8] Defence expenditure has therefore been reduced to a *per capita* figure — i.e. the expenditure per member of the total armed forces, active component only. High *per capita* figures indicate probable high technology and high expenditure on training and maintenance of equipment. It can also of course indicate well-paid troops and high expenditure on the purchase of equipment. It is only a rough guide but it does have relevance, as a study of the figures of known high technology and well-trained and maintained forces, *vis-à-vis* those at the other end of the scale will indicate. *Per capita* defence expenditure is shown for each sub-Saharan African country in the *Appendix*. This illustrates the trend but also shows the obvious exceptions to the general rule — i.e. countries with relatively high *per capita* expenditure but with small, ill-equipped forces and *vice versa*.

Case studies will investigate seven of the larger and better equipped armies, including one each from West, East, Central and Southern Africa. Each of the regions also has other armies worthy of study (for example, Tanzania in East Africa) but, for the sake of brevity, only one has been chosen per region (with the exception of Southern Africa). The countries selected are Nigeria, Kenya, Cameroon and South Africa. In addition to these, three further case studies have been included: Zimbabwe, because it is a relatively powerful army in the Southern African Development Community (SADC); and Namibia and Botswana, as these two neighbours are roughly in the same category (population, gross domestic product (GDP) and development) but are following very different defence policies. The larger defence expenditure of Botswana is producing a more capable force for that country. These different approaches by neighbours are important and are therefore analysed in more detail.

In Chapter 1 a framework was developed relating to both the military and the non-military factors that should be considered when determining military power and potential. This chapter is aimed at answering a specific question, namely: Is a particular army capable of conventional operations and is it capable of internal security (or COIN) operations? Thus not all the factors will be taken into consideration. The selected non-military factors are population; GDP; area; road density; railways and ports; civil aviation assets; airfields; waterways (where present);

telecommunications, and economic development (major imports, major exports, major industries, agriculture and arms industry). The following military factors have been selected; namely, defence expenditure; active strength of the total armed forces; defence expenditure *per capita* of the members of the armed forces, and army strength. The ground forces are then discussed in more detail by looking at major formations and units; principal equipment; higher military training establishments, and recent operational and peace-keeping experience. This is followed by an analysis of the respective military capability of each of the countries included in the case studies.

5.1 West Africa: Nigeria

Nigeria has a well-developed system of higher military training establishments, including the Nigerian Defence Academy, the National War College and the Command and Staff College.[9]

The Nigerian military has considerable peace support experience, including deployment in Angola, Bosnia, Croatia and Iraq/Kuwait — in all, 23 deployments since 1960, mainly as part of observer missions.[10] Recent operational experience includes deployment in Liberia (9 000 troops) and Sierra Leone (10 000 troops), nominally in a peace support role, but especially in the latter case and as part of the Economic Community of West African States Monitoring Group (ECOMOG) force, to reinstate the civilian government overthrown in a military *coup*.

Nigeria's army is one of the very few in Africa organised at the divisional level, although operationally it has deployed at battalion level. From a study of available equipment it would seem that the armoured and mechanised brigades are not very well served with either tanks or armoured personnel carriers (APCs), although up to 200 BMP-2 infantry combat vehicles (ICVs) are reported to be in service. On the other hand, the number of guns available indicates a well-equipped force, especially in respect of 105mm and 122mm categories. Air defence is not of the same standard but has some good armament (ZSU 23 - 4 and SAMs). Some of the equipment for the reconnaissance battalions is good (Fox and Cascavel) but the AMLs are largely obsolescent. There is not enough information available about the engineers and their equipment to be able to comment.

The Nigerian ground forces represent a reasonably well-organised and equipped force that should be capable of conventional operations. There are, however, shortcomings: with a budget cut of 50 per cent between 1996 and 1997 and a consequent low *per capita* defence expenditure of $10 390 it is probable that serviceability has declined and that training has suffered. (There is, however, an impressive training structure of military schools and colleges.) The amphibious brigade would indicate that Nigeria has the capability of transporting its forces for operations at a distance — i.e. that it has reach. But a study indicates that the navy does not have operational equipment for this role. Nigeria has however deployed troops in Liberia and Sierra Leone, which does exhibit a capability to project power. The parachute force is relatively small (a battalion) and is not capable of significant operations. There is a considerable civil air capacity for moving troops.

The civilian infrastructure of Nigeria should be able to support its armed forces in operations, but the arms industry (the Defence Industries Corporation)[11] seems to be elementary. With its considerable mining sector, there should be a developed engineering industry to back-up defence needs. However, without specific evidence to the contrary, it would appear that the armed forces are not capable of conducting conventional operations for any prolonged period; but they are adjudged fully COIN-capable. In spite of the negative comments, Nigeria has one of the most noteworthy armies in sub-Saharan Africa.

5.2 Central Africa: Cameroon

When the available military equipment in Cameroon is compared to the order of battle, certain discrepancies emerge. It is for instance difficult to envisage the available air defence equipment being distributed among six batteries. The armoured car battalion in the Presidential Guard must be somewhat underequipped even if all armoured vehicles are assigned to it. A significant item of weaponry is the four SA343 L HOT-equipped helicopters; and the air force appears to have sufficient aircraft for the deployment of the airborne/commando battalion. There does not appear to be any field headquarters above the unit level. Accordingly, employing a brigade-sized field force might present problems, although the military regional headquarters might be able to take on this role. The ability of the army to maintain and service its equipment must be in some doubt due to the relatively low budget, especially when expressed as a *per capita* figure. The national infrastructure does not appear to provide any major engineering industry to act in support of the armed forces. There is no known arms industry. The air force has an adequate transport component (although it would operate under similar maintenance constraints), but basically the army does not have any major capability for operating outside national boundaries.

Divisions between the inhabitants of north and south, and between those using French and those using English, are probably reflected in the armed forces and presumably lead to a partially divided military. Cameroon has been involved in border disputes with Nigeria, at times leading to violence (for example, February 1994). Overall its army does not appear to be a match for that of its very large neighbour, Nigeria. It is probably not capable of conventional operations but can conduct COIN operations. The nature of the economy is such that, should the armed forces conduct conventional operations, they would be able to do so only for a very limited period.

5.3 East Africa: Kenya

Kenya has a higher military training establishment in the form of the Kenya Defence Staff College, and has considerable peace support experience — in Namibia, Angola, Croatia, Iraq/Kuwait and Liberia.[12]

The Kenyan army appears to be underequipped in several areas. The number of tanks is insufficient for three armoured battalions, although one is possibly a reconnaissance rather than an armoured battalion. There are enough vehicles for such a reconnaissance unit, though the AMS 60/90 must be considered obsolescent. The available artillery (no medium guns) seems to be insufficient for the three brigades, but possibly the 120mm mortars are used in this role. The force is weak in air defence equipment which is limited in range and hitting power. While the engineering allocation looks inadequate, the engineers do have a bridge-building capability. There appears to be no field headquarters higher than brigade level; consequently the ability of the force to operate at divisional level must be in doubt.

One striking feature of the army is the air cavalry battalion — thought it is not clear whether the aircraft are provided by the air force or the army (sources differ). However, it is a potent force in the sub-Saharan context, with 11 Hughes 500MD with TOW; 8 Hughes 500ME and 15 Hughes 500M. In addition there is a respectable transport fleet (9 IAR 330, 3 SA342). If well used this helicopter force could be of great value on any battlefield. The L118 105mm light gun is said to be air portable by helicopter. But the air force seems to be underequipped for transporting an airborne battalion. The army and armed forces have a limited ability to operate at a distance — limited reach — because of a lack of air and sea transportation assets. However Kenya has borders with five countries, which gives it reach in a geographical sense. The low road density indicates that large-scale movements within the country would be slow.

The standard of individual training is by all indications good. There are, however, ethnic strains in the armed forces, with tribalism evident. This, one would expect, would negatively influence efficiency.[13] The low *per capita* defence expenditure places a question mark over serviceability of equipment, and economic development seems to be such that the economy can probably give only limited support to the armed forces. Consequently any conventional operations would have to be of short duration. There is no known arms industry, but the country has been involved in discussions to purchase a munitions plant (small arms ammunition) from Belgium. To sum up, a force capable of limited conventional operations and the full spectrum of COIN operations.

5.4 Southern Africa

5.4.1 Namibia

The Namibian Defence Force is newly constituted (established in 1989). There do not appear to be field headquarters above unit level, and it is not a well-equipped force. The equipment that it has is obsolescent and probably expensive to maintain, both financially and in terms of manpower. There appears to be a complete lack of guns for fire support, and the anti-tank and air defence equipment is outdated. The acquisition of 23mm anti-aircraft guns mounted on vehicles has, however, recently been reported. Although the *per capita* defence expenditure is relatively low, the army is very lightly equipped, and so it might be sufficient. Namibia has some experience of peace support operations in Angola.

It has a limited capacity for the manufacture of APCs (the Wolf) and has reportedly ordered a number.[14] No doubt other armoured vehicles (for example, reconnaissance vehicles) could be successfully manufactured. With its existing engineering capability, civilian industry can give limited support to the armed forces, in the form of light armoured vehicles and in general transport manufacture and maintenance. However, it is unlikely that any prolonged conventional type operations could be conducted, although a limited COIN capacity exists.

5.4.2 Botswana

Officers of the Botswana Defence Force attend staff training courses in Egypt, Kenya, the United Kingdom and Zimbabwe. Experience in peace support operations has also been gained in Somalia, Mozambique and Rwanda.[15]

The Botswana Defence Force was formed in 1977. It is a relatively balanced force and is reportedly to expand to 10 000 personnel. It is, in sub-Saharan Africa terms, well funded at $33 066 *per capita*, the highest in the region. The force is at present a purchaser of major equipment which would partially account for this; F5s have, for instance, been purchased for the air wing.[16] Botswana is definitely in the market for tanks: an earlier attempt to buy Leopard 1s from the Netherlands was blocked by Germany.[17] It will be interesting to see whether a relatively high expenditure *per capita* continues; if it does it would indicate that equipment purchased is being maintained in a serviceable condition. The equipment is not over-generous for two brigades. For example, only three batteries are available (if the 120 mm mortars are considered a battery) and each brigade would have only two infantry battalions. Engineers too, seem to be in short supply (one battalion for the two brigades). However, the envisaged expansion to 10 000 men may be aimed at making provision for these shortcomings. The state of training appears to be good, with the United States and the United Kingdom reported as being involved, *inter alia*, in combined training exercises within Botswana. The national economy does not seem capable of lending much support to the armed forces; consequently any possible conventional (or, more likely, semi-conventional) operations would presumably be of short duration. A force capable of COIN operations and very limited conventional operations.

5.4.3 Zimbabwe

Zimbabwe has a higher military training establishment in the form of the Zimbabwe Staff College, which conducts both junior and senior (joint) command and staff courses.[18]

The Zimbabwean army was formed in 1980, and has been deployed in Mozambique to protect the Beira Corridor against former RENAMO dissidents. As for peace support operations, it sent a battalion to Angola and Somalia, and observers to Rwanda, Mozambique and Angola.[19]

Zimbabwe is, within the Southern Africa sub-region, a country of note in terms of GDP, defence expenditure, and defence expenditure *per capita* of the armed forces. Even in the larger sub-Saharan region, its defence expenditure is noteworthy (fourth, after Botswana, South Africa and Nigeria). In addition Zimbabwe has, in African terms, a well-developed infrastructure and economy. All these facts mean that militarily it is a country with considerable potential, but also at present with severe monetary problems. Looking at the armed forces, more particularly the army, the potential is not quite realised. The mechanised brigade is lightly equipped and organised: an armoured company (there is sufficient equipment available) instead of the expected battalion; with one mechanised infantry battalion (again there is sufficient equipment) instead of the expected two. The artillery organisation (two battalions) is insufficient for a force of five brigades (i.e. excluding the Presidential Guard brigade) and there are insufficient guns to equip the two battalions (sufficient for only two gun- and two mortar batteries). There is a surfeit of multiple rocket launchers (MRLs) but these cannot really make up for the deficiency in guns (because of differing characteristics). There also appears to be a shortage of engineers for the required (at least) five battalions. The air force's 11 CASA 212-200 transport aircraft do not have sufficient capacity to lift a parachute battalion (in practice probably not more than approximately two light companies). There is thus little "reach".

Zimbabwe Defence Industries is a government-owned munition and filling operation. Ammunition up to 19 mm can be produced, and mortar bombs (60, 81 and 120 mm) are cast and filled. There are also clothing and webbing manufacturing facilities. A contract has reportedly been placed with Plessey for a new communications system, and it is intended to produce much of the equipment internally. Zimbabwean heavy industrial and engineering concerns collaborate in weapons production.[20]

The army is underequipped for its organisational composition. On the other hand, with a small arms industry and a relatively well-developed industrial base, the economy should be able to give the armed forces some support during operations. The army is consequently adjudged as being capable of limited conventional operations and the full spectrum of COIN.

A recent report, however, suggested that much of the military equipment is unserviceable or unreliable. A reduction of military personnel is also under consideration.[21]

5.4.4 South Africa

South Africa has a well-developed system of higher military training establishments, including a Military Academy, a SA Defence College, and colleges for each of the four service arms.

The South African (SA) army is a force integrated from members of the former *Umkhonto we Sizwe* (MK); African People's Liberation Army (APLA); the armies of the former Transkei, Bophuthatswana, Venda and Ciskei (TBVC) and the South African army. These forces have varying experience. Of the three, the former South African army had the most experience of semi-conventional and conventional warfare (in Angola), while certain MK units had some; the SA army also engaged widely, the TBVC armies to a limited extent, in COIN operations; and MK and APLA participated in insurgency. In the process of integration, large numbers of experienced personnel have left the army, and in the pending rationalisation more will probably do so. The army has an on-going internal security role and is constantly involved in operational deployment in both rural and urban areas. It has developed (and kept current) an own doctrine of land warfare which it disseminates to units and individuals through a well-developed system of basic military training, schools, colleges and field training facilities.

The army has no experience of peace support operations, although it has participated in training exercises for them in Zimbabwe.

Of the countries included in the case studies, only South Africa maintains a system of organised reserves. It comprises two forces, the Citizen Force (with units principally allocated to conventional forces but some to COIN duties), and the Commandos (all of them for rear area protection, which includes COIN duties). These two forces were, in the past, fed by a system of conscription applied to young white males who, after two years' service with the regular forces, were transferred to one of them. There were also volunteers who either joined *ab initio* or extended their compulsory service likewise in one or other of them. Since 1994 government policy has discontinued conscription (although the *Defence Act* still makes provision for it) and the Citizen Force and Commandos are now manned by volunteers only. In practical terms this means that very few units are at strength and thus would not be able to carry out their operational tasks. When it is further taken into account that, having volunteered, the individual cannot (in terms of present policy) be forced to report if called up, it is apparent that the system is not trustworthy. But, the SA National Defence Force (SANDF) is eager to maintain it; and once the present rationalisation phase has ended, and should the government commit itself to an even (over a number of years) budget, it is expected that the organised reserves will once again operate efficiently.

The SANDF has been functioning under a constantly decreasing budget since the early 1990s, which has negatively affected planning. Until rationalisation has been completed (in the next three years) this state of uncertainty will probably continue. The total force is to be cut from 95 000 to some 75 000 active (full-time) members,[22] and much experience will be lost. At the same time units are being closed down, equipment is being phased out and the amalgamation of units and functions is being planned. It is in fact a major re-organisation of the SANDF and of the army in particular, and it will inevitably have a marked effect on morale, organisation and efficiency. As in all re-organisations, the intention is to emerge more efficient, "leaner and meaner". How successful this will be remains to be seen. In addition, the integration of the former MK, APLA, TBVC armies and the former South African Defence Force (SADF) has to be coped with. The army has integrated the greatest number of personnel; and the administrative aspect of integration, although beset with problems, has been relatively successful. However the process of truly becoming a single like-minded organisation, in which the vast majority of personnel feel comfortable and accepted, has a long way to go. It is unlikely that integration will be able to make real progress until rationalisation is completed. It will probably take years.

The South African economy is capable of giving the armed forces considerable support. The country had a well-developed arms industry, but it has been very negatively affected by the major cuts in defence expenditure. Nevertheless, it still has the capacity to manufacture weapons (from 155 mm guns down to small arms); to produce most (if not all) types of ammunition (bombs, shells, cartridges) needed; and to produce armoured vehicles (light, medium, heavy) and most of the electronic equipment called for. (There is also a considerable aviation and naval arms industry.) But without foreign sales the industry will continue to shrink; and given an international industry with similar problems, selling abroad is no easy task. However, in sub-Saharan Africa there is no other arms industry approaching South Africa's.

The *per capita* expenditure indicates that most equipment should be maintained in a serviceable condition, although not without difficulty. Further cuts in the budget (such as that envisioned for the financial year 1998/99 (to R9,201 billion from R9,5 billion) might have a negative influence on serviceability.[23] A major purchasing programme is planned (mainly for the air force and navy). One of the objectives of rationalisation is to increase funds available for capital expenditure from 18 per cent to 30 per cent of the budget.[24] A smaller personnel strength will also free more funds for maintenance.

When the equipment of the army is compared with the formal organisation, it appears that the units can be equipped according to requirements. Although little information is available, it is believed that the army engineers are well provided with bridges – including vehicle-launched assault bridges – mine breaching equipment and common engineering plant. One area of vulnerability in the army is air defence equipment; adequate mobile anti-aircraft guns and missiles are lacking. The tanks, although adequate, should be replaced if at all possible. The Ratel ICV is approaching the end of its life and should also be replaced, by approximately the year 2005. The parachute brigade (with both active and reserve units) is capable of airborne assault operations of limited size. The air force has a significant transport capability.

To summarise, the South African army is a force with good equipment (in African terms) and with adequate support from the economy and the arms industry. On the down side, it is a force, both full-time and part-time, undergoing major restructuring with consequent negative results. A further negative factor is the failure of the government to support defence policy with an adequate and stable financial allocation.

The force is adjudged to be equipped and organised for conventional operations, even if it is not capable of conducting them at present. It should, with a reasonably short period of training, be able to attain again its former expertise in this field. In spite of present shortcomings, it is the most capable of sub-Saharan conventional forces. It is also fully capable of carrying out COIN operations.

6 CONCLUSION

There are in reality very few "armies" in sub-Saharan Africa. The vast majority are what Cline called "police forces", whose true task is the control of their own population.[25] Even the few that are capable of conventional operations ("true armies") have a limited capability.

One of the principal problems of sub-Saharan armies is in the logistic field. The technical ability to use, and especially maintain, equipment is restricted; and generally little financial provision seems to be made for carrying out the function of logistics.

If African countries really wish to develop a conventional capability, they will have to accept the costs not only of raising and equipping but also of maintaining a suitable force. Whether there is any real need for such a capability is, of course, a question worthy of debate. In view of the relative absence of interstate warfare in the sub-Saharan region and of the relative frequency of intra-state conflict, "police armies" are probably what most states need; but determining the needs of particular states is a study of a different nature. (An example of one is the analysis by Brian MacDonald.[26] MacDonald, in answering the question "how much is too much?", studies a number of countries in the sub-Saharan region, including Zimbabwe and Kenya. By means of a strategic threat analysis, he determines the force needed in order to answer the question posed.) This chapter has, as already stated, looked at a force in the light of organisation, equipment and budget against the background of the national infrastructure and economy in order to determine what type of force a country has and to venture an opinion on its probable effectiveness.

A role that sub-Saharan armies have often accepted is that of peace support operations, in conjunction with the United Nations and with regional bodies (e.g. Economic Community of West African States). This provides valuable experience in both command and control, and should lead to less violent internal security operations within national territory — since these two types of operation have similarities. With so much emphasis being placed on peace support, one can expect further contributions from sub-Saharan armies in this context in future. Much effort is spent on training; it often involves other armies, and this should contribute to a general raising of the standard of the forces that participate.

Sub-Saharan armies also have what is called by the South African Department of Defence "collateral utility". This term encompasses tasks for which they are suited but which are not usually considered when designing, organising and equipping fighting forces. They can vary from flood relief, providing water in times of drought, aid in health campaigns — for example, vaccination and inoculation — and adult education. The list is almost endless. Many African armies are involved in such tasks and, in the light of experience even in developed nations, will continue to be.

Because of Africa's underdevelopment, another role is precisely in the field of development. Ngari, for instance, sees an educative and social function for armed forces, in that the personnel who pass through them should leave them as better citizens. Military service should lead to the acquisition of skills and moral values and to intellectual growth.[27] A further developmental role can be the integration of diverse ethnic and racial groups into a national whole. But this is a difficult balancing act; if it is not well managed, divisions may be aggravated. However it is generally accepted that when the groups are brought together under controlled conditions — when members of one can meet those of another — mutual confidence can be built. To what extent this ideal is being achieved in sub-Saharan armies (and armed forces as a whole) is an open question. It should remain an objective.

REFERENCES

1. Cline, R S, *World Power Trends and US Foreign Policy for the 1980s*, Westview Press, Boulder, Colorado, 1980, p 121.

2. Barber, W E, "National Security Policy", in Louw, M H H, *National Security: A Modern Approach*, Institute for Strategic Studies, University of Pretoria, 1978, pp 60-61.

3. *African Defence*, December 1990.

4. Barber, W E, *op cit*, p 60.

5. Moyse-Bartlett, H, *The King's African Rifles*, Gale and Polden Ltd, Aldershol, 1956, pp 412-415.

6. Slim, F M Sir William, *Defeat into Victory*, Cassel and Company Ltd, London, 1956, pp 165-166; p 353; and pp 458-459.

7. The figure of 7 000 (the strength of the armed forces of Botswana) was chosen as the Botswana Defence Force is an example of a small but well-equipped defence force with a satisfactory *per capita* defence expenditure.

8. "Of Guns and Diamonds - Sierra Leone", *Strategy African Defence*, Vol 2, Issue 3, illustrates this well. The government forces had, among other equipment, only one Mi-24E helicopter and two BMP.2 armoured infantry fighting vehicles available. This was, however, a markedly superior force when compared to the insurgents whose inventory included one 60 mm mortar (no

ammunition), one 12,7 mm and one 14,5 mm heavy machine gun (latter reportedly inoperable).

9. Malan, M, et al, *African Capabilities for Peace Operations*, ISS Monograph Series, No 17, Nov 1997, pp 84-89.
10. *Ibid*, pp 88-83.
11. "Nigeria's Rapid Deployment Force: How Viable?", *African Defence*, December 1989.
12. Malan, M, et al, *op cit*, pp 33-34; and 37-39.
13. "Kenya - A Presidential Army?", *Africa Confidential*, Vol 36, No 9, 28 April 1995.
14. *African Armed Forces Journal*, September 1997, "Sitrep".
15. Malan, M, et al, *op cit*, pp 107-108.
16. *African Armed Forces Journal*, September 1995, "Sitrep".
17. "Balked Botswana deal stirs MBT market", *Strategy Africa Defence*, Volume 2, Issue 3.
18. Malan, M, et al, *op cit*, pp 45-49.
19. *Ibid*.
20. "ZDI - Zimbabwe Defence Industries", *African Armed Forces Journal*, June 1995.
21. *Business Day* (Johannesburg), 8 May 1998.
22. "Transformation: A New Structure?", RSA, *Department of Defence Bulletin*, No 82/97, 9 December 1997.
23. *Ibid*.
24. *Ibid*.
25. In this regard see the views expressed by General I Ngari to a seminar on defence equipment co-operation. In discussing the reasons for the establishment of armed forces, he lays emphasis on this internal security role. It should be noted that he continues to propagate a development role while also stating a conventional role. See Ngari, I, "African Military Perspectives", *African Armed Forces Journal*, Dec/Jan 1995, pp 12-14.
26. MacDonald, B S, *Military Spending in Developing Countries: How much is too much?*, Carleton University Press, Ottawa, 1997.
27. Ngari, I, *op cit*, p 14.

APPENDIX:
SUB-SAHARAN *PER CAPITA* DEFENCE EXPENDITURE: 1997

(Arranged lowest to highest, US dollars)

Guinea Bissau	864	Mali	5 986
Ethiopia	1 058	Senegal	6 217
Chad	1 449	Central African Republic	6 666
Madagascar	1 571	Burkina Faso	6 900
Rwanda	1 661	Côte d'Ivoire	7 842
Eritrea	1 739	Kenya	8 471
Equatorial Guinea	1 742	Mauritius	8 888
Sudan	2 007	Cameroon	10 316
Djibouti	2 395	Nigeria	10 389
Angola	2 669	Mozambique	12 857
Burundi	2 727	Namibia	13 103
Tanzania	2 752	Zimbabwe	13 457
Uganda	2 884	Lesotho	16 500
Zambia	2 963	Gambia	18 750
Cape Verde	3 636	Ghana	18 714
Togo	4 317	South Africa	22 015
Niger	4 339	Seychelles	25 000
Malawi	5 600	Gabon	25 106
Guinea	5 670	Botswana	33 066
Benin	5 883		

The following countries have not been included in this table due to insufficient data: Congo Brazzaville, Congo Kinshasa, Liberia, Sierra Leone, Somalia. The figures have been calculated using the formula: Defence Budget (or expenditure) ÷ Total Active Strength of Armed Forces.

Source: Based on: International Institute for Strategic Studies, *The Military Balance 1997/98*, Oxford University Press, London, 1997.

Chapter 5

THE CHALLENGE OF EFFECTIVE AIR POWER IN SUB-SAHARAN AFRICA

Michael Hough

1 INTRODUCTION

It has been stated that for any independent state wishing to protect itself against external threats, air power will have to be capable of performing the following minimum tasks:

- surveillance and intelligence gathering
- deterrence of aggression
- capability for rapid reaction
- protection of economic zones of interest
- aid to the civil power
- defence of national air space
- ability to operate independently
- capability for joint operations with other forces
- international peace-keeping operations
- international humanitarian activities
- the training of friendly forces

Underpinning these would be mobility; sustainability; command, control and communications; and research and development.[1]

The comparative emphasis placed by any nation on these components will of course depend on a number of variables, including the nature of threats, terrain, human resources, and the political, economic and technological situation that prevails. Air force design can also not be separated from broader defence policy, military strategy and force design.

In the African context, it has been stated that the predominantly domestic nature of threats against African states; the relatively low risk of interstate armed conflict; and the vulnerability of African states to non-military threats, are some of the key factors that impact on the requirements for and application of air power.[2]

The first area of impact is on conventional military (and specifically air power) capabilities, which may need to be adapted to the fact that conflict in Africa tends to be primarily domestic, and that financial constraints necessitate affordable and realistic capability goals. The second area of impact is the collateral utilisation of air power. The increased prominence of domestic security concerns, implies that greater importance be attached to these roles. Third, the idea of collective security and regional co-operation should be taken into account in planning.[3]

Also to be taken into account is that domestic conflict in Africa is increasingly involving neighbouring states (for example, Angola's intervention in Congo Brazzaville), and hence the line between domestic and interstate conflict is blurred.

In the following analyses, an overview of the historical development of air power in selected countries in sub-Saharan Africa is given; followed by an analysis of contemporary air power in sub-Saharan Africa with specific emphasis on combat capability. The chapter concludes with a discussion of secondary roles and regional co-operation as far as air forces are concerned. The emphasis is predominantly on military air power.

2 HISTORICAL DEVELOPMENT: AN OVERVIEW

It has been stated that the role of air power has expanded in African countries since independence, due to the vast distances involved and physical obstacles such as rivers and deserts, as well as a lack of a proper road infrastructure.[4]

While many African countries such as Nigeria and Sudan attempted to diversify the obtaining of equipment, others were linked almost exclusively to a single source, as is the case with for instance Libya. The legacy of equipment from the colonial era was supplemented by equipment which in some cases reflected changing political allegiances. Ethiopia shifted during the 1970s from a predominant United States (US) supply to Soviet equipment. Multiplicity of sources can of course create logistic and maintenance problems, while relying on a single supplier can create the problem of continued assistance if political allegiances change.[5]

During the 1980s, older aircraft acquired at independence were supplemented by "second-line" aircraft. Countries such as Mozambique and Tanzania received MiG-21 and MiG-17 aircraft, and the Northrop F-5 fighter was supplied to Kenya, Sudan, Morocco and Ethiopia. Countries such as Algeria and Libya, and eventually also Angola, obtained more advanced aircraft such as the MiG-23 and MiG-25, due to political considerations and the ability in some cases to pay in hard currency.[6]

A selection of case studies, representing some of the larger air forces in sub-Saharan Africa, gives some indication of the historical development of African air forces as set out above.

2.1 Angola

Following the withdrawal of the Portuguese in November 1975 with the granting of independence to Angola, the People's Air and Air Defence Force of Angola (FAPA/DAA) was established in January 1976 with some of the aircraft abandoned by the Portuguese Air Force and eight MiG-21 MFs supplied by the Soviet Union. The last remaining airworthy ex-Portuguese Fiat G91R 4s were withdrawn from service by the mid-eighties. Some Alouette III's left by the Portuguese, however, remained in service.[7]

The civil war in Angola affected recruitment and force development in the FAPA/DAA. In this context, it was stated:

> These unusual circumstances affected both recruitment and force development. FAPA/DAA's pilots, mostly in their mid-twenties, got combat experience immediately. Moreover, given FAPA/DAA's virtually instantaneous creation, its long-term dependence on external assistance was inevitable. Soviet, Cuban, and other communist forces provided pilots and technicians to fly and maintain FAPA/DAA's growing, diversified, and increasingly complex air fleet. The principal tasks of this new branch of the Angolan military were to protect the capital, guard major cities and military installations in the south against South African air raids, and extend the air defence network and combat operations southward to confront UNITA forces and South African invaders.[8]

2.2 Nigeria

The Nigerian Air Force was established in 1964 with West German assistance. Initially, Dornier DO27s and two Nortatlases were supplied, as well as Piaggio P149D trainers and LET L29 Delfins supplied by Czechoslovakia.[9]

The civil war of the 1960s led to considerable expansion of the air force, and included the delivery of MiG-17s, MiG-15 UTIs and

Iluyshin I128 bombers. The latter were flown by Egyptian crews seconded to Nigeria. Subsequent deliveries included MiG-21J fighters; and 24 Alpha jet trainers in the 1980s. Apart from Europe and the Middle East, Nigeria is also one of the few countries to purchase and operate the BAC Jaguar obtained from Great Britain.[10]

By 1990 Nigeria ranked eighth among African states in the number of combat aircraft. Budgetary constraints had, however, started limiting air force procurements. Currently the serviceability of most combat aircraft and armed helicopters in Nigeria is in doubt.[11]

3 CONTEMPORARY AIR POWER IN SUB-SAHARAN AFRICA

Contemporary air power in sub-Saharan Africa will be discussed by means of a comparative table (Table 1) indicating features such as combat aircraft and personnel. This is followed by a selection of case studies pertaining to the role and expansion of air forces in sub-Saharan Africa, and examples of the operational application of air power in conflict situations.

From the comparison, it appears that only Angola, Nigeria, Sudan, South Africa, and to some extent Zimbabwe, have relatively modern air forces in the sub-Saharan African context. In the case of, for instance, Nigeria and Sudan, the serviceability of some aircraft is, however, in doubt. In some other cases, the serviceability of all aircraft (for example Congo, Togo and Guinea) is in doubt.

The problem of serviceability is also exemplified in Table 2. In certain cases (as has for instance been reported regarding South Africa) some equipment has also been moth-balled due to a lack of funds to deploy it.

TABLE I:
AIR POWER IN SUB-SAHARAN AFRICA: 1997*

Country	Combat aircraft and attack helicopters	Main supplier/ maker of combat aircraft	Personnel	Relative modernity of air force	Serviceability of aircraft
Angola	27 combat aircraft (MiG-21 MF, MiG-23, SU-22, SU-25) 26 attack helicopters (MI25/35, SA-365M, SA-342)	Soviet Union/Russia	11 000	Yes	In doubt
Benin	No combat aircraft		150	No	In doubt
Botswana	38 combat aircraft (F5-A, F5-B)	Canada	500	No	Yes
Burkina Faso	5 combat-capable trainers	Italy	200	No	Yes
Burundi	6 combat-capable trainers	Italy	100	No	Yes
Cameroon	15 combat aircraft (Alpha Jet, CM-170, MB-326) 4 attack helicopters (SA-342L)	France/Germany	300	No	Some doubt
Central African Republic	No combat aircraft		150	No	Yes
Chad	4 combat-capable trainers	Italy/Switzerland	350	No	Yes
Congo	12 combat aircraft (MiG-21)	Soviet Union/Russia	1 200	No	In doubt
Côte D'Ivoire	5 combat aircraft (Alpha Jet)	France/Germany	700	No	Some doubt
Democratic Republic of Congo	Following the civil war in 1997, only some helicopters remain operational				Some doubt

The challenge of effective air power in sub-Saharan Africa

Country	Combat aircraft and attack helicopters	Main supplier/ maker of combat aircraft	Personnel	Relative modernity of air force	Serviceability of aircraft
Djibouti	No combat aircraft		200	No	Yes
Equatorial Guinea	No combat aircraft		100	No	Yes
Eritrea	6 combat-capable trainers	Italy		No	Yes
Ethiopia	85 combat aircraft (MiG-21MF, MiG-23BN, MiG-27 and F-5) 18 attack helicopters (Mi-24)	Soviet Union/Russia and US		Yes	Some doubt
Gabon	9 combat aircraft (Mirage 5) 7 combat-capable trainers 5 attack helicopters (SA-342)	France	1 000	No	Yes
Ghana	15 combat-capable trainers	Czech Republic	1 000	No	Yes
Guinea	8 combat aircraft (MiG-17F, MiG-21)	Soviet Union/Russia	800	No	In doubt
Guinea-Bissau	3 combat aircraft (MiG-17)	Soviet Union/Russia	100	No	Yes
Kenya	30 combat aircraft (F-5) 34 attack helicopters (Hughes 500 MD, ME and M)	US	2 500	No	Yes
Madagascar	12 combat aircraft (MiG-17F, MiG-21FL)	Soviet Union/Russia	500	No	Yes
Malawi	No combat aircraft		80	No	Yes

Country	Combat aircraft and attack helicopters	Main supplier/ maker of combat aircraft	Personnel	Relative modernity of air force	Serviceability of aircraft
Mali	16 combat aircraft (MiG-17F, MiG-21)	Soviet Union/Russia	400	No	Some doubt
Mozambique	43 combat aircraft (MiG-21) 4 attack helicopters (Mi-24)	Soviet Union/Russia	1 000	No	Some doubt
Namibia	No combat aircraft			No	Yes
Niger	No combat aircraft		100	No	Yes
Nigeria	92 combat aircraft (Alpha Jet, MiG-21, Jaguar)	Soviet Union/Russia France/ Germany and France/UK	9 500	Yes	Some doubt
Senegal	8 combat-capable trainers	France	650	No	Yes
Seychelles	No combat aircraft		20	No	Yes
South Africa	114 combat aircraft (Impala II, Mirage F-1AZ, Cheetah C)	RSA Atlas France	11 140	Yes	Some doubt
Sudan	56 combat aircraft (F-5, PRC J-5, J-6, F-7)	US, People's Republic of China	3 000	Yes	Some doubt
Tanzania	24 combat aircraft (F-5, PRC J-5, J-6, J-7)	People's Republic of China	3 600	No	Some doubt
Togo	15 combat aircraft (Alpha Jet, EMB-326G)	France/Germany/ Brazil	250	No	In doubt
Uganda	2 combat aircraft			No	Some doubt

Country	Combat aircraft and attack helicopters	Main supplier/ maker of combat aircraft	Personnel	Relative modernity of air force	Serviceability of aircraft
Zambia	63 combat aircraft (J-6, MiG-21 MF)	Soviet Union/Russia and People's Republic of China	1 600	No	Some doubt
Zimbabwe	56 combat aircraft (Hunter, Hawk, PRC F-7)	UK and People's Republic of China	4 000	Yes	Yes

Sources: IISS, London, *The Military Balance 1997/98*; press clippings; and *SIPRI Yearbook 1997: Armaments, Disarmament and International Security*.

*Updated to mid-1997. Aircraft types are only given for combat aircraft and attack helicopters. Training aircraft considered to be combat-capable are included in totals for combat aircraft where the latter exist. Countries where no air force is indicated, or fledgling air forces such as that of Cape Verde with one aircraft, are not included in the tables, and neither are countries such as Liberia and the Somali Republic where no active national armed forces are currently indicated. Unserviceability mainly pertains to combat aircraft and attack and armed helicopters, indicated as "some doubt", while "in doubt" refers to all aircraft. Only in the case of Ethiopia and South Africa do indications currently exist regarding planned expansion/modernisation of combat aircraft. South Africa recently announced that the SAAB Gripen is to be purchased. Reports of recent purchases of *inter alia* helicopters, and combat aircraft by Zimbabwe to support its intervention in the DRC have appeared in the press.

TABLE 2:
SOUTHERN AFRICA: AIR POWER RELATED ASSETS - MILITARY

Assets	Numbers	Types	Serviceability
Fighters	± 328	17	30%-50%
Transport	± 216	30	50%-60%
Helicopters	± 263	20	50%-60%
Trainers	± 162	16	40%-55%
Totals	**± 969**	**83**	
Radars	± 250	All	10%-80%
Air Defence — SAM's — AAA	± 36 ± 600	8+ 15+	0%-35% High
Airfields	70		Low-High
Personnel	40 000 - 50 000		

Source: Presentation by Chief of the South African Air Force, Lt Gen W H Hechter, SD, SM, MMM, at the Sir Pierre van Ryneveld Air Power Symposium on *Air Power in Southern Africa: A collective asset*, 15 September 1997.

3.1 Analysis

It has been stated that the acquisition of equipment is severely limited by financial considerations in almost every country in Africa, and that considerations of national prestige sometimes tend to dominate the obtaining of more appropriate equipment to counter long-term threats. The motives for and the conditions of sale or transfer stipulated by supplier countries are also factors affecting equipment acquisition. This was especially the case during the Cold War period, when *inter alia* ideological rivalry determined the source of arms supplies to countries such as Ethiopia, Angola and Mozambique.[12]

It has, however, also been noted that due to few sub-Saharan African countries having sufficient technical personnel to operate and maintain more advanced weapons, they have had to recruit foreign technicians and instructors. In this regard, factors such as logistical constraints, burdensome bureaucracy, differing standards of flight discipline and the generally low level of education in Africa lead to frustrations for supplier countries.[13]

As for organisation of air forces and personnel, air forces in Africa are often subservient to army direction and sometimes called an "air wing". In this regard it has been noted that: "With the relatively small size of most African air forces and with the support of the army being the primary function of many of them, it usually is more efficient and effective to have an army-dominated air force".[14]

Concerning personnel, it has been noted that air crews in African air forces, especially in sub-Saharan Africa, generally lack air-to-air combat experience, as combat air activity has predominantly consisted of tactical bombing and transport.[15]

3.2 Combat aircraft and attack helicopters in future African markets

It has been stated in various studies that few air forces in Africa can afford even to consider the replacement of their existing combat aircraft, however outdated and in poor shape they may be. The combat elements within the air forces of many African countries are therefore seen to be in crisis. Africa's climatic conditions add to the decline in operational readiness of aircraft.[16]

A significant number of sub-Saharan African countries are equipped with combat aircraft supplied by the former Soviet Union or China, and many of these aircraft are seen as obsolete and not worth the investment needed for an upgrade. Russia currently demands hard currency for spares, and is not always seen as a reliable supplier. Therefore, "there must come a point at which the investment of the time and money necessary to maintain the MiG-17 in flying condition can no longer be justified". The MiG-21 is, however, seen as suitable for upgrading, and a number of companies have developed upgrade programmes. (It has recently been reported that Russia intends establishing a facility in Angola for the refurbishing of military equipment, including aircraft.) Some views hold that it is unlikely that any African air force with fewer than 40 MiG-21s in service could fund a modernisation programme.[17]

Other aircraft seen as potentially upgradeable in the African context are the Northrop F-5s.[18]

An alternative to upgrading is the increasing availability of combat aircraft withdrawn from service with major powers under treaty provisions. The Alpha Jet is such an example, and is already operated by a number of African countries in a ground attack role. Other aircraft mentioned in this regard include the British Aerospace Hawk, already serving as an advanced trainer and combat aircraft for Kenya and Zimbabwe. Multirole fighters such as the SAAB JAS 39 Gripen represent more advanced technology, but may be too costly for most African countries.[19]

These options also apply to transport aircraft, and "African countries should consider the possibility of picking up bargains, even if some further investment in upgrading is necessary", should they not be able to afford purchasing new aircraft.[20]

As far as attack helicopters are concerned, three distinct roles are emerging on the battlefield — transport, reconnaissance and attack. It has been stated that the market for attack helicopters in Africa is steadily growing, and that since 1980 the ratio of attack helicopters to other helicopters deployed has risen.[21]

Two options exist in this regard. Weaponry can be added to existing reconnaissance or transport aircraft, or purpose-built designs can be developed. Cost is, however, a major factor as far as the latter option is concerned. The conversion of small multirole/observation helicopters or transport helicopters to the attack or escort role, is seen as the cheaper solution. Nigeria, for instance, uses the BO-105D and Gabon the SA-342.[22]

In the above regard, it has been observed that "The attack helicopter based upon the lightweight multirole designs seems likely to become the basis of the African attack helicopter market for the foreseeable future, although dedicated conversions of observation aircraft ... may offer alternative solutions".[23]

As far as air defence radars are concerned, limited resources again point to shorter range tactical radars (mobile), rather than ground radars facilitating long-range interception being deployed. Some countries such as Angola do, however, have a varied collection of radars supplied by the former Soviet Union.[24]

Three case studies regarding the expansion of air forces in sub-Saharan Africa will now briefly be discussed.

3.2.1 Zaire Air Force report

In a research report published in 1988 concerning future missions of the (former) Zaire Air Force, the emphasis fell on externally-supported armed rebellion as the main threat. The air force (and ground forces) had a major role to play in countering this, operating both inside their own territory as well as destroying "rebel sanctuaries" in neighbouring states and countering the regular forces of those countries. Helicopters for troop transport were seen as significant as this would deny mobility to insurgents and, combined with the mass use of armed helicopters, would be the most effective way to counter insurgency. Helicopters would also be deployed in escort and search-and-rescue roles. It was not foreseen that "rebel forces" would have any significant anti-air firepower.[25]

Passive navigational equipment should be fitted to these helicopters, the report suggested, due to the lack of ground features to lock on. Fixed-wing aircraft such as the Hercules C-

130 would supplement helicopter transport, especially in a long-distance transportation role involving large numbers of troops and quantities of equipment. Transport helicopters should be armed with machine guns or rockets.[26]

Attack helicopters should function in conjunction with their fixed-wing counterparts, and it was proposed in the report that the Zaire Air Force should possess a substantial number of transport and attack helicopters. Attack helicopters could provide overhead cover; visual reconnaissance; direct fire support; escort; and search and rescue. The latter role would be supplemented by fixed-wing aircraft.[27]

The report also expressed concern over military buildups in neighbouring states, and especially over surface-to-air missiles. Training in the Zaire Air Force should therefore emphasise low-level navigation, dogfight techniques and SAM evasions if electronic countermeasures are not affordable.[28]

As far as combat aircraft are concerned, a need for expansion is expressed in the report, but with the qualification that the (former) government could not afford this. "This dilemma is faced by most African leaders. In order to enlarge their armed forces, therefore, they usually enter into doubtful arrangements with an outside supplier, who, in turn, demands reciprocation usually in money, political allegiance or military facilities. For most black Africans, strong military ties with a supplier means loss of a part of their independence".[29]

The report then assessed that Zaire needed a small but efficient air force, with the following key features:[30]

- strategic air bases distributed in at least three air regions
- three squadrons of interceptors
- three squadrons of fighter bombers
- three squadrons of COIN aircraft (helicopters, jets and turbo-propeller)

- a fleet of heavy transports
- a fleet of STOL transports
- training and liaison aircraft

Finally, certain specific problems regarding military campaigns, and specifically the use of the air force, are identified in the report:

> Most black African nations cannot afford long, resources-consuming wars. The war must be won or lost in a matter of weeks if there is no external intervention in the war, the nation in possession of the Air Force well trained to interdict the flow of supplies to reach the battle support will win without any doubt.
>
> In Zaire's armed forces, an issue of particular importance for the future is the problem of close air support. Often in the past ground forces did not receive timely close air support. CAS aircraft were shooting at the wrong place and even shooting at friendly forces.
>
> That is a problem that the Air Force and ground forces must try to resolve as quickly as possible for the benefit of the two services. The two main problems are target designation by ground troops and clear two-way communication between the aircraft and the ground. How can these two problems be eliminated?[31]

3.2.2 French fighter industry in Africa

A study undertaken in 1993 on the potential sales of the French fighter aircraft Rafale through the year 2010, stated that:

> With the end of the Cold War, many of the nations which had been wooed by the two superpowers in the 1970s and 1980s have been facing drastic cuts in expenditures on armament as a condition for economic aid. This is particularly the case in the Horn of Africa, in Ethiopia and Somalia, as well as in sub-Saharan Africa. At the same time, international lending

organizations such as the World Bank or the International Monetary Fund have been increasing their pressures on those African nations heavily indebted to reduce their spending in the defense sector. The drastic changes which have occurred in the Republic of South Africa will also help decrease regional tensions and reduce the need for additional platform equipment for the surrounding nations.

Those factors, compounded with the desire of many African nations to see their despotic governments toppled, will certainly lead to a drastic decrease in the number of fighter aircraft deployed in most of Africa.[32]

As far as sub-Saharan Africa is concerned, countries such as Nigeria, Sudan, Angola, Mozambique, South Africa, Zambia and Zimbabwe were identified as requiring modernisation of their fighter capability.[33]

The study, however, came to the conclusion that only South Africa would be in the market (as it currently is), in the short- to medium-term, for high-end fighters. Some countries, such as Zambia, were identified as being potential buyers of light strike fighters, with assistance from the potential supplier. Angola would also require considerable aid to be able to afford high-end fighters, and would also probably choose a mix of American and Russian rather than French makes.[34]

Factors that determined the preceding assessment include the economic situation of African countries; a decrease in tensions in areas such as Southern Africa, which could reduce the incentive to purchase additional expensive weapons; continued civil strife in certain countries, which would put the emphasis on counter-insurgency equipment rather than sophisticated aircraft; and policy limitations on arms sales to countries such as Sudan which are seen as being involved in international terrorism.[35]

3.2.3 South Africa

The *Defence Review* presented to the cabinet and parliament during 1997, as far as force design is concerned, formulated four options for the South African National Defence Force (SANDF). Option one, which is the preferred option in the shorter term due to financial restrictions, is viewed as the growth-core for the maintenance of military capabilities and skills. Option two is seen as the most prudent force design in the long term.[36]

As far as the South African Air Force (SAAF) is concerned, option one states the following regarding its role in landward defence:[37]

- The SAAF is an important participant in landward defence, and this involves fixed-wing aircraft as well as helicopters.

- Fighter aircraft are the most important means for ensuring a favourable air situation over an area of operations, and for enabling aerial support to own ground forces. Both medium and light fighters are included in Option 1 as set out above (32 and 16 aircraft respectively).*

- Option 1 provides for 16 light reconnaissance aircraft, four electronic warfare aircraft and a squadron of remotely piloted aircraft for purposes of aerial surveillance.

- As far as air mobility is concerned, Option 1 provides for 44 transport aircraft of various types, nine VIP aircraft, 96 transport helicopters and nine voluntary squadrons.

As far as air defence is concerned, it is stated that this is the primary task of the SAAF, and that flexible air defence is provided for in this force design option through a combination of airspace control radars (both static and mobile), point defence

---

* The number of combat aircraft has been reduced from 48 to 24, to enable the purchase of 24 jet trainers to replace the Impalas (See: *Beeld*, (Johannesburg), 27 November 1998).

missile systems and aircraft.[38] Regarding the function of medium multirole fighter aircraft (referred to earlier), the *Defence Review* states that:

> Medium fighters are an essential component of the Air Force's air defence capability. Obsolescence and defence cutbacks have led to a reduction in medium fighter numbers from 89 in 1989 to a present level of 51 aircraft. The F1's were to be phased out in 1999 subject to annual review, while the Cheetah C will stay in service until 2012. The Option 1 requirement is for 32 medium multi-role fighters.[39]

The Mirage FI AZ was eventually phased out earlier, at the end of 1997.

Two of the "strategic gaps and risks" identified in the option one force design, and pertaining to air power, are identified as "limited strategic reconnaissance capabilities in the air force", and "insufficient air defence capabilities for a classical defensive counter air posture".[40]

3.3 Selected examples of the operational application of air power in sub-Saharan Africa

With reference to the civil war in Angola (1975-1976); the Ogaden war between Ethiopia and Somalia (1977-1978), and the war between Tanzania and Uganda (1978-1979), Thom notes that "modern weapons, including jet combat aircraft, were used with varying effectiveness in all three conflicts". Ethiopia, especially, demonstrated the effective use of air power.[41]

Colestock notes that up to the mid-eighties "the bulk of the combat air activity has been tactical bombing and transport". He cites Morocco's air strikes on the Polisario Front; Ethiopia's air strikes against Eritrean positions; South Africa's strikes in southern Angola; and Libya's attacks in Chad as all involving air-to-ground attacks and a ground-based defence. Air transport during combat operations has been relatively successful but has frequently been supplemented by external powers – for example, French and United States assistance in Chad in 1983, and Soviet and Cuban assistance to the Angolan government in the 1980s.[42]

South Africa's participation in the Angolan civil war in the 1970s and 1980s did involve incidents in which Angolan MiG-21s were shot down by South African Mirage-FI fighters.[43] South African suppressive attacks were also launched on the Angolan air defence networks. Cuban pilots and combat aircraft were seconded to the Angolan Air Force in this period.

The resuming of hostilities in Angola's civil war during 1992 saw a new wave of airborne missions launched by the government in Luanda against the UNITA rebel movement. South African mercenary pilots are alleged to have *inter alia* flown MiG-23 fighters and Mi-17 helicopters in these missions.[44]

More recently, Angolan MiG-21 jets were deployed out of Luanda to provide air support to the ground forces of former President Nguesso (who has since taken over power), and were reported to have bombed positions in Brazzaville in the attack which resulted in the take-over of the presidential palace. The air support was supplemented by Angolan ground forces. In turn, Congo Brazzaville forces of the then government of President Lisouba carried out air raids by Mi-24 helicopters over northern parts of the capital held by supporters of Nguesso.[45]

In the recent conflict in the former Zaire, which led to Mobutu's overthrow, Mobutu is reported to have acquired Russian-made jet fighters and helicopter gunships which flew air strikes against rebel-held areas. Civilian targets were alleged to have been bombed in these attacks.[46]

In the conflict between rebels of the Revolutionary United Front (RUF) and the National Provincial Ruling Council of Captain Valentine Strasser which erupted in Sierra Leone in 1991, an Mi-24E helicopter was used for armed reconnaissance in support of Mi-17 heliborne operations. South African mercenary pilots and an aircrew from Belorussia are reported to have been involved in the airborne operations. In December 1997 a Nigerian Alpha jet was reported to have bombed villages in Sierra Leone as part of the campaign to oust the military junta which seized power in May 1997. Similar aerial bombings by Eritrea and Ethiopia on civilian targets were reported in the war between these two countries during 1998, with accounts of some aircraft being shot down by ground fire. Angolan and Zimbabwean jets and helicopters also bombed rebel positions in the Democratic Republic of Congo (DRC), when they intervened to support the regime of President Laurent Kabila against the Tutsi-led rebellion that is still continuing. The rebels alleged that civilians were targeted.[47]

It is difficult to assess the contribution of air power to the outcome of the conflicts here discussed. Ultimately, the main roles were still played by ground forces; in many cases there was heavy dependence on foreign and mercenary pilots; ground-based defence — such as that of UNITA in Angola in the early 1990s — the lack of suitable airfields from which airborne attacks could be launched, and the seemingly sporadic nature of air attacks, *inter alia*, limited the use and effectiveness of air power. In 1992 UNITA was reported to have destroyed almost all of Angola's eight new Mi-24 helicopters, while some transport aircraft were damaged in mortar attacks or shot down with surface-to-air missiles.[48]

With reference to the use of aircraft in armed conflict, the following has been noted:

> Although the switching of suppliers causes severe disruptions in capabilities, the use of aircraft in warfare places even more difficult demands on African air forces. Without an indigenous production capability, Africans sometimes have insurmountable problems in dealing with the equipment attrition of warfare. Heavy utilization rates, maintenance

failures, logistic problems, and combat losses can quickly put an African air force near zero effectiveness in a war.[49]

3.4 Collateral roles

Certain collateral roles have increased in importance as a result of domestic security concerns in African countries. With reference to the South African situation, it is stated:

> In dealing with domestic security concerns, whether natural or insurrectionary, the applications of air power are derivatives of the surveillance and mobility functions. It includes the distribution of emergency relief, border patrol to monitor the movement of refugees and to combat illegal cross-border activities of various kinds, and search and rescue. Domestic security operations could also require the rapid movement of security forces and specialised surveillance. Should domestic security support be requested by another state, the mobility function will come heavily into play in order to transport security forces and to provide the necessary logistical support. Generally speaking, the capabilities required to execute these tasks would be a subset of the capabilities required to fully accommodate the needs of such collateral applications.[50]

The SANDF has increasingly become involved in combating crime in support of the South African Police Service (SAPS). During 1997 the SAAF executed 1 285 operational flying hours to prevent crime; an additional 2 882 hours patrolling South Africa's borders; and an additional 307 hours to assist the South African Navy (SAN) in patrolling the coast. Cuts in the defence budget could, however, have drastic implications for the SANDF role in assisting the police.[51]

4 REGIONAL CO-OPERATION: THE SOUTHERN AFRICAN EXAMPLE

Co-operation among air forces is exemplified by the Standing Aviation Committee (SAC) of the Inter-State Defence and Security Committee (ISDSC) in the Southern African region. It is envisaged that the ISDSC, which is a ministerial committee of the former Frontline States, will eventually be one of the institutions of the Southern African Development Community (SADC) Organ for Politics, Defence and Security, established in 1996.[52]

The inaugural meeting of the SAC was held in Zimbabwe during June 1995, and it is a regional sub-subcommittee of the ISDSC, comprising air force chiefs and air wing chiefs of the member states of the SADC.[53]

Two of the most important objectives of the SAC have been identified first, as the promotion of regional stability, *inter alia*, through supporting and contributing to regional air force co-operation; ensuring freedom of maritime, land and air communication lines, and providing rapid response to humanitarian crises; and second, prevention of aggression and *coups d'ètat* by maintaining and improving combat capability and by establishing and maintaining a rapid crisis response capability.[54]

Despite uncertainties regarding certain issues and structures involving the SADC Organ, the SAC meets annually; but ultimately its success or failure will largely depend on the success or failure of the SADC Organ.

5 CONCLUSION

As to future developments regarding African air forces, the following had already by 1986 been noted:

> Much of the future of African air forces depends upon the economic decisions of individual countries. Although it would

be easy to predict a slow but steady increase in these forces as technology and equipment are acquired, growth is more likely to be erratic and not always positive. Many African air forces have lapsed into disrepair, with more derelict aircraft than operational ones. Most African governments keep enough aircraft in flying condition to maintain the psychological benefits of having an air force (the air displays during military parades, the ability to move troops rapidly about the country, the aerial visibility of the country's forefront of technology).

As much as Africans want to maintain and expand their air forces, they will be almost exclusively dependent on external suppliers. These suppliers often offer second-line or used equipment at concessionary prices. In some instances, this is a "dumping" process, but more often than not it is what the donor perceives as a rational approach to starting or continuing an air force building program.[55]

The nature and future of most African air forces are primarily determined by their ability to pay for external assistance. Other factors such as the changing security environment in Africa and initiatives regarding collective security will also exert some influence.

As far as effectiveness is concerned, it has been noted:

> Manpower and materiél figures provide only rough — and often deceptive — indicators of military capabilities, however, and changes in the size and equipment inventories of African armed forces do not necessarily signify like changes in effectiveness.[56]

Human resources, logistics and mobility, followed by firepower and manpower have, in descending order, been described as the key ingredients that determine the levels of military capability in African states.[57]

Sub-Saharan Africa has been described as a region short of modern combat aircraft. Unserviceability of whole air forces or certain components of them are indicated for many of the countries; some have no combat capability but only a measure of transport and helicopter capability; where combat capability does exist, it is often based on combat-capable trainers; and air forces are primarily tactical.[58]

A recent assessment of the Zambian Air Force, for instance, concludes:

> Because of lack of spares and flying hours by its pilots, the air force is little more than a fair weather force. Able to transport troops and cargo, it is judged incapable of defending Zambian airspace against any military threat. Rotary wing aviation seemingly enjoys a better lot, their pilots and ground crew being more current with their mounts.[59]

A related problem, with implications for military aircraft as well, is the declining standard of air traffic safety. During 1996 77 near-misses were reported, mostly in the western sector of Africa.[60]

In conclusion, it appears that a mix of helicopters (both for attack and transport); fixed-wing aircraft for COIN, transport, reconnaissance, and search-and-rescue missions; and light fighters, would be the most appropriate for most sub-Saharan African countries. Littoral states will require some maritime patrol capability. Maintenance costs will be a crucial factor. Upgrading of existing equipment will also remain important, although this does have limitations. For the foreseeable future, financial constraints are likely to be one of the main factors limiting expansion and modernisation — which in any case cannot be undertaken by indigenous industries alone, where such industries exist. South Africa is a partial exception to this rule. In general, it has even been observed: "While some African countries aim to produce pilots that are capable of getting the best out of combat aircraft, it must be said that many more maintain an air force largely to provide the government with transport and communications services."[61]

REFERENCES

1. Knight, M (Sir), "Air power in developing countries", in *Air power in developing countries with consideration of the RSA in a regional role*, Ad hoc Publication No 30, Institute for Strategic Studies, University of Pretoria, October 1993, pp 7-8.

2. Kriel, J (Lt Gen), "The South African Air Force after integration", in Hough M, and A du Plessis, *The future application of air power with specific reference to Southern Africa*, Ad hoc Publication No 32, Institute for Strategic Studies, University of Pretoria, May 1995, p 9.

3. *Ibid*, pp 9-12.

4. Colestock, H E, "African Air Forces", in Arlinghaus, B E and P H Baker, *African Armies: Evaluation and Capabilities*, Westview Press, Boulder, 1986, p 141.

5. *Ibid*, p 145.

6. *Ibid*, p 146.

7. Brent, W A, *African Military Aviation*, Freeworld Publications, Nelspruit, 1994, p 12.

8. Internet document (Angola) at: http://lcweb2.loc.gov/cgi-bin/query2/r?frd/cs:@field(DOCID+ao0159.

9. Brent, W A, *op cit*, p 156.

10. *Ibid*, and Internet document (Nigeria) at: http://lcweb2.loc.gov/cgi-bin/query2/r?frd/cstdy:@field(DOCID+ng0145.

11. Internet document (Nigeria), *op cit*.

12. Colestock, H E, *op cit*, p 145.

13. *Ibid*, p 146.

14. *Ibid*, p 147.

15. *Ibid*, p 144.

16. Durwen, S, "Combat aircraft for Africa: A low-scale priority", *Strategy African Defence*, Vol 2, No 1, 1996, p 30.

17. *Ibid*; and *African Armed Forces*, September 1998, p 9.

18. *Ibid*, p 32.
19. *Ibid*, p 34.
20. "Transport Aircraft", *Strategy African Defence*, Vol 2, No 2, 1996, p 26.
21. Roberts, J, *African Defence Journal*, No 104, April 1989, p 42.
22. *Ibid*, pp 42-45.
23. *Ibid*, p 46.
24. Walters, B, "Air defence radars: The options for Africa", *African Defence Journal*, No 119, July 1990, p 42.
25. Biangala, E (Lt Col), *Zaire Air Force: Future Missions*, Air War College, Air University, Alabama, May 1988, pp 6-9.
26. *Ibid*, p 10.
27. *Ibid*, pp 11-14.
28. *Ibid*, pp 24-25.
29. *Ibid*, p 32.
30. *Ibid*, p 33.
31. *Ibid*, p 26.
32. Simon, Y, *Prospects for the French Fighter Industry in a Post-Cold War Environment*, Rand, Santa Monica, 1993, pp 142-143.
33. *Ibid*, pp 142-164.
34. *Ibid*.
35. *Ibid*, pp 142-143 and p 152.
36. RSA, *Defence Review*, First and Second Reports, 26 May 1997, p 82.
37. *Ibid*, pp 67-68.
38. *Ibid*, p 69.
39. *Ibid*, p 70.
40. *Ibid*, p 75.
41. Thom, W G, "Sub-Saharan Africa's changing military environment", *Armed Forces and Society*, Vol 11, No 1, 1984, pp 54-55.
42. Colestock, H E, *op cit*, pp 144-145.

43. Van Loggerenberg, J P B (Lt Gen), "The role of air power in Southern Africa", *Strategic Review for Southern Africa*, Vol XIII, No 1, May 1991, pp 42-43.

44. Venter, A J, "Mercenaries fuel next round in Angolan civil war", in *Jane's International Defence Review*, 1996, p 1.

45. *Business Day* (Johannesburg), 16 October 1997; and *The Star* (Johannesburg), 2 September 1997.

46. *Weekly Mail* (Johannesburg), 21-27 February 1997.

47. Hooper, J, "Of guns and diamonds — Sierra Leone", *Strategy African Defence*, Vol 2, No 3, 1996, p 29; Internet document (Sierra Leone News Archives - December 1997 - Sierra Leone Web) at: http://www.sierra-leone.org/slnews1297.htm; and *Business Day* (Johannesburg), 12 June 1998; 26 August 1998 and 8 September 1998.

48. Venter, A J, *op cit*, p 5.

49. Colestock, H E, *op cit*, p 148.

50. Kriel, J, *op cit*, p 11.

51. SANDF, media statement, 21 January 1998.

52. Hough, M and A du Plessis (eds), *Africa: Selected documents on political, security, humanitarian and economic issues, Ad hoc Publication No 33*, November 1996, pp 32-35.

53. Shikapwashya, R S (Lt Gen), "The Standing Aviation Committee of the Inter-State Defence and Security Committee of the Southern African Region", *ISSUP Bulletin 8/95*, Institute for Strategic Studies, University of Pretoria, 1995, p 4.

54. *Ibid*, pp 4-6.

55. Colestock, H E, *op cit*, pp 147-148.

56. Barrows, W L, "Changing military capabilities in Black Africa", in Foltz, W J and H S Bienen, *Arms and the African*, Council on Foreign Relations, 1985, p 101.

57. *Ibid*, p 102.

58. IISS, *The Military Balance 1997/98*, Oxford University Press, London, 1997, p 234 and further.

59. Quintana, M, "Zambia Defence Expenditure", *Africa Defence Journal*, October 1997, p 5.

60. *The Star* (Johannesburg), 16 September 1997.
61. Walters, B, "Training tomorrow's pilots", *African Defence Journal*, No 116, April 1990, p 44.

Chapter 6

THE CHALLENGE OF EFFECTIVE SUB-SAHARAN MARITIME DEFENCE

Louis du Plessis

1 INTRODUCTION

If countries in the continent worst hit by violence since the beginning of the nineties are also experiencing socio-economic underdevelopment, it may be asked whether they have any ability to protect their national interests. Furthermore, if their maritime ability is so limited that they cannot patrol and police the areas off their coasts, one may expect that such states will be vulnerable to the foreign exploitation of their marine and mineral resources.

In fact, this is exactly the situation most African states south of the Sahara currently find themselves in. Without some form of maritime defence, they are unable to protect their vital national interests.

The aim of this chapter is to identify the maritime challenges facing sub-Saharan African states at the end of the twentieth century.

By way of a conceptual introduction, the general nature of navies is characterised, before exploring the seven broad categories within which sub-Saharan navies could be classified. Since the pre-dominantly Arab Mediterranean and adjacent states find themselves in a strategic position often very different from sub-Sahara, they have been excluded from the study.

After describing some basic features of the present African maritime environment, the external and internal challenges facing African maritime defence are outlined. Special attention is given to the exploitation of African resources by foreign powers and to the political, social and economic obstacles to maritime development. Within this context, comments on the abilities and shortcomings of a few specific sub-Saharan navies are made.

Finally, the paper differentiates between functional and material dimensions by exploring the maritime roles and equipment required by sub-Saharan states to guard national security. Some main conclusions are drawn.

2 CHARACTERISING NAVIES

To distinguish between the various maritime challenges confronting states, a few remarks on the general nature of navies must be made. All navies share at least the following important characteristics: a common medium; common organisational characteristics that emphasise hierarchical discipline; common sources and types of armament — primarily from industrialised states; and a common goal of protecting offshore national security.[1]

2.1 Roles of navies

Although the roles of navies can be defined and classified in various ways, their very essence is their military character. Their ability to use force provides the means to perform other essential tasks. Flowing from their military capability, navies can also perform a diplomatic role to support a state's foreign policy without actually employing violence, but by practising so-called gunboat diplomacy. A third, policing, role concerns the preservation or extension of sovereignty, securing activities related to the exploration and exploitation of own resources and the maintenance of law and order.[2]

In addition to these fundamental roles, navies in modernising societies normally contribute to the enforcement of internal stability and the promotion of nation building.[3]

These fundamental roles are often linked to the inevitable basic missions practised by all navies: constabulary and regulatory missions; territorial or coastal defence missions; and force projection at sea.[4]

From these roles and missions follows maritime strategy. The strategic importance of the sea lies in the access it provides to non-adjacent areas. Maritime strategy is about the use of the sea — its use to a country's own advantage and the prevention of its use by others that would be to its detriment, both in time of war and peace.[5] In fact, the primary question of maritime strategy is: To what end does a country want to, or need to, use the sea?[6]

2.2 Utilising the sea

Concerning the use of the sea for security purposes, a distinction can be made between the following two categories:

- **Projection of military power ashore**. The impact of naval forces on land can manifest itself in three forms: amphibious operations — from a raid, at one end of the scale, to full-scale invasion at the other; coastal bombardment; and seaborne air operations. The deployment of some 50 000 Cubans in Angola during 1988 is a manifestation of the projection of power ashore.[7]

- **Deployment of naval forces**. The sea may also be used to deploy naval forces to secure a country's own use of the sea or to prevent an adversary from doing so to the country's disadvantage. Examples are the French deployments in the

Southern Indian Ocean and the United States deployments in the Arabian Sea and Persian Gulf in the 1990s.

Maritime self-defence depends upon an ability to project power, and is related to sea control and to the ability to prevent the use of the sea by opponents. Maritime self-defence is also related to sea denial.

- Sea control is related to Mahan's doctrine of "command of the sea". The objective is to use the sea for a country's own purposes, while preventing the enemy from doing so. Eighteenth-century Britain is a classical example of this capability.

- Sea denial prevents the enemy from utilising the sea for his purposes, and can be regarded as an aspect of sea control. The best-known example of a sea denial strategy is the use of the German U-boats in the two world wars. Modern attack craft are often well suited for this role, but submarines are even better suited.

- These strategies for sea utilisation can be illustrated by the course of the Falklands War. One of the main reasons why Argentina lost the war for the Malvinas and Falklands is because it failed to secure sea denial, while Britain won sea control. This control included the defensive aspects of sea denial to enemy forces as well as the offensive aspects of projecting power ashore.[8]

- A country may be said to practise maritime defence effectively when it possesses and employs an adequate sea control (including sea denial) capability to defend its strategic interests.

2.3 Measuring maritime power

An argument frequently put forward is that reach — a navy's ability to operate effectively further afield than during coastal sea denial — is the ultimate measure of maritime power. It is this aspect of maritime power that separates the major navies from the others.[9]

Four categories of navies may be identified in terms of operating radius:[10]

- **Global navies.** Global navies have the capability to maintain forces on a protracted and worldwide basis and to discharge priority missions simultaneously, without denuding forces required for maritime defence in contiguous seas. The United States Navy falls into this category. The Russian Navy also belonged here, but its capability is currently declining.

- **Ocean-going navies.** Ocean-going navies have the strength to contest the sea against all but the most powerful opposition in pursuit of their interests in distant waters, but are unable to attempt more than one such operation without support. The navies of France and the United Kingdom fall into this category.

- **Littoral navies.** Littoral navies have little or no capability to operate outside contiguous waters.

- **Coastal navies.** Coastal navies extend territorial law enforcement and present some challenge to potential intruders, but have a minimal capability to cope with even a modest naval threat. Their primary function is coastguard duties. For maritime protection they have to rely on allies.

Given these concepts of sea power, the following questions may be asked: Where does the maritime capability of sub-Saharan states fit into the broader picture? And: In which strategic maritime environment do these African states need to assert their interests?

3   CLASSIFYING SUB-SAHARAN NAVIES

Although the vast majority of the world's navies are limited to operations in those areas of the ocean falling under their national jurisdiction, specifically the exclusive economic zone (EEZ) established by the 1982 Convention on the Law of the Sea,[11] the African naval hierarchy is unique among the Third World regions in its preponderance of ineffective navies. This holds true even when the northern Arab-African navies are included. The number of minor vessels grew between independence in the 1960s and the mid-1980s. Since then, there has been a gradual decline in all sizes of vessels in sub-Sahara; and even the initial increase during the first decades after independence added little to the combat potential of the many weak navies.[12]

In addition to their limited mobility and firepower, there is a lack of clarity in their overall orientation: in particular, their definition of missions, patterns of acquisition, logistic adequacy, maintenance capability, and the quality of their training and operational experience.[13]

Consequently, most sub-Saharan navies can be considered either as at an embryonic stage of development, such as Namibia's, or at a stage of stagnation or decline, such as Mozambique's. They are generally regarded as little more than "incipient coast guards".[14]

Adding more recent data[15] and some qualitative considerations to an adapted Morris hierarchy of navies,[16] a rank framework of the maritime capability of the 44 sub-Saharan countries is developed. (See Table 1.)

The above classification shows that there are no maritime forces in Africa south of the Sahara in the two top ranks. Only one qualifies for Rank 4, namely littoral navies; two possibly for Rank 3, namely coastal navies; and seven for Rank 2, namely constabulary navies (see map). The remaining 18 sub-Saharan nations with some or other maritime ability have "token" navies.

TABLE 1:
RANK FRAMEWORK OF MARITIME CAPABILITY OF SUB-SAHARAN COUNTRIES

SUB-SAHARAN MARITIME RANKS

Rank	Capability	Total	Countries in regions					
			West Africa	Southern Africa	Horn of Africa	East Africa	Central Africa
6 Regional force projection navies	Such navies have impressive territorial defence capabilities and some ability to project force into the adjoining ocean basin.	0	0	0	0	0	0
5 Adjacent force protection navies	Such navies have impressive territorial defence capabilities and some ability to project force offshore (beyond the EEZ).	0	0	0	0	0	0
4 Littoral navies	Such navies have considerable offshore territorial defence capabilities that fall within EEZ limits.	1	0	South Africa	0	0	0
3 Coastal navies	Such navies provide a primarily inshore territorial defence, with a limited offshore defence capability.	2	Nigeria	0	0	Kenya	0
2 Constabulary navies	Such navies have a certain ability to prevent the exploitation of own coastal waters, but the emphasis is on constabulary functions.	7	Ghana, Guinea, Guinea-Bissau, Senegal	0	Eritrea	Mauritius, Tanzania	0
1 Token navies	Such navies are unable even to patrol national territorial seas effectively. They are impotent in the EEZ.	18	Benin, Côte d'Ivoire, Sierra Leone, Togo	Angola, Malawi, Mozambique, Namibia	Djibouti, Sudan	Madagascar, Seychelles	Cameroon, Cape Verdi, Congo Brazzaville Congo Kinshasa, Equatorial Guinea, Gabon
0 No navies	For practical purposes, no maritime capability	16	Burkino Faso, Gambia, Liberia, Mali, Niger	Botswana, Lesotho, Zambia, Zimbabwe	Ethiopia, Somalia	Uganda	Burundi, Central African Republic, Chad, Rwanda

Sources: Adapted from International Institute for Strategic Studies, *The Military Balance 1997-1998*, Oxford University Press, London, pp 236-263; *Africa South of the Sahara 1997*, Europa Publications, London, 1997, pp 137-1111; and Morris, MA, *Expansion of Third World Navies*, Macmillan, London, 1987, pp 22-66.

Sixteen have virtually no maritime capability at present.[17] (Compare this framework with sub-Saharan maritime manpower and craft, as analysed in Table 2.)

From a normative viewpoint of maritime defence, this framework becomes particularly disturbing when it is seen against the background of the modern strategic environment in which sub-Saharan nations have found themselves during the closing years of the twentieth century.

4 FEATURES OF THE SUB-SAHARAN MARITIME ENVIRONMENT

The low maritime ranking of sub-Saharan nations, described above, can be coupled to a lack of historical interest in, or even awareness of, the importance of maritime issues. Also, many African societies have associated the sea and ships with colonialism and the slave trade.

For many years the great shipping nations travelled to and around Africa on their way to trade with the East or Australia, to fetch slaves or to colonise and develop markets. As a result of these activities many well-known harbours and ports were developed along the sub-Saharan coast, such as Dakar, Luanda, Cape Town, Durban, Maputo, Beira, Dar-es-Salaam and Mombasa, all of which profited from maritime travel and trade.[18] However these activities did little to encourage an interest in maritime affairs. Some observers claim that Africa is still "watching from the shore" while others exploit the sea around her coast.[19]

Several universal trends currently impact on Africa's maritime environment. They are associated with the utilisation of the sea, technological development, international political transformation, the sea routes around the continent and the provision of assistance by Western financial institutions.[20]

Problems of feeding rapidly growing populations in the Third World, especially in Africa south of the Sahara, coupled to the exhaustion of resources on land, have resulted in a relative increase in the importance of maritime assets and in the commercial exploitation of the sea. Fishing, as a means of securing food, is growing in importance globally and has become a primary source of protein or income in many countries.[21] In fact, competition for fish resources has contributed to major diplomatic and economic conflicts, including the Cold War.

The number of small navies has increased drastically since 1950. Many of the new independent coastal states that have emerged since the Second World War are described as "inexperienced, ambitious and often resentful"; as constantly "seeking redress for real or imaginary wrongs and injuries to their status".[22] Considerable quantities of destructive modern weapons, including submarines and attack craft armed with missiles, have been acquired by these small navies. Moreover, since industrialised states, such as the United States and France, have been downsizing their forces in the 1990s, more second-hand vessels have been available for purchase. These craft and armaments, linked to national ambitions, have increased the probability of armed conflict in several unstable regions.

The post-Second World War period saw rapid technological progress. Although the smaller navies do not have nuclear weapons or nuclear propulsion, the acquisition of modern conventional weapons technology has multiplied their firepower. Particularly the anti-ship missile, which can be launched from a wide range of platforms, has strengthened the growing self-confidence of the smaller navies.[23]

Also after the Second World War, maritime attention became increasingly focused on Africa. As it forms part of the coastal region of both the Atlantic and Indian Oceans, the continent in general and Southern Africa in particular was regarded as the gateway between them. Given the vulnerability of the Suez and

Panama Canals in times of crisis, this region was recognised as a major choke point.[24] Strategically the Cape sea route became one of the world's most important trade routes and still is. By the mid-1990s approximately 30 per cent (154 million tonnes) of Middle East oil, bound for Europe and the Americas, was conveyed *via* the Cape. The number of tankers rounding the Cape every month varies from 35 to 50.[25] Over the past three decades African ports have became indispensable elements in trading with the continent.

Since the second half of the eighties, a stable bipolar international situation has been replaced by an unstable multipolar one with an increased potential for local or regional conflict. This instability may be ascribed to factors such as ethnic nationalism, religious intolerance or territorial claims. At the same time a gradual shift in economic power from the West to the Far East is slowly but surely becoming discernible. In the absence of global East-West competition, the major powers have started to re-channel aid from sub-Saharan states to other priority areas.

These external changes have obliged Third World, especially African, leaders to emphasise policies of self-sufficiency. Several states that have poured funds and equipment into the region over a period of several decades, as part of their global alliance building, have begun to divert these sources. The former Soviet Union has withdrawn its aid and support, while many Western states are hesitant to supply Third World states with military main armament. The growing absence of superpower support and mounting pressure have obliged African states to direct their own development. Countries in the region are grasping the fact that they must increasingly rely on themselves for progress and security.[26]

As regards maritime security, the position of the major naval powers has changed. The only two that have permanent naval deployments in the Southern African region are France and the United States. The French Navy provides the largest, albeit somewhat unobtrusive, regular presence: mainly in the Indian Ocean but with occasional visits to francophone states in West Africa. Although the United States Navy also maintains a large permanent presence in the Indian Ocean, concentrated in the Gulf and off Somalia, it has had no direct influence on the maritime forces of the southern African states.

Despite the decisive importance of African sea routes, sub-Saharan Africa has, since the end of the eighties, become increasingly marginalised in terms of the world's consciousness and willingness to provide assistance. This is largely because of the inability of the states in the region to generate internal economic growth or to maintain internal law, order and representative government. Also, the post-Cold War relaxation in superpower competition brought an end to their setting one side off against the other and securing lucrative financial arrangements as a result. Western financial institutions at present perceive far more attractive opportunities in regions such as Eastern Europe and the Far East than in Africa, which has experienced more than 30 years of miserable post-colonial rule.[27]

If the growing maritime threats to the needs of sub-Saharan societies are linked to these factors, a series of external, as well as internal, challenges emerge.

5 EXTERNAL CHALLENGES TO SUB-SAHARAN MARITIME DEFENCE

For geographical reasons nations on the African continent are oriented towards one of three different ocean basins: the north African (or Arab-African) nations, towards the Mediterranean; sub-Saharan west coast nations towards the Atlantic, and east coast nations towards the Indian Ocean.[28] Consequently, the Indian Ocean Rim Association for Regional Co-operation (IORARC) and the Zone of Peace and Co-operation in the South Atlantic (ZPCSA) have emerged.

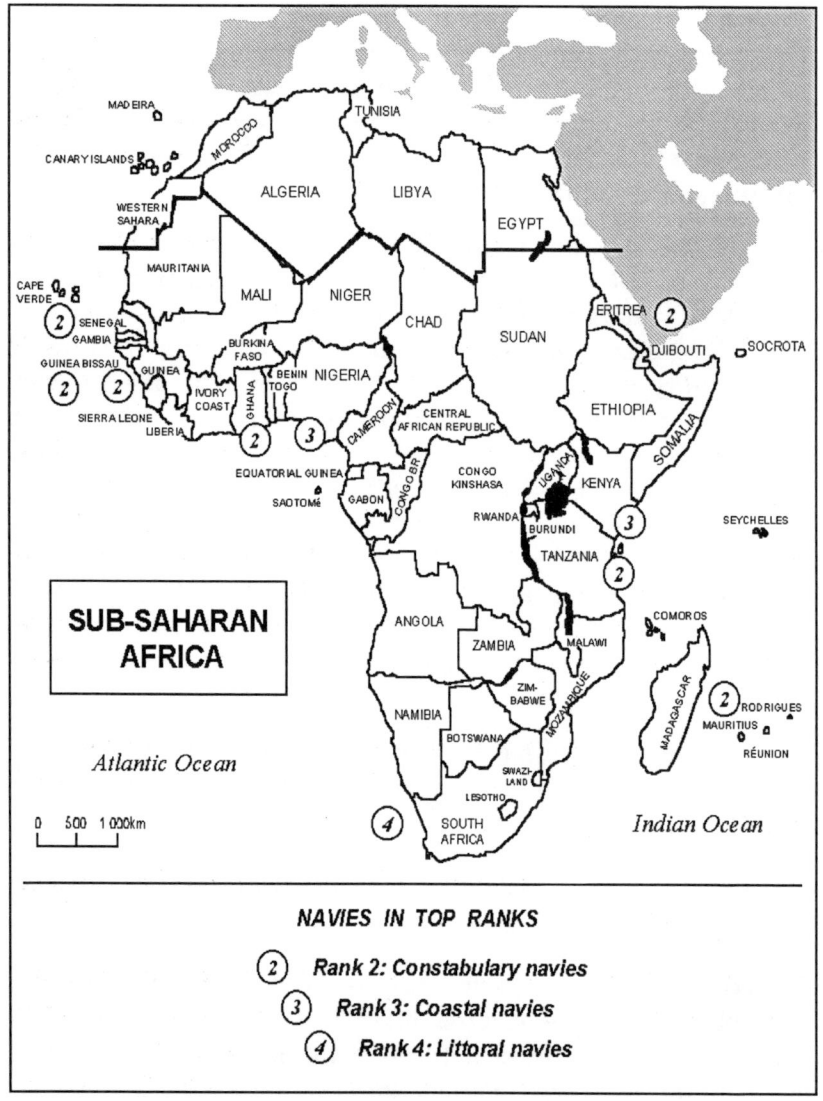

The external challenges to Africa's maritime security gain significance when placed in the context, first, of protecting national assets in territorial waters and in the exclusive economic zone against foreign exploitation of natural resources such as fishing and minerals; and, second, of handling ecological threats such as pollution.

The exclusive economic zone (EEZ) is the most prominent example of the global trend towards more extensive national control of ocean zones. The trend also applies to African countries, since most of them signed the United Nations Convention on the Law of the Sea (UNCLOS) and have come to recognise the significance, in economic and security terms, of the 200 nautical mile EEZ concept, one of the important provisions of UNCLOS.[29]

While the territorial sea and airspace extends over the first 12 nautical miles, the EEZ includes the sea-bed, the water column and the airspace extending between 12 and 200 nautical sea miles offshore, and generally also the bulk of the continental shelf. The EEZ thus ensures control over offshore resources. Moreover, a coastal state is entitled to carry out any military activities within its EEZ and is granted exclusive authority to protect the resources within this space.[30] Although landlocked states have certain rights to marine resources, coastal states have the exclusive right to authorise the construction of installations within their EEZs.[31]

The EEZ entails a long list of tasks and hazards for most sub-Saharan states, since the inshore and offshore territorial defence capabilities of their navies are, at best, weak and often non-existent, and even their EEZ surveillance potential is questionable. The locating of EEZ violators by them is problematic, and the enforcement of their EEZ rights in the face of opposition is even more difficult.[32]

The protection of sea routes is of utmost importance to Africa's developing economies, particularly given their dependence on commodity exports. All the states, littoral and landlocked, depend to some degree on the Atlantic and Indian Ocean seaboards. In South Africa 80 per cent of the value and more than 90 per cent of the tonnage of its imports and exports flow through its ports, and it can be assumed that similar figures obtain for the rest of sub-Saharan Africa.[33] However none of the states, not even South Africa which is blessed with both eastern and western coastlines, fully benefits from access to these oceans and to their potential wealth.[34]

The many small and weak sub-Saharan states are vulnerable to a number of foreign influences. This vulnerability is associated with the vast length of the African coastline; with the fact that major shipping routes pass through each of the continent's ocean basins, and with the richness in natural resources of the continent and some of its offshore regions.[35]

Fisheries worldwide are being increasingly overexploited. According to the United Nations Food and Agriculture Organisation (FAO), this is true of one-quarter of all fish stocks.[36] And the economies of many sub-Saharan littoral states depend on fishing or offshore mining for their survival. For example, over 95 per cent of Angola's export is offshore oil. Such dependence implies that the protection and development of harbours, and of mineral and marine resources, is imperative: sub-Saharan navies should best focus their meagre resources on this essential requirement. The fact is that economic prosperity can be ensured only if a state can police its natural assets.

Fishing is an economic activity that has obvious maritime implications. Of the littoral states, Benin, Cameroon, Congo, Côte D'Ivoire, Gabon, Ghana, Madagascar, Mozambique, Namibia, Nigeria, Senegal, Sierra Leone and South Africa have sizeable fish catches.[37] This is a lucrative industry in the richer southern Atlantic Ocean. For poor countries, like Mozambique, it is one of the few growing industries.[38]

However, as the chief of the South African Navy indicates, prospects for growth in the fishing industry are not favourable, since fish resources have already been overexploited. Nonetheless, the protection and management of this resource, which South Africa shares with other Southern African countries, is of utmost importance.[39] If sub-Saharan societies fail to protect their vast maritime resources, literally billions of dollars' worth of seafood alone — not to mention the wealth that still stands to be exploited below the sea-bed within the EEZ (be this oil or gas or minerals) — will be lost.[40] The societies will also forfeit tourist revenue earned from activities such as game fishing and diving. Countries with no maritime ability to control the areas and resources off their coasts leave a vacuum and create an opportunity for exploitation.[41] For instance, with the possible exception of South Africa, Kenya and Nigeria, the navies are unable to protect the unauthorised foreign exploitation of Africa's rich fishing grounds.

In 1997 poachers caught half-a-billion rands' worth of Patagonian toothfish in South African territorial waters off the Prince Edward Islands. According to the South African government, the South African Navy was powerless to stop the plunder. The South African Deputy Minister of Defence, Ronnie Kasrils, identified the current theft of maritime resources as sub-Saharan Africa's greatest security threat: "This will continue until fishing stocks have been totally plundered or until a regional naval presence calls a halt to what amounts to daylight robbery. The more fish lost, the more hungry stomachs on land and the fewer jobs. Those thousands of kilometres of open sea and coastline beckon the gunrunners, the drug smugglers, the international mafia, the terrorists and the pirates of all nationalities, who are fast becoming the greatest security threat of our time."[42]

Furthermore, while only South Africa and Namibia are involved in large-scale offshore diamond mining, several states have offshore oil and gas fields. These include: Congo Brazzaville, Congo Kinshasa, Gabon, Cameroon, Benin, Côte d'Ivoire, Nigeria, Namibia, South Africa and Mozambique. In the case of Nigeria, oil exports account for 90 per cent of foreign exchange, and 20 per cent of federal government revenue. In Southern Africa, Mossgas has recently gathered steam in South Africa, while in Angola during the 1980s the Cabinda fields earned 90 per cent of exports, 50 per cent of state revenue and 30 per cent of GDP.[43]

Another challenge arises from the realities of pollution. With 300 000 to 500 000 tons of oil being transported along the Southern African coast daily, there is the constant danger of oil spills, should an accident occur.[44] Such accidents are most likely to increase, given the ageing tanker fleet and the notorious sea conditions around the African coast.[45] A major oil spill also presents serious pollution problems to neighbouring countries, due to the prevailing sea currents. Another pollution threat is the dumping of toxic and nuclear waste in African waters. This possibility has angered many sub-Saharan leaders and has stimulated renewed concern for the environment.[46]

These problems, which demand an expansion in maritime capability, are exacerbated by internal difficulties linked to economic, political and security preferences.

6 INTERNAL CHALLENGES TO SUB-SAHARAN MARITIME DEFENCE

Since the beginning of the nineties Africa has been one of the regions of the world worst hit by violence. Of the 30-plus civil wars that occurred across the world in the mid-nineties, seven were in sub-Saharan Africa.[47]

The internal civil strife in African societies that threatens state security is rooted in economic causes. Africa has an annual economic growth rate of a mere 1,5 per cent — the lowest among the world's continents — against a population increase rate of 3,2 per cent. This poor economic performance has been exacerbated by conditions of environmental and agricultural degradation; drought; disease (especially Aids and cholera); rampant corruption and mismanagement; refugee crises (which relate to conditions of civil strife and famine); intensified ethnic conflict; and a debilitating debt burden of 290 billion dollars, some 90 per cent of the continent's GDP (110 per cent for sub-Saharan Africa).[48]

The majority of the populations south of the Sahara live below the subsistence level, many in extreme poverty. The fact that the population growth rate by far exceeds the economic growth rate, results in an inexorable decline in income *per capita*. Given these realities, the priorities are not maritime. The socio-economic obstacles oblige the states to choose rice rather than rockets, "shelters rather than ships".[49]

The maintenance of a navy, by its very nature, is a capital-intensive and technology-intensive undertaking. Consequently, the few sub-Saharan societies experiencing economic growth in conditions of relative political stability are also those identified above with some kind of maritime capability. Comparative comments will be made about a few maritime forces.

- Nigeria's naval growth, for example, has benefited from its fairly large and diversified economy, by African standards. However, in practice, only about a third of its listed vessels can go to sea.

- Kenya has one of the best equipped, best trained and most professional navies in sub-Sahara. In reach, firepower and combat effectiveness it overshadows Nigeria, and is second only to South Africa, which has the leading sub-Saharan navy.[50]

- Although South Africa still "continues to ignore the escort role in favour of pure self-defence",[51] it maintains a well-managed naval infrastructure. Preston correctly indicates that the industrial sector is capable of manufacturing the most advanced maritime components and that ships of the South African Navy have recently been overhauled with new locally-manufactured electronics and upgraded sonars.[52] This technological expertise enables the South African Navy to play a substantial role in annual international naval exercises.[53]

- Moreover, South Africa, Kenya and Nigeria have naval support capabilities with some operational outreach and sustainability.[54] In addition to the South African Navy's seaborne logistic support, two other characteristics contribute to its position in the fourth rank of navies; namely, its regular blue water deployment and its submarine warfare potential. However these capabilities are in a state of decline as a result of severe budget constraints.

In countries that experience economic decline and political instability, the navies face serious problems, including those previously placed in naval rank 2. At the beginning of the nineties, the Ethiopian Navy was ageing rapidly, and the country's continuing involvement in land-based conflicts precluded any emphasis on naval development. Since April 1993, when Eritrea declared itself independent and took over most of the Ethiopian naval assets, the frail infrastructure of the new Eritrean Navy has made the development of a modern maritime force very difficult.[55] Obstacles in the way of Ghana's naval development include limited resources and serious problems with economic growth.[56] In contrast, the constabulary Mauritius Coast Guard, with direct Indian naval support and with the French naval presence, is quite effective. In general, however, these and the other maritime forces in Rank 2 — those of Tanzania, Guinea, Guinea-Bissau and Senegal — have a very limited ocean-going capability and very seldom venture beyond the radar range of their own coasts.

Most sub-Saharan states find themselves in the predicament that the maritime infrastructure required to support and maintain naval systems and military air surveillance elements does not exist and is unlikely to be developed in the medium term. This is acknowledged by naval officers of most states. According to the commander of the Tanzanian Navy, for example, his navy is not only small but finds it "difficult to counter the losses of the country's natural resources and to counter environmental hazards".[57] According to the Namibian Defence Force it is only now developing plans for a small maritime wing. "Namibia does not have much to contribute at present but we nonetheless have a legitimate interest in what our neighbours are doing."[58]

The present economic, social and political conditions confronting most sub-Saharan countries, including Tanzania, Congo Kinshasa, Angola and Mozambique, have rendered their navies almost superfluous. Where some kind of navy does exist, as in the case of the seven "constabulary navies" (Table 1) they often relapse into offshore coastal defence organisations, such as the 20 labelled as "token navies".

Furthermore, most sub-Saharan states have no ship-building industries. This means that they must acquire their platforms from countries such as the United States, Great Britain, France, Spain, China, and previously the Soviet Union. But they face a permanent problem of finding enough foreign currency to buy vessels and spare parts from overseas shipyards.[59]

Maritime issues also tend to be a low priority within sub-Saharan security establishments. No African state has allocated even a third of its national defence budget to the navy —

generally a minimum in the case of leading naval powers such as the United States, Russia, France and the United Kingdom. In sub-Sahara the emphasis is on the army and possibly the air force; naval development is deferred and delayed. Armies and air forces are often needed to maintain domestic order, whereas the irrelevance of navies in this context has made them appear a somewhat less pressing national priority to many national policy-makers.[60]

A low level of modernisation is linked to a lack of military professionalism. Underdevelopment and weak national institutions tend to draw sub-Saharan armed forces, including naval forces, into much greater involvement in domestic economic, political and social life than is the case with most navies of developed societies. Instead of focusing on maritime efficiency, naval officers are inclined to spend much of their time on internal politics. Even where professionalism is emphasised, politicisation tends to occur.[61]

Finally, a fundamental security need is to guard national resources and ensure national security more efficiently by expanding maritime capability. At present however, even by Third World standards, Africa south of the Sahara lags behind all other regions in naval development — both in qualitative and quantitative terms.[62]

In attempting to answer the question as to what the main sub-Saharan maritime priorities should be to address these grave challenges, it is necessary to differentiate between functional and material dimensions. The first refers to the roles navies play in guarding national security interests; the second, to the type of equipment needed to fulfil these roles.

7 DEFINING THE FUNCTIONAL DIMENSION

When protecting their maritime interests, sub-Saharan nations inevitably perform maritime functions at both the regional and the national level – levels that are interdependent and difficult to separate.

Sub-Saharan prosperity depends on stability and also on the unhindered flow of trade into and out of, as well as within, the region. Trade invariably points to the importance of sea lines of communication, of the freedom to operate ports and of the efficiency of the roads and railways that link them to their respective hinterlands. It also implies an interdependence among the members of the region, especially from the point of view of the landlocked states.[63] The problems of one state tend to become the problems of its neighbours.

Having acknowledged this international truth, the Organisation of African Unity (OAU) Council of Ministers as early as February 1988 resolved that African nations should work in closer collaboration to provide maritime services, in order to increase their participation in the world's seaborne trade. Since then a series of contacts at regional and sub-regional level have been initiated to attain this goal.[64]

The readmittance of South Africa to the community of nations in the nineties has opened up exciting prospects for trade in the ocean areas to the east and west of the country, thus stimulating the expansion of overall trade south of the Sahara. An Indian Ocean trade bloc, along the lines of the North American Free Trade Agreement and the Asian Pacific Economic Forum, could create a market of over 1 400 million people – one of the largest in the world. Such a bloc should significantly benefit the littoral states on the east coast of Africa.[65]

A similar prospect for trade is offered by the establishment of a South Atlantic Rim, which could encompass Argentina, Brazil and Uruguay on the western side of the rim, with the littoral states of the western seaboard of Africa on the eastern side.[66] Such expansion in trade and the resulting socio-economic growth of sub-Saharan societies depends in many ways on the ability of the littoral states to keep sea lines of communication open so as to ensure commercial intercourse.

A fundamental principle of maritime policy is to guarantee the security of coastal and territorial waters. Any visiting vessel — whether it has travelled across the ocean, around the world or only from a neighbouring port — must have the assurance that, when it enters the territorial and coastal waters of a particular country, it will be safe.[67] Insurance is also related to safety. If an area is not secure, insurance premiums for ships are higher. A sub-Saharan example of the mid-1990s was Lloyd's warning to ships to stay out of the unsafe Sierra Leone area or risk losing their insurance.

An efficient maritime structure should adhere to a series of navigational and safety requirements.[68]

- All harbours must be clear of obstacles, regularly dredged if required, and competently marked and buoyed.

- Adequate lighthouses and marked shipping lanes should be provided.

- Current mapping, aerial photography and particularly hydrographic services must be available on demand.

- Guaranteed sea search-and-rescue facilities must be provided. This should include an adequate 24-hour radio watch and reliable weather forecasts.

- To ensure the peace of mind of all honest visiting ships, coastal patrols by the navy, police or coast guard of the country in question — aimed at combating piracy, illegal immigration and smuggling — are imperative.

Another important principle is the utilisation of the EEZ to the advantage of the citizens of a coastal country. This includes the controlled exploitation of fishing resources, offshore oil and mineral mining, and deep-sea salvage.[69]

Coupled to economic development, emerging sub-Saharan navies could play a significant role in all activities aimed at water space management. Examples are:[70]

- Assistance with the protection of marine resources, notably fishing, the protection of the marine environment and the ecology, and pollution control, including oil spills and the dumping of toxic waste at sea.
- Disaster relief and ensuring the safety of life at sea.
- Hydrography and the support of scientific research.

African nations are not totally devoid of expertise and resources for these roles. South Africa, Nigeria and Kenya have proven expertise in the fields of training, hydrographic surveying, knowledge of the maritime environment and the exploitation of offshore oil, gas and mineral resources.[71]

As can be deduced from the above-mentioned growing external maritime challenges to African states, policing — that is, the enforcement of state authority — is a function of high priority. With the 1982 *Convention on the Law of the Sea* having come into effect in the mid-1990s, the need for naval policing capabilities is now greater than ever before.[72]

Neighbouring countries could consider bilateral or multilateral agreements so that certain policing tasks, such as operations against smugglers and dealing with oil spills, could be shared.[73] Policing functions demand well-established national legal systems including adequate legislation, efficient courts and the effective collection of fines. The South African Navy has, for instance, already assisted the Namibian and Mozambican governments in law enforcement against illegal fishing vessels.[74]

Furthermore, when piracy, drug smuggling and illegal immigration are combated, foreign coast guards, such as those of the United States and Norway, can provide African navies with

TABLE 2:
MARITIME PROFILE OF SUB-SAHARAN COUNTRIES

SUB-SAHARAN NAVIES: MANPOWER AND CRAFT					
Region and country	Manpower	Craft	Region and country	Manpower	Craft
WEST AFRICA			HORN OF AFRICA		
Benin	50	1	Djibouti	120	8
Côte d'Ivoire	950	8	Eritrea[5)]	Unknown	19
Ghana	850	4	Sudan[6)]	900	29
Guinea	400	9	EAST AFRICA		
Guinea-Bissau	350	8	Kenya	1 200	11
Nigeria[1)]	5 600	37	Madagascar	450	4
Senegal	700	17	Mauritius[7)]	600	39
Sierra Leone	140	5	Seychelles[8)]	300	4
Togo	110	2	Tanzania	1 050	14
SOUTHERN AFRICA			CENTRAL AFRICA		
Angola	2 500	9	Cameroon[9)]	1 250	31
Malawi[2)]	220	2	Cape Verde	120	2
Mozambique	650	3	Congo, Brazzaville	800	6
Namibia[3)]	100	3	Congo, Kinshasa[10)] (ex Zaire)	1 000	19
South Africa[4)]	7 200	59	Equatorial Guinea	120	2
			Gabon	515	7

Note 1: In the table the term "craft" refers to patrol and coastal combatants, mine warfare and support vessels. These are ships and craft whose primary role relates to the protection of the sea approaches and coastline of the state. Included are corvettes (1 for Nigeria), missile craft (with permanently fitted missile-launcher ramps and control equipment), torpedo craft (with an anti-surface-ship capability) and amphibious ships (procured to disembark troops and their equipment over unprepared beachheads). It does not refer to principal surface combatants (such as frigates, destroyers, cruisers and aircraft carriers) or submarines.

Note 2: The data should not be considered in isolation. In this chapter the quantitative information is linked to an analysis of naval functions and to qualitative considerations to create a classification of sub-Saharan navies.

Table 2 continued

Note 3: The following facts about specific countries are noteworthy:[1] *Nigeria*: The navy also includes 1 frigate. The 37 craft listed above include 1 corvette but also 26 patrol boats.[2] *Malawi*: The maritime wing of the army.[3] *Namibia*: A coast guard.[4] *South Africa*: The navy also includes 3 submarines.[5] *Eritrea*: The navy also includes 1 frigate.[6] *Sudan*: The 29 vessels include 20 inshore patrol craft and 7 supply ships.[7] *Mauritius*: A paramilitary coast guard. The 39 vessels include 35 patrol craft.[8] *Seychelles*: A paramilitary coast guard.[9] *Cameroon*: Of the 30 vessels, 26 are river patrol craft.[10] *Congo Kinshasa*: Of the 19 vessels, 10 are river patrol craft.
Note 4: The following sub-Saharan countries are not listed in the table because, for practical purposes, a maritime capability is virtually non-existent, in many cases because they are landlocked states. In West Africa: Burkina Faso, The Gambia, Liberia, Mali and Niger; in Southern Africa: Botswana, Lesotho, Zambia and Zimbabwe; in the Horn of Africa: Ethiopia and Somalia; in East Africa: Uganda; and in Central Africa: Burundi, the Central African Republic, Chad and Rwanda.
Sources: *Jane's Fighting Ships 1997/98*, Butler and Tanner, London, 1997; International Institute for Strategic Studies, *The Military Balance 1997/98*, Oxford University Press, London, 1997, pp 236-263; *Africa South of the Sahara 1997*, Europa Publications, London, 1997, pp 137-1111.

practical examples of a combination of professionalism in maritime law enforcement and the simultaneous maintenance of maritime defence readiness.[75]

According to the chief of the South African Navy, any regional peace-keeping efforts in sub-Saharan African littoral and island states "would require not only land forces but the use of maritime forces as well". He underlines the fact that, in this regard, the high accessibility of a large number of sub-Saharan countries through naval diplomacy or naval projection of power should be borne in mind.[76]

Because adequate funds are a constant problem in implementing sub-Saharan policies, cost-effectiveness is a key consideration when planning state authority enforcement in the EEZs, and it demands closer regional co-operation. In fact, even the most modest maritime surveillance asset can quickly absorb the economic benefits of the resource it is designed to protect.[77]

From the point of view of cost-effectiveness, it is also essential that organisational structures be developed to facilitate co-operation in maritime areas. Southern Africa is currently taking the lead in establishing structures for regional security co-operation. Among a number of initiatives is the Inter-State

Defence and Security Committee (ISDSC) and the Standing Maritime Committee (SMC) of the Southern Africa Development Community (SADC). Related organisations are the Port Managers' Association of Eastern and Southern Africa (PMAESA) and the Port Managers' Association of Western and Central Africa (PMAWAC). However, the regional focus is not yet on maritime affairs.[78]

Some of the main fields in which structures for sub-Saharan maritime co-operation are regarded as urgent are: policing the EEZs, combating the increasing invasion of the region's waters by unlicensed fishing fleets, tackling the danger of pollution which threatens both tourism and marine life, sharing information such as hydrographic surveys and oceanographic studies, exchanging intelligence on maritime criminal activities, such as arms smuggling by sea, and training sub-Saharan peace-keeping forces.[79]

Joint training is often discussed, and it was suggested that a joint maritime academy be formed; serving at first South Africa, Angola, Namibia, Kenya, Tanzania, Mozambique and Madagascar, and later, naval communities further north. Central aims are to promote a maritime consciousness and the standardisation of approaches to maritime matters.[80] Officer training at existing sub-Saharan naval institutions — such as those in Nigeria, Kenya and South Africa — will furthermore, be a relatively inexpensive way of improving relations and reducing suspicions about the motives of the regional players.[81]

Sub-Saharan states will be able to perform this series of essential roles in protecting national interests only if they can procure the required hardware. Consequently, the remaining issue is to explore the material dimension: What are the most essential categories of equipment required for these maritime roles?

8 EXPLORING THE MATERIAL DIMENSION

The systematic creation of efficient, but inexpensive and unpretentious, naval forces in sub-Saharan states is a first prerequisite. The fact of the matter is that most littoral states have either relatively young or emerging navies, or older — but also small — stagnating or declining navies. In general, no African state has the financial or technical wealth to maintain a navy as well as a separate coast guard.[82] The thrust of any effort toward development and co-operation should thus be to establish a naval capability where one does not exist, and to assist in its improvement where it does. The next step would be to maintain such navies and to create the facilities to make them self-sufficient.[83]

In considering realistic alternatives, the Nigerian analyst, Oladimeji, wisely argues that the first present priority for African navies is "effective offshore policing capabilities" before they can "move into blue water". "To do otherwise in the near term is to indulge in pipe dreams."[84] Effective naval capabilities can be developed only incrementally.

A further suggestion to stimulate a maritime consciousness is for the South African Navy or the South African private sector to contribute to the fishing industries of the continent's littoral states by refurbishing or supplying fishing vessels. In one survey, for example, it was found that only 87 of 263 trawlers in Angola were operational.[85] A more advanced possibility is that the private arms sector could supply small (Namacurra-type) simple, robust coastal patrol vessels to sub-Saharan states, while the South African Navy could play a role in training the crew members.

The socio-economic conditions south of the Sahara necessitate a prudent and discerning policy on the purchasing of vessels. The following is a case in point: Nigeria was one of the first African countries to acquire a modern capability to counter mines, by buying two Italian Lerici class vessels. However, the utility value of such specialised craft was widely questioned. Their sophisticated equipment only added to Nigeria's existing heavy maintenance burden, and by themselves they were of little security value.[86]

South Africa, with its limited naval resources, indicated that it was willing to play a role in providing maritime equipment, "not as a dominant Big Brother but on the basis of partnership and co-operation".[87] The Ministry of Defence stated that the country's ship-builders were geared to producing the type of coastal vessels the embryonic navies or coast guards of Africa require.[88]

Since maritime problems are shared by the sub-Saharan states and since they require the same type of strong inshore patrol vessels, a joint acquisition programme by several states would achieve economies of scale, while each state could still equip its vessels to suit individual operational requirements.[89]

When Deputy Defence Minister Ronnie Kasrils proposed that the South African Navy could become the "leading edge" of the South African National Defence Force in promoting economic development in Southern Africa, he argued that it could assist not only in the above-mentioned establishment of neighbouring navies but also in developing African ports, such as Luanda, Mombasa and Dar-es-Salaam.[90] The suggestion was that naval officers might give experienced advice to private maritime engineering firms. The landlocked states have a special strategic interest in the security of the ports they use for imports and exports. In the mid-1990s, for example, relief and food aid from the European Union to Uganda, Burundi, Rwanda and the eastern region of Congo Kinshasa was offloaded in Mombasa or Dar-es-Salaam. And consider the strategic importance of Beira to Zimbabwe, and potentially of Lobito to the Zambian and Zairian copperbelts. In South Africa the Gauteng economic heartland would grind to a halt within weeks if ports such as Durban were closed.[91]

When exploring the type of craft that embryonic navies require, it must be emphasised that the very first priority of a small navy is safeguarding the state's interests and enforcing its authority in territorial waters. This priority is heightened by the immense importance of the EEZ in the light of the previously-analysed growing nutritional and mineral exploitation of the sea. The point is this: a navy must have the capability to police state-regulated maritime regions and to prevent infringements. Such capability entails off-shore surface patrol and aircraft surveillance — relatively inexpensive commercial aircraft can be converted for surveillance.[92] The emphasis is on this task of surveillance, and on policing territorial waters and protecting off-shore facilities.

What is required for these functions is not so much submarines, combat vessels, and strike aircraft that can inflict lethal damage and fight intense wars at sea; it is ships and planes that, on the one hand, can undertake quick reconnaissance missions and, on the other, can perform a variety of patrolling, policing and demonstration functions and tailor force to operations at the lower end of the spectrum of violence.

All coastal states are concerned with preserving their own use of the sea, at least within their home waters, as a means of communication. Accordingly, the minimum sea-control requirement is obviously to keep ports open, even if small states must rely on a Big Brother for the protection of their trade. In this respect, providing mine counter-measures, an unglamorous aspect of naval operations, plays a crucial role in small navies that plan to deny adjacent seas to intruders.[93]

However, when eventually these navies have "found their feet" in the water and are established as professional forces, they should bear in mind that small missile boats are something that

Preston calls "great little equalisers". But impressive though they are in terms of sheer firepower, they provide poor surveillance and need considerable co-ordination and targeting information if they are to function effectively. Radar surveillance and target data can best be provided by larger units or from a shore base.[94] Moreover, a cramped strike-craft, with every man needed to keep the system operating, is not very suitable for training and is also relatively expensive.

Thus, although a pure sea-denial force may package remarkable anti-surface firepower in fast attack craft, the small size of the craft simply does not allow sufficient room for the multimission capabilities required, specifically antisubmarine capabilities. They are also unable to accommodate helicopters or the necessary command, control and communications facilities.[95]

Sub-Saharan navies will eventually realise that, to cope with the complexity of sea control, a budding contiguous-sea navy cannot simply increase its number of small ships; it will soon experience a need for bigger ships: corvettes or small frigates. To become big navies, small navies need large ships.[96] This need motivated the South African cabinet in November 1998 to approve the procurement of four corvettes, three submarines and four maritime helicopters from European consortiums. As navies grow they simultaneously shift from an emphasis on patrol and surveillance to sea denial, and then to sea control.[97]

The smaller sub-Saharan navies necessarily place more emphasis on patrol craft than on sea-denial or sea-control forces. With the increase in the number of large patrol craft and aircraft, the now larger navies focus less on small patrol craft and shore-based helicopters, as more suitable vessels, capable of taking helicopters to sea, start appearing.[98] This development is linked to the crucial need for squadrons of dedicated maritime patrol aircraft able to cover a vast surveillance area at a much greater speed than naval vessels.[99]

Another comment on regional co-operation should be made in the context of the material dimension: it is that the establishment and the development of sub-Saharan maritime forces are alike promoted by standardisation. Standardisation implies similar equipment for combined operations, necessarily linked to an agreement on command and control structures, on communication procedures, and on common doctrines.[100] The variety of craft, languages and training procedures makes this a major challenge; nevertheless the navies of South Africa, Kenya and Gabon co-operated quite effectively in the mid-1990s. An ultimate goal is to achieve a high degree of interoperability among medium-sized vessels of reasonable sophistication. In fact, interoperability, especially standard operating procedures, is paramount.[101]

Eventually, technological development could offer the sub-Saharan maritime forces the opportunity to participate in OAU, Commonwealth or UN-initiated ventures in the region. The additional benefit, of course, is that it would also afford the forces a high degree of mutual maritime security.[102]

Final conclusions will be drawn, based on a brief summary of the main argument.

9 CONCLUSION

This chapter commenced with a conceptual framework, defining the general nature of navies; distinguishing between their military, diplomatic and policing roles; identifying the essence of maritime strategy; and analysing the nature of sea control, sea denial and maritime defence. The importance of an operating radius or reach was emphasised.

The framework of seven ranks that was developed revealed that no sub-Saharan navy can be placed in the top two categories. Only one is in rank 4 – littoral navies; two in rank 3 – coastal navies; seven in rank 2 – constabulary navies; and the other eighteen in rank 1 — token navies. Of the 44 sub-Saharan countries, 16 have virtually no maritime capability at present. The sub-Saharan naval hierarchy is unique among Third World regions in its preponderance of weak navies, not only in mobility and firepower but also in training experience and maintenance capability. In fact, most are regarded as coast guards.

Trends that currently impact on Africa's maritime environment relate to the utilisation of the sea, technological development, international political transformation, the sea routes around the continent and the provision of assistance by Western financial institutions. The growing marginalisation of sub-Saharan states in the international consciousness and the decline in international support have obliged them to promote policies of self-sufficiency.

After defining a coastal state's right to protect national assets in its territorial waters and exclusive economic zone, several external challenges to African maritime defence were identified. It was pointed out that the sub-Saharan states are vulnerable to foreign exploitation of their marine and mineral resources, such as fish, oil and gas, and to threats of pollution and the dumping of toxic waste. At the same time they are also confronted by a series of internal challenges to maritime defence. Africa has an economic growth rate of 1,5 per cent — the world's lowest — exacerbated by disease, agricultural degradation, crime, rampant corruption and intensified ethnic conflict. Consequently, and understandably, its priorities are not maritime. The few sub-Saharan societies experiencing economic growth are also those that possess some kind of maritime capability, especially Kenya, Nigeria and South Africa.

Referring to specific countries, it was indicated that, without the efficient maritime infrastructure required to support and maintain naval systems, most navies face such serious problems of ageing that they may degenerate and lapse into offshore defence organisations. Related internal problems are the general irrelevance of navies relative to the rest of the armed forces, and the emphasis on the politicisation, rather than the professionalism, of naval officers.

These external and internal threats to maritime defence in particular, and national interests in general, confront sub-Saharan nations with serious challenges that are manifested in two related spheres: functional and material.

In protecting their maritime interests, sub-Saharan nations will inevitably have to fulfil maritime functions at both the regional and the national level. A fundamental principle for a beneficial maritime policy was identified as guaranteeing the safety and security of coastal and territorial waters. Any visiting vessel, whether it has travelled across the ocean or only from a neighbouring port, must have the assurance that, when it enters the coastal waters of a particular country, it will be safe. In this context this chapter explored a series of navigational and safety requirements.

An argument was put forward that emerging sub-Saharan navies could play a significant role in water space management, such as: assistance with the protection of marine resources, notably fishing; disaster relief and ensuring the safety of life at sea; and hydrography and the support of scientific research. The essence is to keep the sea lines of communication open.

With the 1982 *Convention on the Law of the Sea* having come into effect in the middle of the 1990s, policing — that is, the enforcement of state authority — will necessarily be a high priority function. Moreover, regional peace keeping will also require maritime forces.

Referring to initiatives such as the Inter-State Defence and Security Committee, it was argued that the establishment of effective structures for sub-Saharan maritime co-operation was essential and, furthermore, that joint maritime training may promote a maritime consciousness and the standardisation of approaches to maritime matters.

With respect to the material dimension, most littoral states have limited economic resources and only an emerging maritime capability. The objective of co-operation should be to establish a naval capability where it does not exist, and to assist in its improvement where it does. The emphasis should be on procuring robust patrol vessels to enable states to enforce their authority in territorial waters. A joint sub-Saharan acquisition programme for several states would achieve economies of scale.

The conclusion was reached that this function does not require ships that can fight intense wars at sea, but ships and planes that can undertake quick reconnaissance missions and that can patrol effectively. The smaller sub-Saharan navies will necessarily place more emphasis on patrol craft than on sea-denial or sea-control forces. This is linked to a need for squadrons of dedicated maritime patrol aircraft that are able to cover a vast area at a much greater speed than naval vessels.

When the sub-Saharan navies have eventually succeeded in asserting their authority in coastal waters, as the South African Navy does, larger units such as corvettes or small frigates will be required.

From a regional perspective, the ultimate goal is to standardise sub-Saharan maritime equipment and to achieve a high degree of interoperability among medium-sized vessels of reasonable sophistication. This will enable sub-Saharan maritime forces to defend their national and regional interests more effectively.

Finally, this chapter began by defining the roles of navies. The framework of seven naval ranks illustrated the maritime weakness of sub-Saharan nations. The features of the African maritime environment, as well as a series of external and internal problems, indicated that, should sub-Saharan states wish to maintain national and regional security, they will face severe challenges.

However the challenges can be transformed into opportunities. This will happen if, in the functional dimension, sub-Saharan states concentrate on a series of policing tasks for ensuring safety in their territorial waters and for keeping the sea lines of communication open; and, in the material dimension, if they focus on procuring robust craft and aircraft for quick reconnaissance missions and patrols. Activities and structures for closer regional co-operation will improve maritime expansion substantially. Sub-Saharan Africa will then develop a maritime defence capability to protect its national and regional interests efficiently.

REFERENCES

1. Morris, M A, *Expansion of Third World Navies*, Macmillan, London, 1987, p 271.
2. Sass, B, "The challenge for African states", in Mills, G, *Maritime Policy for Developing Nations*, The South African Institute of International Affairs, Johannesburg, September 1995, pp 208-209.
3. *Ibid*, p 209.
4. Morris, M A, *op cit*, p 271.
5. Groenewald, E P, "The requirements of small navies with specific reference to the RSA", *Strategic Review for Southern Africa*, Vol XI(1), May 1989, p 56.
6. *Ibid* p 71.
7. *Ibid* p 74-75.
8. *Ibid* p 57-59.
9. *Ibid* p 51-52.
10. *Ibid* p 53-54.
11. *Ibid* p 51.
12. Morris, M A, *op cit*, pp 243-244.

13. Oladimeji, O A, "Where are the African navies going?", *Proceedings*, March 1990, p 101. Oladimeji is a naval captain and the director of information for the Nigerian Navy.
14. Kasrils, R, "Regional maritime partnership – opening address", *The Southern African Naval Conference on Regional Maritime Co-operation*, Cape Town, 18-21 October 1994, p 9. Ronnie Kasrils is the South African Deputy Minister of Defence.
15. International Institute for Strategic Studies, *The Military Balance 1997-1998*, Oxford University Press, London, pp 236-263; *Africa South of the Sahara 1997*, Europa Publications, London, 1997, pp 137-1111.
16. Morris, M A, *op cit*. See especially Chapter 2: The Hierarchy of Naval Capability, pp 22-66. For a summary, see pp 25-26, 34-35.
17. Morris, M A, *op cit*, p 242; and Oladimeji, O A, *op cit*, p 101.
18. Sass, B, *op cit*, pp 196-198.
19. *Ibid*, p 198.
20. Groenewald, E P, *op cit*, pp 60-61; and Simpson-Anderson, R C, "The maritime interests and policy of the Republic of South Africa", *The Southern African Naval Conference on Regional Maritime Co-operation, op cit*, pp 72-73. Vice Admiral R C Simpson-Anderson is the Chief of the South African Navy.
21. Groenewald, E P, *op cit*, p 60.
22. *Ibid*, p 61.
23. *Ibid*, p 61.
24. Compare Simpson-Anderson, R C, *op cit*, p 72.
25. *Ibid*, p 72.
26. Kibwana, J R E, "Kenya's maritime interests and policy, and the requirements for regional maritime co-operation", *The Southern African Naval Conference on Regional Maritime Co-operation, op cit*, p 52. Major General J R E Kibwana is the Kenya Navy Commander.
27. Mills, G, "The nature of Africa's insecurities: A regional dimension?", *The Southern African Naval Conference on Regional Maritime Co-operation*, Cape Town, 18-21 October 1994, p 26.
28. Morris, M A, *op cit*, p 242.
29. Oladimeji, O A, *op cit*, p 102.

30. Morris, M A, *op cit*, pp 132-133.
31. Sass, B, *op cit*, p 200.
32. Morris, M A, *op cit*, p 142.
33. Mills, G, *op cit*, p 27.
34. Kasrils, R, *op cit*, p 9.
35. Morris, M A, *op cit*, pp 246-247.
36. Mills, G, *op cit*, p 27.
37. Ongobo, F, "The Congo's maritime interests and policy: the need for regional maritime co-operation", *The Southern African Naval Conference on Regional Maritime Co-operation, op cit*, p 39. Capt (Navy) Fulgort Ongobo is the Congo Navy Commander. Also see Shalli, M, at the same *conference on maritime co-operation*, p 63. Brigadier General Martin Shalli is the director of operations, plans and training of the Namibian Ministry of Defence.
38. Mills, G, *op cit*, p 28.
39. Simpson-Anderson, R C, *op cit*, p 74.
40. Kasrils, R, *op cit*, p 12.
41. Sass, B, *op cit*, p 207.
42. Kasrils, R, *op cit*, pp 9-10. See De Villiers, C, "Poachers in Patagonian toothfish plunder", *Sunday Times Metro*, 30 Nov 97, p 2.
43. Mills, G, *op cit*, p 28.
44. Simpson-Anderson, R C, *op cit*, p 74.
45. Ongobo, F, *op cit*, pp 39-40.
46. Oladimeji, O A, *op cit*, p 102.
47. Compare (a previous edition) of International Institute for Strategic Studies, *The Military Balance 1994-1995*, Brassey's, London, p 223.
48. Mills, G, *op cit*, p 25.
49. Oladimeji, O A, *op cit*, p 102.
50. Morris, M A, *op cit*, pp 243-244.
51. Preston, A, "Africa's navies – a look ahead for the 1990s", *Naval Forces*, Vol XIII (11), 1992, p 36.

52. *Ibid*, pp 34-35; compare Jakobsen, J, *An Assessment of the South African Navy*, report for the Centre for Southern African Studies. University of the Western Cape, May 1994.
53. Simpson-Anderson, R C, *op cit*, p 76.
54. International Institute for Strategic Studies, *The Military Balance 1997-1998*, Oxford University Press, London, pp 254, 258-259.
55. *Ibid*, p 244.
56. Morris, M A, *op cit*, p 243.
57. Sande, L G, "Tanzanian maritime interests and policy and the requirements for regional co-operation", *The Southern African Naval Conference on Regional Maritime Co-operation, op cit*, pp 66-67. Brigadier L G Sande is the commander of the Tanzanian Navy.
58. Shalli, M, *op cit*, pp 63-4.
59. Oladimeji, O A, *op cit*, pp 101-102.
60. Morris, M A, *op cit*, pp 272-273; also compare Wright, I, "Recent development in African navies", *Naval Forces*, Vol 9-2, 1988, pp 86-89.
61. Morris, M A, *op cit*, p 272.
62. Oladimeji, O A, *op cit*, p 101.
63. Simpson-Anderson, R C, *op cit*, p 77.
64. Oladimeji, O A, *op cit*, p 102.
65. Simpson-Anderson, R C, *op cit*, p 73.
66. *Ibid*, p 73.
67. Sass, B, *op cit*, pp 199-200.
68. *Ibid*, pp 200-201.
69. *Ibid*, p 201.
70. Simpson-Anderson, R C, *op cit*, p 78.
71. Sass, B, *op cit*, p 212.
72. "Law of the Sea", *United Nations Yearbook*, 1992, pp 996-1003.
73. Kibwana, J R E, *op cit*, pp 48-49.
74. Sass, B, *op cit*, p 212.
75. Oladimeji, O A, *op cit*, p 103.

76. Simpson-Anderson, R C, *op cit*, p 77.
77. Kibwana, J R E, *op cit*, pp 48-49.
78. Sass, B, *op cit*, p 211.
79. Kibwana, J R E, *op cit*, pp 49-50; and Sande, J G, *op cit*, p 67.
80. Sass, B, *op cit*, p 212.
81. Mills, G, *op cit*, p 31.
82. Sass, B, *op cit*, p 208.
83. Simpson-Anderson, R C, *op cit*, p 77.
84. Oladimeji, O A, *op cit*, p 103.
85. Mills, G, *op cit*, p 30.
86. Preston, A, *op cit*, p 36.
87. Kasrils, R, *op cit*, pp 10-11.
88. *Ibid*, pp 10-11.
89. *Ibid*, p 12; and Kibwana, J R E, *op cit*, pp 50-51.
90. Compare Kasrils, R, "The role of the SA Navy", *Conference on South Africa and International Naval Co-operation*, by SAIIA and IDP, Cape Town, 9 August 1994.
91. Kasrils, R, *Maritime partnership...op cit*, p 10.
92. Groenewald, E P, *op cit*, p 62.
93. *Ibid*, p 63.
94. Preston, A, *op cit*, p 38.
95. Groenewald, E P, *op cit*, p 64.
96. *Ibid*, p 65.
97. *Ibid*, p 65-69; Mbeki, T, "Statement on defence acquisition package", *Department of Defence Bulletin*, 18 November 1998.
98. *Ibid*, p 67-68.
99. Mills, G, *op cit*, p 30.
100. Kasrils, R, *Maritime partnership...*, *op cit*, p 13.
101. Simpson-Anderson, R C, *op cit*, pp 77-78.
102. *Ibid*, p 78.

Chapter 7

PARTICIPATION IN SUB-SAHARAN PEACE SUPPORT OPERATIONS

Theo Neethling

1 INTRODUCTION

The end of the Cold War has not resulted in worldwide peace and stability. The shift from a bipolar to a multipolar and multi-faceted world has, in fact, reduced the risk of conventional interstate wars, but has been the cause of several intrastate armed conflicts with an even higher risk of regional instability. Such conflicts and the and the realities of new threats or dangers have produced a dramatic growth in peace-keeping requirements since the end of the previous decade. Between 1988 and 1994, the engagement of the United Nations (UN) in preventive diplomacy missions grew by over 350 per cent.[1]

In sub-Saharan Africa, conflicts have always been complex and extremely difficult to resolve. However, the end of the Cold War has added another dimension, as the end of bipolar politics has led to a paradoxical situation for the continent: While a loss in the continent's strategic importance eroded the interest of the international community in Africa to some extent, intrastate conflicts on the continent have escalated.[2]

As a result of support for the notion of peace support operations[3] worldwide, a clear international message has emerged against the backdrop of greater international ambivalence towards Africa's problems in particular and towards peacekeeping specifically.[4] In this context the international community has signalled that African countries should begin to take charge of their own peace-keeping requirements and find solutions to their own conflicts.

It is therefore widely accepted that African leaders, as represented in the Organisation of African Unity (OAU) and the various sub-regional organisations, have to accept an increased burden of responsibility for conflict-resolution and management on the continent. Peace keeping, peace enforcement and even conflict termination have become most important as secondary functions of African armed forces, especially since the conflicts in Angola, Mozambique, Rwanda, Somalia, the Democratic Republic of the Congo (DRC) and Congo Brazzaville have all proved that, when a state suffers as a result of acute internal conflict, instability and threats to security can be experienced across an entire region.

In the following analysis, an overview of the management and conducting of multinational peace support operations is given. The international peace-keeping system, sub-Saharan African contributions to peace support operations, as well as the general framework for security co-operation and related developments in sub-Saharan Africa, are especially assessed. This is followed by an analysis of the challenges to the successful conducting of peace support operations, with specific emphasis on the perils associated with such operations in the sub-Saharan African environment.

2 CONDUCTING MULTINATIONAL PEACE SUPPORT OPERATIONS

To ensure success, peace support operations are critically dependent on the extent to which international authority underpins them and on the political will of participating member states. This kind of authority is necessary to assist in reducing political pressure on the countries responsible, to avoid international isolation of the participating countries if the operation "goes wrong" and to prevent overextending the capabilities of any country's armed forces.[5]

Success in any peace support operation therefore depends upon a broad political process. Such missions never comprise only military exercises. In fact, military operations play a distinctly supportive role, and may even produce few obvious results as regards the outcome. Of significant importance is the broad political apparatus or institutional framework created to manage co-operative security and to co-ordinate peace missions. Such political apparatus and institutional framework entails a complex amalgam of political, diplomatic, military and economic measures at both a domestic and broader level.

2.1 United Nations

The first of the objectives of the UN listed in its Charter is "[t]o maintain international peace and security, and to this end: to take effective collective measures for the prevention and removal of threats to the peace, and for the suppression of acts of aggression or other breaches of the peace, and to bring about by peaceful means, and in conformity with the principles of justice and international law, adjustment or settlement of international disputes or situations which might lead to a breach of the peace".[6]

Concrete measures to be taken by the UN Security Council, the principal organ which was vested with the primary responsibility for the maintenance of international peace and security to achieve this purpose are set out in Chapters VI and VII of the Charter. Chapter VI provides that international disputes "likely to endanger the maintenance of international peace and security" can be brought to the attention of the Security Council or the General Assembly. If the Security Council determines that a threat to the peace, breach of the peace or act of aggression exists, the Council may use the broad powers given to it in Chapter VII of the Charter. Should the Security Council regard it necessary, it may take, under Article 42, "action by air, sea and land forces as may be necessary to maintain or restore international peace and security".[7]

The 15 member states of the Security Council — not the Secretary-General — create and define peace support operations. The UN Charter specifies that the Council has primary responsibility for the maintenance of international peace and security. Each of the five permanent Council members can veto any decision on peace support operations.[8]

As already mentioned, the end of the Cold War has not reduced threats to peace and has in fact seen the transformation (or mutation) of classical peace-keeping operations into multidimensional conflict management activities. Accordingly, the UN requested its Secretary-General, Dr Boutros Boutros-Ghali, to prepare a report containing "... an analysis and recommendations on ways of strengthening and making more efficient within the framework and provisions of the Charter the capacity of the United Nations for preventive diplomacy, for peacemaking and for peace keeping". As a result, his report titled *An Agenda for Peace* was submitted in 1992 and has since served as a broad framework for peace support operations.[9]

Because the UN is the source of authority for types of peace support operations, its set of terms and definitions is of importance. An *Agenda for Peace* has sought to identify a new approach to UN peace keeping. It suggested that it was no longer appropriate to consider peace keeping in isolation, and presented the concepts of preventive diplomacy, peacemaking, peace keeping and post-conflict peace building as a range of options to be considered in the context of peace support activities. None of these concepts were really new, but were presented as a range of options for the first time. In the report, the terms "preventive diplomacy", "peacemaking", "peace keeping" and "post-conflict peace building" were defined as follows:[10]

- Preventive diplomacy is action to prevent disputes from arising between parties, to prevent existing disputes from escalating into conflicts and to limit the spread of the latter when they occur.

- Peacemaking is action to bring hostile parties to agreement, essentially through such peaceful means as those foreseen in Chapter VI of the Charter of the UN.

- Peace keeping is the development of a UN presence in the field, hitherto with the consent of all parties concerned, normally involving UN military and/or police personnel and frequently civilians as well. Peace keeping is a technique that expands the possibilities for both the prevention of conflict and the making of peace.

- Post-conflict peace building is action to identify and support structures that will tend to strengthen and solidify peace in order to avoid a relapse into conflict.

It is noteworthy that "peacemaking" refers to the use of diplomatic means to persuade parties in conflict to cease hostilities and to negotiate a peaceful settlement of their dispute. As with "preventive diplomacy", or "preventive action", as it is currently referred to by the Secretary-General of the UN, the UN can play a role only if the parties to the dispute agree that it should do so. Peacemaking thus excludes the use of force against one of the parties to enforce an end to hostilities, an activity that in UN parlance is referred to as "peace enforcement".[11] The notion "peace support operations" is now widely used in doctrine (for example, in NATO documents) to cover all "peace keeping", "peace enforcement" and related operations.

Another significant development relates to the fact that co-operation between the UN and regional organisations has greatly increased in the 1990s. Yet, the concept of co-operation is not entirely new. The UN Charter has provided for the involvement of "regional arrangements or agencies" for maintaining international peace and security along with the UN since 1945. Article 53 of the Charter even refers to enforcement action by regional bodies under UN authority.[12] However, it is important to note an increase in UN practice to devolve responsibility to regional bodies that are situated within the affected area — i.e. the North Atlantic Treaty Organisation (NATO) in Europe, the Organisation of American States (OAS) in the Americas and the OAU in Africa.

The independent states that are signatories to the UN Charter form the resource base of the organisation, and the military personnel who serve in peace support operations are provided by the member states on a voluntary basis.[13] Sub-Saharan African countries have been players in UN peace support operations throughout the last 20 years.

2.2 Sub-Saharan African contributions to peace support operations

Participation in peace support operations is thus not something new to sub-Saharan African countries. Beginning with the Korean conflict (in which South Africa and Ethiopia took part) they have regularly contributed to UN multinational operations inside and outside the African continent. Over the past 20 years, sub-Saharan African forces have participated in numerous prominent peace support operations. Forces from Ghana and Nigeria took part in peace missions in Israel and Lebanon. Representatives from Ghana, Kenya, Nigeria and Senegal served on the UN Iraq-Kuwait observer mission. In the 1990s, soldiers from Ghana, Kenya and Nigeria participated in the multilateral peace mission in the former Yugoslavia. Furthermore, forces from Ghana, Cameroon, Namibia and Senegal participated in UN operations in Cambodia.[14]

Africans have also played key roles in UN operations in sub-Saharan Africa. For instance, UNAVEM-I, the UN Angola Verification Mission in Angola from 1989 to 1991, was commanded by a Nigerian. UNAVEM-II from 1991 to 1995 was successively commanded by a Nigerian and a Zimbabwean, and UNAVEM-III from 1995 by a Zimbabwean. In addition, the deputy commander of ONUMOZ, the UN Operations in Mozambique from 1992 to 1994, was a Botswana Defence Force Officer.[15] Africans were also in command of UNOMIL, the UN Observer Mission in Liberia, from 1993 and 1997.[16]

During 1995, 18 OAU member states provided the UN with more than 6 000 peacekeepers. Ghana, Chad, Egypt, Sudan, Senegal and Zambia have joined the 36 countries from other continents participating in the UN Standby Arrangements System. This mechanism is intended to provide a pool of forces for deployment anywhere in the world for UN peace-keeping duties on request of the Secretary-General.[17]

In 1998 the 69 countries that have officially expressed their willingness to participate in standby arrangements include, Niger, Senegal, Ghana, Tanzania, Zambia, Sudan, Tunisia, Zimbabwe, Botswana, Chad, Egypt, Kenya and Nigeria.[18]

It is therefore clear that a substantial number of African countries have participated in international peace support operations and related initiatives of the UN structure. At the same time it should be noted that regional and sub-regional peace initiatives have become an increasingly important aspect of the development of an African framework for co-operative security with a view to managing Africa's scourge of conflict.

2.3 Regional and sub-regional peace initiatives in sub-Saharan Africa

It is commonly known that the UN is overextended in terms of resources and capacity to perform effectively the many peace support tasks it has assumed over the last decade. Having reached a critical point, this has called for an appropriate division of responsibilities between the UN and other role-players in the sphere of peace support operations. In sub-Saharan Africa, prospects for managing conflict by means of peace support operations are closely linked to the dynamics of regional and sub-regional peace initiatives.

2.3.1 Regional peace initiatives

Conflict resolution and the issue of peace, security and stability have been major concerns of the OAU since its inception in 1963, when it was confronted with three categories of threat to peace and security:

- disputes involving only its members

- situations involving members with colonial regimes, and

- situations resulting from relations between members and states outside Africa.

The first category concerns territorial and other disputes between member states. Internal disputes were outside the sphere of the OAU or the UN until as recently as 1993, except when there were international implications. Since then the OAU has helped in finding solutions to the conflicts in Chad and Nigeria. Both the OAU and the UN have been involved in the second category, for example in Namibia. In such cases there has been great reliance on the UN. The third category relates to experiences, such as in the Congo in 1960-64 and Nigeria in 1967-70, where there was large-scale outside interference.

Ad hoc arrangements were in effect the order of the day in OAU dealings with interstate conflicts, while intrastate conflicts were largely left to each member state to handle.[19] Another factor of concern in this context relates to certain core principles of the OAU, which member states are pledged to "observe scrupulously". They are:

- the sovereign equality of all states
- non-interference in the internal affairs of states,
- respect for the sovereignty and territorial integrity of each state and its inalienable right to independent existence.

These provisions mean that unless the government of the state in question decides to ask for international support for conciliation in interstate or intrastate conflicts, or the UN Security Council decides that intervention is required, there are no coercive instruments to address any incipient crises. In addition to *ad hoc* arrangements, these provisions have constantly posed particular difficulties in conflict management and resolution in African states wracked by civil war or other forms of violent dissent.[20]

In 1991 the OAU committed itself to deploying greater efforts towards the creation of an enabling environment for conflict prevention, management and resolution.[21] The *Kampala Document* of 23 May 1991 represented the first concerted African call for a continental peace-keeping body in Africa. Although not an official OAU document, it nevertheless carried considerable weight.

In the *Kampala Document* it was suggested that Africa should institute a continental peace-keeping machinery as an important instrument for the preservation of peace in instances which potentially or actually threaten the security of African state(s) or the continent as a whole. In order to realise the establishment of a continental peace-keeping body, each participating member state was called upon to implement special training measures in peace support operations for a contingent of its armed forces. In view of this, a continental peace support operation was regarded as an *ad hoc* operation through rapid mobilisation of pre-agreed manpower and financial contributions from member states.[22]

Another important milestone was the establishment of the OAU's Mechanism for Conflict Prevention, Management and Resolution in Cairo in 1993. This was a less ambitious initiative and should be seen as a departure from the OAU's earlier *ad hoc* arrangements for conflict management. However it confirmed African leaders' determination to work together and assume greater responsibility for the maintenance of peace, security and stability on the continent.

In establishing the mechanism, the African heads of state and government were guided *inter alia* by the following principal considerations:[23]

- The UN should clearly remain the pre-eminent international authority with the responsibility for dealing with international peace and security, including internal crises which threaten regional stability in Africa.

- The UN, together with regional and sub-regional organisations, should form a partnership in framing new approaches to crisis prevention, management and resolution in the post-Cold War era.

- Regional and sub-regional organisations on the one hand, and the UN system on the other, should endeavour to share proportionately the burden relating to the maintenance of worldwide peace, security and stability.

- As a regional organisation, the OAU should realise the need for it to take primary ownership of its own problems, especially those relating to issues of peace, security and stability.

It was declared that the primary objective of the mechanism was the anticipation and prevention of conflicts. In circumstances where conflicts had already occurred, it would be its responsibility to undertake peacemaking and peace-building functions to facilitate their resolution.[24] The OAU has, accordingly, spent a lot of energy in assuring that the mechanism becomes fully operational. Yet it cannot be stated that it is without its shortcomings.[25] At the same time it can safely be argued that significant work was done to address Africa's peace-keeping challenges in an overarching way.

In the interim the United States and some European nations have started to support the idea of an African response capability of some kind, staffed and commanded almost exclusively by Africans. As a result, the *African Crisis Response Force* and the *African Crisis Response Initiative* have successively been tabled as the American answers to Africa's peace-keeping challenges. The former was introduced in 1996 and related to the institution of a standing African force tasked with a peace-keeping responsibility, but was not met with a great deal of enthusiasm within Africa and elsewhere.[26] The latter was a reaction to the lukewarm African response and can be regarded as a long-term plan; a first step in a programme to encourage and assist African countries in training and capacity building to develop or establish a response capability of some form.[27]

In the light of previous debates on the issue and as a result of these initiatives, the OAU Council of Ministers decided in February 1998 to accept the principle of an African peace force of some kind that will carry out peace support operations under UN and OAU auspices. They have also acknowledged the efforts and initiatives of the US, France and Britain to improve the ability of African forces to conduct peace support operations in Africa.[28] However, many questions remain unclear, especially as regards the following:[29]

- What will the generic objectives governing African involvement in peace support operations be?

- In what kind of peace support operations will such a force be prepared to engage?

- How will the financial arrangements for peace support operations be determined in the light of the cumbersome nature of UN bureaucracy?

- How will African entry and exit criteria be determined and who should be the key role-players in setting the necessary parameters?

- What should be done in the fields of interoperability of equipment; formulation of common doctrines; allocation of responsibilities to different participating states; command responsibilities within combined forces, and many more?

An integrated African (OAU) and sub-regional policy on peace support operations seems to be imperative. At the same time it should be kept in mind that peace support operations are international endeavours, endorsed by the UN and conducted in accordance with the internationalist ethos of the UN Charter.[30] Against this background it can be argued that the ideal arrangement will be one in which the OAU is fully involved in all aspects of the preparation of African forces for UN operations on the continent. The OAU should furthermore be in a position to deploy peace missions in African conflicts, based on a UN mandate and with sufficient political and financial backing from the world body.[31]

As far as funding of sub-Saharan peace support operations is concerned, it must be noted that a special fund, known as the "OAU Peace Fund", was created in the wake of the adoption of the OAU Mechanism for Conflict Prevention, Management and Resolution. The purpose of this fund is to provide exclusive support to OAU operational activities relating to conflict management. Contributions to it will be used for OAU activities undertaken within the framework of conflict anticipation and prevention, peacemaking, peace building and peace keeping.[32]

The fund is supported by an annual five per cent contribution from member states and sources outside Africa. From its inception in 1993 to March 1996, African countries contributed approximately five million US$, of which about one million came voluntarily from Algeria, Lesotho, Egypt, Mauritius, Ethiopia, Namibia and South Africa. Over the same period, approximately six-and-a-half million US$ was contributed by the following countries: Indonesia, China, Germany, the US, Belgium, Sweden, Italy, Denmark, the United Kingdom, Norway, Spain and Korea. That means that Africa's contributions to the OAU Peace Fund made up approximately 50 per cent of the total received during this period.[33]

The above figures should be seen in the context of the cost of peace support operations. For example, in August 1996 the UN's Department of Peace-keeping Operations estimated the cost of running UNAVEM III (the UN mission in Angola) at approximately 940 000 US$ a day.[34]

In conclusion, it is stipulated in the UN Charter that regional problems should, *ipso facto*, have regional solutions. There is thus a pressing need for regional organisations such as the OAU to take care of their own security problems and to bear the burden of conflict. In addition, it is believed today that sub-regional organisations should also endeavour to share the burden of maintaining worldwide peace and security proportionately.

2.3.2 Sub-regional peace initiatives

The OAU was entrusted with the responsibility of promoting the unity and solidarity of African states and ensuring the peaceful settlement of disputes by negotiation, mediation, conciliation or arbitration. It has had this responsibility for peace keeping since its inception in 1963. Its first real peace-keeping test was the Chadian imbroglio which was handled in 1981 by the OAU heads of state;[35] and since then it has dealt with many and varied forms of conflict.[36] However the OAU, like the UN at the top of the pyramid, is experiencing financial problems as recalcitrant members neglect to pay their dues on time.[37]

A devolution of responsibility from the UN to regional or sub-regional organisations, such as the Southern African Development Community (SADC), should be seen in this light. It alleviates the capacity problems of the cash-strapped UN by assuming or sharing some of its peace support duties. Also, sub-regional organisations have a particular knowledge of, and responsibility for, their region; and they have great potential as building blocks in volatile parts of the world.[38]

The model here should be perceived in the context of the realisation that African states and organisations will have to accept an increasing burden of responsibility for conflict prevention and resolution on the continent, and that this can best be achieved by co-operation at sub-regional level.[39]

If regional organisations are primarily responsible for dealing with their own security problems, it does not imply a diversion from UN guidance and control. Regional organisations and arrangements on the one hand, and the UN system on the other, should endeavour to share the responsibility of maintaining peace. They should form and maintain partnerships and act decisively and expeditiously when framing new plans for crisis prevention, management and resolution. However the UN, with its cumulative experience, should remain the pre-eminent international authority for dealing with international peace and security, and with internal crises that threaten regional stability, particularly in Africa.[40] It is an approach that assigns peace-keeping responsibilities to regional or other organisations according to current UN policy.[41]

In graphic terms, the partnership between the UN and the OAU with its sub-regional organisations may be viewed as a pyramid. The UN, which is the world body and the supreme organ responsible for peace and security worldwide, is at the top of the pyramid; in the middle is the OAU as a regional entity for conflict management; at the base are the sub-regional organisations.

The great advantage of positioning a regional organisation midway in the hierarchical model is that it is neither too far from, nor too close to, theatres of conflict. It is ideally positioned to co-ordinate all activities relating to conflict management.

At sub-regional level the most prominent sub-Saharan organisation involved in peace operations thus far is notably the one created for the Liberian conflict by the Economic Community of West African States (ECOWAS). Initially termed a Monitoring Group, this military organisation is now generally known by its acronym, ECOMOG. It developed in August 1990 out of the military forces deployed into Liberia in an attempt to put an end to the civil war there. Over the period of its existence, it has included contingents from eight West African and two East African states.

ECOMOG has since its inception largely been controlled by Nigeria. Critics of the organisation often complained that it was a thin veil for Nigerian hegemonic ambitions. This generally accompanied accusations that Nigerians controlled all the key staff positions and unfairly diverted resources to their fellow countrymen. There were also allegations that Nigeria was not neutral; and this led to a severe degrading of ECOMOG's credibility as a role-player in the Liberian conflict.[42]

Then, in 1997, ECOMOG made international headlines when it intervened in Sierra Leone to reverse a military *coup* and restore power to elected President Ahmad Tejan Kabbah. Again Nigerian domination was prominent as hundreds of Nigerian troops were sent in with a view to driving out the military regime.[43] The military junta was successfully ousted in February 1998. ECOMOG was commended by the Secretary-General of the OAU for its initiative,[44] although Nigeria had engaged in the conflict under the banner of ECOMOG without any official mandate.[45] Peace has, however, not been restored in this conflict-ridden country.

Another significant example of changing responses to African crises in West Africa relates to the two-year-old conflict in the Central African Republic and the formation of the Inter-African Mission to Monitor the Bungui Accords (MISAB). Provided with a UN mandate, MISAB formally became the buffer between the combatants on 12 February 1997. Comprising just over 1 000 soldiers from six African countries at its peak, the force was commanded by a Senegalese officer and supported by French logistics. Although small in size and posture, and perhaps insignificant in world politics, MISAB has reduced the tensions and security problems in the Central African Republic in its exercise in indigenous multinational peace keeping. MISAB has proved that there is a political will towards contributing to peaceful conflict resolution in certain parts of sub-Saharan Africa.[46]

A further meaningful development in West Africa relates to a military exercise held in Senegal in March 1998 which featured a mock operation to protect civilians in war zones, fly them to safety and organise refugee camps. Senegal, Mauritania and Mali organised and commanded the exercise in which soldiers from Guinea, Guinea Bissau, Ghana, Gambia and Cape Verde took part. France supplied the equipment and was responsible for the logistics, while the US and Britain sent troops. The exercise also enjoyed the support of the Secretary-General of the UN and can clearly be regarded as part of capacity building efforts to establish a regional or sub-regional response capability of some kind.[47]

In Southern Africa the initiatives of the SADC are an important step in the development of regional solutions to regional problems. Its Organ for Politics, Defence and Security at political level, and the Inter-State Defence and Security Committee (ISDSC) at technical level, will possibly provide the future framework for co-operation and assistance in peace support and security operations in Southern Africa.

The objectives of the SADC Organ for Politics, Defence and Security place a heavy emphasis on the development of political and diplomatic skills to deal with the prevention and resolution of intra- and extra-regional conflict; a commitment to a common regional (Southern African) approach to all issues of mutual concern; and undertakings to foster democratic institutions and practices within member states. Of particular concern are the aims to develop a collective security capacity; to conclude a mutual defence pact for responding to external threats; and to create a peace-keeping capacity in national armies that could be called upon within Southern Africa or elsewhere on the continent.[48]

An approach to what appears to be the future model for peace support operations in Southern Africa is that they will be undertaken by the SADC as a sub-regional organisation; that they will be politically and morally fully sanctioned and backed by the OAU; and that the UN will provide the necessary international support and endorsement.

It has already been indicated that such an approach would be in accordance with UN policy. The UN has come to share responsibilities for peace support operations with regional organisations; for example, in Georgia with the Russian Federation, and in the former Yugoslavia with the North Atlantic Treaty Organisation (NATO) as a military alliance.

In pursuance of efforts to develop regional defence and security co-operation in Southern Africa, the ISDSC initiated discussions on certain issues in 1995. They include:[49]

- responsibilities of various countries according to geographical location
- doctrine and standard operations procedures
- command-and-control
- training
- tasks
- standardisation of equipment
- logistic support
- medical services, and
- communication and signals.

On a practical level, the armed forces of eight Southern African countries (including a contingent of the SANDF) participated in Exercise Blue Hungwe (Fish Eagle), a multinational peace support exercise held early in 1997 in Zimbabwe, and assisted and facilitated by British military experts.[50] With this exercise the sub-region came closer to sharing peace support responsibilities on the African continent.

However the progress made in 1996 with the establishment of the SADC Organ on Politics, Defence and Security has come under pressure; problems are being experienced in the actual realisation of objectives and in the structuring of the various proposed institutions. There is still a need for proper structural arrangements, skills and resources.[51] The main difficulty evidently relates to differences between the heads of state — especially between South Africa and Zimbabwe — over the political control of the organ.[52] Much will depend on efforts to resolve such problems, and on the measure of future political cohesion in SADC.

3 CHALLENGES TO THE SUCCESSFUL CONDUCTING OF PEACE SUPPORT OPERATIONS

In sub-Saharan Africa peace support operations are an even greater challenge than in most other parts of the world. In fact, the problems and the perils of UN peace-keeping missions in Somalia, Rwanda, Mozambique and Angola seem to have resulted in an increasing unwillingness on the part of the major powers and traditional contributors to peace support operations to deploy their forces on the African continent any longer. In Rwanda, for example, a three-year UN "peace-keeping" operation failed to halt ethnic strife that resulted in between 500 000 and one million deaths: in spite of the UN's efforts to restore peace, a silent genocide continued.[53]

In general, the successful conducting of peace support operations needs prompt, effective and sustained action, without loss of momentum through a lack of resolve. The essential elements may include the following:[54]

- **Clarity and consensus**: The primary effect of enforcement powers should be a deterring one. This is possible only if a mandate with clear goals exists, together with appropriate and transparent criteria so formulated that the precise nature of the response to be decided upon can be determined on a case-by-case basis.

- **Political resolve**: The lack of staying power in the face of adversity severely weakens the credibility of international enforcement. For collective security to be effective, a credible force must be mustered, with adequate financing from states that have sufficient political resolve to stay the course.

- **Resources**: A credible deterrent and enforcement capacity depends on the reliable availability of adequately equipped and trained forces. Such a capability must be provided by all participating parties and member states.

- **Command and control**: Unity of command and control must be assured to meet the overriding concerns of mission integrity and the maximum safety of personnel.

In addition to the above, the following four issues can be listed as a set of requirements for effective action during peace support operations, namely:[55]

- sound intelligence
- the training of peace-keepers for peace support operations
- interaction between the peace mission and the media, and
- the status of civil-military relations during peace missions.

Both past and current peace support operations in sub-Saharan Africa have resulted in certain lessons that require careful analysis and study. This is necessary for an understanding of the challenges to the successful conducting of peace support on the continent.

3.1 Nature of internal conflict in Africa and parameters of engagement

It is an indisputable fact that Africa is the continent most plagued by conflict. In Africa the nature of recent and current threats relates less to conflict between than to conflict within states. Such conflict is rooted in one or more of the following:

- religious and ethnic differences or tensions
- religious fundamentalism
- disputes over traditional boundaries and scarce resources
- inequitable distribution of political and economic power

- struggles for the reform and democratisation of political and economic systems

- negative legacies of colonial rule, and

- ethnic competition stemming from the collapse of the old patterns of relationships that once provided a framework for collaboration among ethnic groups.[56]

Some observers argue that conflict and insecurity in Africa are simply and primarily products of poor governance and the politics of exclusion — typically of ethnic or religious minorities. Poor governance is accompanied by poor administration where the elements of state and society are not well served by the state. In such circumstances governments are likely to lose control over substantial parts of society, and their monopoly of power becomes eroded, proliferating downwards into the hands of warlords.[57]

Civil wars, fuelled by deep-seated hatred and involving armed factions and the availability of weapons and ammunition (common in Africa), present peace forces with serious challenges and an untenable operational environment. In addition, since the late 1980s and early 1990s, it has become clear that the UN needs action that will restore, maintain and keep peace; cease-fires that did not last were reached, sometimes repeatedly, by the parties at operational and tactical level. This happened in the former Yugoslavia and in Somalia.[58]

Moreover, terminating conflicts where there is no peace to keep, and where men and boys with guns prevent the distribution of the most basic humanitarian supplies, has become part of conflict resolution challenges in Africa. Peace enforcement then bears little similarity to peace-keeping and humanitarian operations, where the military's role is that of a support force, not an active combatant.[59] In such volatile situations peace-keeping mandates must provide for sporadic change in the nature of peace missions and the action to be taken by peace forces.

This highlighted the need for clear mandates and rules of engagement. A survey of the UN's involvement in the former Yugoslavia, Cambodia and Somalia shows sharp differences in the circumstances of the operations undertaken: a mixture of international and civil war involving radicalised ethnic groups in the former Yugoslavia; the implementation of a comprehensive political settlement in Cambodia, and the collapse of governmental authority in Somalia. The experience of the UN forces in each of these theatres emphasises a critical aspect of the contemporary challenge to peace support operations in internal conflicts; namely, the problem of formulating mandates, the humanitarian and political objectives of which are effectively understood and reinforced by the presence of peace-keeping forces.[60]

In Somalia, for example, there was confusion even at political level in the US over the exact parameters of UNOSOM-I. Although at first a peace-keeping mission, it swiftly evolved into a combat operation. This appears to have caused disarray and a lack of understanding between the UN and the participating member states, resulting in the US decision to withdraw from Somalia.[61]

3.2 Implications of financial constraints

Peace support operations present a range of different problems, of which an important one is finding the necessary funds to finance them. Sub-Saharan Africa is currently in need of financial assistance for these operations.[62] As a result of financial constraints, many sub-Saharan African defence forces have logistical and organisational problems. Furthermore, sub-Saharan African armed forces are generally plagued by obsolete and worn-out military equipment, while there are also training difficulties.[63] Lack of resources bears upon sub-Saharan African participation in peace support operations, as most countries experience difficulties with the ground, air or sea transportation required for timely long-distance deployment.[64]

Effective logistic support, as an essential element of peace support operations, cannot be overemphasised. A lack of such support leaves troops feeling abandoned and incapable of operating optimally. Inadequate logistic support provided to peace-keepers in sub-Saharan Africa has consequently been perhaps the most crucial handicap in the past for sub-Saharan soldiers. A number of sub-Saharan contingents, for example, were deployed in Rwanda in 1994: more than six months after they arrived in the area, they had still not received basic items such as tents, flak jackets, ballistic helmets or ambulances.[65]

Similarly, the ECOMOG forces in Liberia have, since their deployment in 1991, experienced a constant need for logistic support. The following note of a senior US army officer illustrates the difficulties and constraints experienced by certain sub-Saharan countries:[66]

> On one occasion in 1993, a US military delegation was attempting to solicit the participation of a southern African country in ECOMOG. The Africans presented a very detailed listing of equipment they would require before the deployment. (The listing included such items as underwear and socks for the troops.) A senior U.S. participant asked if the country were proposing to contribute only "naked troops in boots". Without batting an eye, the Minister of Defence concurred: that, indeed, was the offer.

It should therefore be borne in mind that, with their weak economies, many sub-Saharan states can hardly meet their own domestic demands, let alone provide substantial or any support for peace operations.[67] Moreover, Africa as a whole seems unable to provide the necessary resources for these operations on the continent. This is aggravated by the reluctance of many of the major powers to become directly involved. If Africa is unable to do the funding itself, it follows that whoever does will significantly influence the objectives and conduct of the operations.[68]

Another problem is that sub-Saharan countries are sensitive to invidious comparison. Their decision makers do not want their troops to appear threadbare and ill-equipped in contrast to those of other troop-contributing nations. This might significantly inhibit the willingness of certain sub-Saharan states to participate in peace support operations.[69]

3.3 Command-and-control arrangements

It needs to be pointed out that states participating in an international peace support operation will retain their autonomy and sovereignty. Contending national priorities have the potential to translate into problems of command-and-control, rules of engagement, disciplinary measures and personnel procedures. Differences of opinion in a volatile situation may result in political disagreement between the participating states.[70]

Since the effectiveness of any military operation is inextricably tied to the quality of its in-theatre command-and-control arrangements, all NATO member states have worked to establish NATO STANAGs (or memorandums of agreement covering joint tactics, operations and techniques). This has resulted in a "certain level of comfort" among NATO allies.[71]

In Somalia, several co-ordination problems between the internal components of the peace operation were experienced. There were often conflicting national and international interests among the contributors to these peace processes. Furthermore, the large number of participating countries in UNOSOM II led to a fragile command-and-control framework, and to indirect, slow and vague command-and-control channels. The operation also suffered from a lack of joint doctrine. As a result, directing and coordinating civilian and military field operations became especially difficult, if not impossible.

UNTAG, the UN Transition Assistance Group in Namibia from 1989 to 1990 and UNAVEM II also demonstrated problems in relation to a lack of

- integrated strategies between the different components of the mission
- integrated command-and-control structures, and
- joint planning mechanisms, and proper communication and reporting systems.

Challenges linked to a lack of co-ordination between and within missions severely impinge on the processes that are often required by their mandates. For example, peace operations that had the worst problems with weapons' management programmes were those that experienced the greatest difficulty in co-ordinating their efforts. The peace missions in Somalia, Angola and Liberia all suffered from ineffective co-ordination.[72]

3.4 Selection of key appointments

The making of key appointments with proper managerial skills and experience is a most important aspect of resource requirements. In the Liberian peace-keeping effort, for example, the failure of the planners of ECOMOG to select officers with adequate training and expertise for vital aspects of the operation undermined the ability of the peace-keepers to arrest the conflict. Officers with no logistic training or experience were chosen to manage logistics, in a bid to achieve a balanced representation of participating countries.

Due to a shortage of high ranking officers, Guinea promoted a lieutenant-colonel to the rank of deputy force commander, whereas a brigadier or a colonel was required for such a position. Further problems were created when a Guinean lieutenant-colonel was promoted to the rank of general upon joining the peace mission. Such appointments were a major factor in eroding ECOMOG's ability to manage the operation successfully.[73]

3.5 Need for meaningful intelligence

Contemporary peace support operations have shown that politically fluid and militarily complex situations may require more advanced resources and procedures for collecting, assessing and distributing intelligence. Intelligence on the military power and disposition of forces, the location of minefields, the level of violence and other features in a deployment area are essential for planning and conducting peace missions.[74] To carry out his mandate effectively, a military commander must be able to detect the movements of the belligerent forces, determine the location of arms caches, and anticipate the plans and tactics of those who intend to violate agreements and jeopardise the execution of the mission mandate.[75]

Problems of control are often related to a lack of meaningful intelligence. Suffice it to say that for any action to succeed, there is a need for adequate intelligence to achieve cohesive planning. In almost all sub-Saharan peace support operations, troops have been dispatched to mission areas with inadequate intelligence on the local inhabitants, their culture, beliefs and customs. Even basic geographic information has been a problem, as few sub-Saharan countries have up-to-date maps — especially maps providing information that is essential for proper military planning.[76]

In addition to tactical warning, strategic warning ensures that the decision makers have a clear overall picture and sufficient quality time to make the necessary decisions. It provides them with regular updates on regional developments. Analysing different pieces of information requires a co-ordinated and concentrated intelligence effort. The sharing of processed information among all potential peace operation participants is a necessity for timely and appropriate response. Here, too, Africa lacks the funding and resources to provide an effective continental service.[77]

3.6 Need for sound civil-military relations

While many military forces have proven capabilities in humanitarian operations, recent experience has revealed an urgent need for improved civilian-military co-ordination in the distribution of essential supplies, the management of refugee movements and the organisation of medical support. Non-governmental organisations (NGOs) may have financial and material resources that peace forces do not have, and at times they have played a valuable role worldwide in saving lives. In many instances during peace missions, however, friction has developed between the peace-keepers and NGOs.[78]

Missions in Cambodia, the former Yugoslavia, Somalia, Angola and Bosnia have all included civilian operations: in Sarajevo and Bosnia there were approximately 112 NGOs serving in one or other capacity. Some of them were really proficient in their duties, while the role of others resulted in strained relations with the peace-keeping forces.[79]

The growing prominence of this juxtaposing of military and civilian operations has often resulted in major command, control and co-ordination problems for which neither contingency planning nor doctrinal guidance really existed. Problems of this nature have been particularly acute in areas of ongoing conflict.[80]

The deployment of a peace force also marks a delicate and critical relationship with the host government and other parties to the conflict, such as the local population. In the case of ONUMOZ, the UN operation in Mozambique from 1992 to 1994, its inability to draft and pass laws frustrated the Mozambican government and was an additional factor to be dealt with. In the urban areas where the ONUMOZ forces frequently mingled with the local population, several incidents of sexual child-abuse, rape and physical aggression by soldiers against civilians were reported. This underscores the sensitive nature of any type of third-party intervention, especially as it recalls the presence of outside forces in colonial times.[81]

The fact that members of a peace-keeping force are often in contact with the local population calls for a great deal of caution and prudence on their part to avoid misunderstandings, tension — or collusion. They must use diplomatic skills, seek compromises by means of negotiation and be tolerant of others; and those are attributes that make additional demands on a soldier's professionalism.[82] Qualified interpreters to liaise with local people are also needed — as the UN acutely experienced in, for example, the Somalia peace mission of 1992 and 1993.[83]

3.7 Role of media coverage

Peace forces must be seen to be efficient and effective. Positive media coverage can enhance such a perception among the peace-keepers themselves, the people in whose area they are deployed, and the public at large. An ability to deal with the media may be crucial in determining how peace initiatives are perceived.[84] The role of the media must therefore be understood and never ignored.

Friction between the military components of peace missions and the media (newspapers, television, radio) has frequently been experienced in the past. Military commanders often choose to ignore them, which is a dangerous attitude because they are there to inform and to educate.[85] When dealt with properly they can be a very powerful instrument in distressful and desperate circumstances.

In Bosnia the role of the media in communicating the situation had in a number of cases a substantial impact on the process of keeping the peace and reducing the level of atrocities, perhaps even more than the actual peace-keepers.[86] In a landlocked country like Rwanda, where borders were sealed off and airports closed, the peace forces would have been completely stranded had the media not portrayed the conditions under which they were operating.[87]

In Angola there was the problem of countering hostile propaganda, banned under the Lusaka Protocol, which usually took the form of unverified charges made by one side against the other. For example, the UNITA radio station tended to broadcast allegations accusing government forces of moving into certain areas, or arming civilians, or committing other cease-fire violations. This alarmed the local population and eroded confidence in the peace process. The problem had to be dealt with by co-operation between the civilian and military information components, and required considerable co-ordination between them.[88]

3.8 Linguistic problems and diverse military cultures

The effective command-and-control of any military operation depends heavily on communication capacity. This is necessary to furnish authorities at all levels with timely information for the direction and co-ordination of all activities at ground level.[89]

In sub-Saharan Africa, the military of the various states have all inherited the languages of the former colonial powers, as well as their various military cultures; and problems of command-and-control during multinational peace support operations were often related to linguistic diversity.[90] For example, the Guinean forces were the only francophone contingent taking part in ECOMOG in 1990. As such, they were unable to communicate properly with other participants.[91] The problem of language was also evident during the UN Assistance Mission for Rwanda, or UNAMIR, where most local trainees were French-speaking. Where bilingual instructors were not available, lectures were given through local interpreters who were not always up to the task.[92]

However, it could also be argued that a peace mission or forces from Africa or any sub-region have a decided advantage over European or Asian troops as far as cultural background, language and knowledge of the continent are concerned. African culture, customs and traditions are often incomprehensible to people from other continents.[93] Consequently, African forces tend to be more compatible with the requirements of peace missions and with the local environment.[94] For example, in the case of ECOMOG the Guinean forces were able to communicate with the Liberians because of the large proportion of Manding speakers in the population of both countries.[95]

Closely related to language is the issue of diverse military cultures. In Liberia, there appeared to be divisions with respect to doctrine. Differences in training for peace keeping were also evident, and were highlighted in the varying approaches to peace enforcement. The background of the Ghanaians served to slow down the operation, because they tended to delay the use of force until diplomacy had been exhausted. In fact, the use of force was not favoured by them at all. (This was probably the result of a philosophy on the part of the Ghanaian head of state that the army had to be kept busy with a view to diverting its attention from politics.) They were so cautious in executing directives that it took them twice as long as some other contingents (e.g. Nigeria and Guinea) to carry out their tasks. Unlike the Ghanaians, the Nigerians were described by a commander as "... a crack force for peace enforcement or outright combat".[96]

4 CONCLUSION

It is clear from what has been said that significant developments have taken place in sub-Saharan Africa in regional and sub-regional initiatives to react to intrastate conflict by means of peace support operations. The OAU is positioned as a regional entity for conflict management between the UN, standing at the apex of the pyramid, and the sub-regional organisations; and the creation of the OAU's Mechanism for Conflict Prevention, Management and Resolution is especially important for coordinating conflict management activities. It is likewise significant that the idea of an all-African Crisis Response Force, or regional response capability, is increasingly being favoured as part of a broader series of political and diplomatic initiatives on the continent. Moreover, developments in Southern and West Africa are especially promising as regards the need to work together and assume greater responsibility for peace, security and stability at sub-regional level.

However, it is a truism that the undertaking of peace support missions in sub-Saharan Africa is by no means a simple task. Africa is a continent that is steeped in conflict, the sources of which are both diverse and endemic. Moreover, past and recent experience worldwide, and in sub-Saharan Africa in particular, has indicated that peace operations present serious challenges and a hostile operational environment to forces that conduct them.

The preceding overview highlights a great, but not exhaustive, number of factors relating to the challenge of undertaking peace support operations on the continent. But it must be noted that some or most of the mentioned problems are not peculiar to sub-Saharan Africa, as many post-Cold War conflicts have shown (e.g. Bosnia and Cambodia). Yet, the real impact of the post-Cold War era is that the burden of resolving conflicts in Africa rests more and more on Africans. They are accordingly compelled to take measures and develop strategies that move beyond conventional peace keeping. What is also different in sub-Saharan Africa is that poverty in a large number of countries reduces the ability to deal effectively with intrastate conflicts. Lack of resources lies at the core of past and recent peacekeeping problems. Operationally, there is also room for improvement. Meanwhile the UN and the Western world are likely to be saddled with at least the material cost of sub-Saharan peace-keeping efforts in the foreseeable future.[97]

Finally, what should be regarded as positive are the calls by African leaders for "African solutions to African problems". Some African heads of state want to show the world that Africa can police itself and be a partner in creating stability.[98] Thus, between 1994 and 1997, during the crises in the Great Lakes region, a group of powerful leaders in the region demonstrated their clear commitment to help find solutions.[99]

In a more technical sense there is also positive evidence in the calls being heard in Africa to address questions of legal and moral authority; to find ways to guarantee financial, technical and logistical support; to identify sources of effective training that will convey relevant knowledge, skills and attitudes; and to define lines of command, and criteria for the composition of forces. Such initiatives will serve to remove ambiguities and policy dilemmas that inhibit effective international action in dealing with regional conflicts, and in developing appropriate responses.[100] In this context, "home-grown" solutions by decisive leaders and a strong element of sub-regional co-operation may, after all, be key elements in the model for conflict-resolution on the African continent.

REFERENCES

1. African Centre for the Constructive Resolution of Disputes (ACCORD), Internet site http://www.accord.org.za/pdf.htm, 1997.
2. Olonisakin, F, "African 'Homemade' Peace-keeping Initiatives", *Armed Forces & Society*, Vol 23, No 3, Spring 1997, p 350.
3. "Peace support operations" is used as a generic term to refer to all types of possible mission support in respect of preventive diplomacy, peacemaking, peace building, peace keeping and peace enforcement.
4. *The Star* (Johannesburg), 30 October 1997.

5. Williams, R, "Peace Operations and the South African Armed Forces", *Strategic Review*, Vol XVII, No 2, 1995, pp 91-92.

6. UN, *Charter of the United Nations*, San Francisco, June 26, 1945.

7. UN, *The Blue Helmets: A Review of United Nations Peacekeeping*, United Nations Department of Public Information, 1990, p 3.

8. UN (Department of Public Information), Internet site http://www.un.org/Depts/dpko/faq.htm, 1998.

9. Boutros-Ghali, B, *An Agenda for Peace: Preventive Diplomacy, Peacemaking and Peace-keeping*, United Nations, New York, 1992, p 1.

10. *Ibid*, p 11. According to *An Agenda for Peace, Supplement* (3 January 1995), certain conditions have led peace keepers to forfeit the consent of the parties concerned. These have been the tasks of protecting humanitarian operations during continuing warfare; protecting civilian populations in designated safe areas; and pressing parties to achieve national reconciliation faster than they were ready to do.

11. UN (Department of Political Affairs), Internet site http://www.un.org/ Depts/dpa/docs/peacemak.htm, 1997.

12. UN, *Charter of the United Nations*, op cit.

13. *Ibid*, p 6.

14. Henk, D, "Peace Operations: Views from Southern and Eastern Africa", *U.S. Army Peacekeeping Institute Occasional Paper*, 1995, p 16.

15. *Ibid*, pp 26-27.

16. UN (Department of Public Information), Internet site http://www.un.org/ Depts/dpko/Missions/unomil_p.htm, 1998.

17. Malan, M, "Foundations for Regional Security: Preparing to Keep the Peace in Southern Africa", *African Security Review*, Vol 5, No 1, 1996, p 7.

18. UN (Department of Peace-keeping Operations), Internet site http:// www.un.org/Depts/dpko/rapid/str.htm, 1998.

19. Nhara, W, "The OAU and the Potential Role of Regional and Sub-regional Organisations", in Cilliers, J and Mills, G, (eds), *Peacekeeping in Africa*, Halfway House, Institute for Defence Policy and South African Institute of International Affairs, 1995, p 103.

20. Steyn, P, "South Africa and Peace Support Operations Limitations, Options and Challenges", paper delivered at a conference *Contemporary Peace Support Operations*, 5 November 1997, Pretoria, p 7.

21. OAU, Central Organ, *OAU's Position Towards the Various Initiatives on Conflict Management: Enhancing OAU's Capacity in Preventive Diplomacy, Conflict Resolution and Peacekeeping*, Min/3(iv), undated.

22. *Kampala Document for a Proposed Conference on Security, Stability, Development and Cooperation in Africa (CSSDCA)*, Kampala, Uganda, May 23, 1991.

23. Nhara, W, "Conflict Management and Peace Operations: The Role of the Organisation of African Unity and Subregional Organisations", in Malan, M (ed), Resolute Partners: Building Peacekeeping Capacity in Southern Africa, *ISS Monograph Series*, No 21, February 1998, pp 33-34.

24. OAU, *Declaration of the Assembly of Heads of State and Government on the Establishment Within the OAU of a Mechanism for Conflict Prevention, Management and Resolution*, Cairo, June 30, 1993.

25. Nhara, W, 1995, *op cit*, p 104.

26. Williams, R, "Don't Hold the African Crisis Response Force Hostage to Unrealistic Demands", *ISS Papers*, No 20, April 1997, p 1.

27. Whitelaw, K, "A Mission for Africa: The West Makes Peacekeeping a Do-it-Yourself Project", *US News and World Report*, 29 September 1997, p 36.

28. *Beeld* (Johannesburg), 28 February 1998.

29. Williams, R, 1997, *op cit*, p 3.

30. *Ibid*, pp 2-3.

31. Vogt, M A, "Cooperation between the United Nations and the OAU in the Management of African Conflicts", paper delivered at a symposium *International Peace and Security: The African Experience*, 21-23 September 1998, Saldanha, p 12.

32. Nhara, W, 1995, *op cit*, p 107.

33. De Coning, C, "The Role of the OAU in Conflict Management in Africa", in Malan, M (ed), Conflict Management, Peacekeeping

and Peace Building: Lessons for Africa from a Seminar Past, *ISS Monograph Series*, No 10, April 1997, pp 23-24.

34. African Centre for the Constructive Resolution of Disputes (ACCORD), Internet site http://www.accord.org.za/conres.htm, 1997.

35. Olonisakin, F, *op cit*, p 351.

36. Nhara, W, 1995, *op cit*, pp 101-102.

37. Arnold, G, "The OAU and Peacekeeping in Africa", *New African*, January 1997, p 33.

38. Cilliers, J and Malan, M, "From Destabilisation to Peace-keeping in Southern Africa: The Potential Role of Southern Africa", *Africa Insight*, Vol 26, No 4, 1996, pp 340 and 345.

39. *Ibid*, p 339.

40. Nhara, W, 1995, *op cit*, p 100.

41. Arnold, G, "The OAU and Peacekeeping in Africa", *New African*, January 1997, p 33.

42. Henk, D, *op cit*, p 13.

43. *Beeld* (Johannesburg), 5 June 1997.

44. *Beeld* (Johannesburg), 28 February 1998.

45. Anon, "Sierra Leone: Koroma's coup", *Africa Confidential*, Vol 38, No 12, 6 June 1997, pp 1-2.

46. McFarlane, F and Malan, M, "Crisis and Response in the Central African Republic: A New Trend in African Peacekeeping", *African Security Review*, Vol 7, No 2, 1998, pp 48, 52 and 57.

47. *Beeld* (Johannesburg), 4 March 1998.

48. Van Aardt, M, "The Emerging Security Framework in Southern Africa: Regime or Community?", *Strategic Review for Southern Africa*, Vol XIX, No 1, May 1997, p 17.

49. Thiart, G, "Training for Peace", *Salut*, Vol 3, No 3, March 1996, p 26.

50. *The Citizen* (Johannesburg), 27 May 1997.

51. Van Aardt, M, *op cit*, pp 17-18.

52. *The Star* (Johannesburg), 23 September 1997.

53. Malan, M, "Treading Firmly on the Layered Response Ladder: From Peace Enforcement to Conflict Termination Operations in Africa", *African Security Review*, Vol 6, No 5, 1997, p 46.

54. Riza, S I, "Parameters of UN Peacekeeping", *The Rusi Journal*, June 1995, pp 19-20.

55. Gamba, V and Potgieter, J, "The Challenges to Multifunctional Peace Support Operations", in Multifunctional Peace Support Operations: Evolution and Changes, *ISS Monograph Series*, No 8, January 1997, p 73.

56. Anyidoho, H, "Lessons Learned during Peacekeeping Operations in Africa", in M Malan (ed), Conflict Management, Peacekeeping and Peace Building: Lessons for Africa from a Seminar Past, *ISS Monograph Series*, No 10, April 1997, p 40.

57. Malan, M, "Treading Firmly on the Layered Response Ladder: From Peace Enforcement to Conflict Termination Operations in Africa", *op cit*, pp 46-47.

58. Gamba, V and Potgieter, J, *op cit*, pp 48 and 54.

59. Malan, M, "Treading Firmly on the Layered Response Ladder: From Peace Enforcement to Conflict Termination Operations in Africa", *op cit*, pp 46 and 48.

60. Berdal, M R, "Whither UN Peacekeeping", *Adelphi Paper 281*, IISS, October 1993, p 27.

61. Roos, J G, "The Perils of Peacekeeping", *Armed Forces Journal*, December 1993, p 15.

62. Arnold, G, *op cit*, p 33.

63. Mwila, B Y, "Equipment Requirements in Africa", *African Armed Forces Journal*, November 1994, p 8.

64. Henk, D, *op cit*, p 19.

65. Anyidoho, H, *op cit*, p 44.

66. Henk, D, *op cit*, p 20.

67. Anyidoho, H, *op cit*, p 44.

68. De Coning, C, "The OAU and Peacekeeping", *International Update*, No 14, 1996, p 2.

69. Henk, D, *op cit*, p 20.

70. Williams, R, "Peace Operations and the South African Armed Forces", *op cit*, pp 91-92.
71. Roos, J G, *op cit*, p 15.
72. Gamba, V and Potgieter, J, *op cit*, pp 62-63.
73. Olonisakin, F, *op cit*, p 360.
74. Berdal, M R, *op cit*, p 27.
75. Gamba, V and Potgieter, J, *op cit*, p 73.
76. Anyidoho, H, *op cit*, p 44.
77. Shelton, G, "Preventive Diplomacy and Peacekeeping: Keys for Success", *African Security Review*, Vol 6, No 5, 1997, pp 5-6.
78. Anyidoho, H, *op cit*, pp 44-45.
79. Thomas, T L, "Russian Lessons Learned in Bosnia", *Military Review*, September-October 1996, p 39.
80. Berdal, M R, *op cit*, pp 9 and 11.
81. De Brito, M, "Relationship between Peacekeepers, Host Governments and Local Populations: A Mozambican Perspective", in Malan, M (ed), Conflict Management, Peacekeeping and Peace Building: Lessons for Africa from a Seminar Past, *ISS Monograph Series*, No 10, April 1997, pp 61-64.
82. Hundt, U A, "Coping with Peacekeeping", *Salut*, Vol 3, No 3, March 1996, p 38.
83. Corum, J S, "Operational Problems in Peacekeeping and Humanitarian Operations", in Shaw, M, and Cilliers, J (eds), *South Africa and Peacekeeping in Africa*, Halfway House, Institute for Defence Policy, 1995, p 124.
84. Shaw, M, "International Peacekeeping — Are there Lessons for South Africa?", *African Defence Review*, No 15, March 1994, p 14.
85. Anyidoho, H, *op cit*, p 45.
86. Mackenzie, L, "Military Realities of UN Peacekeeping", *Rusi Journal*, February 1993, p 23.
87. Anyidoho, H, *op cit*, p 45.
88. Wimhurst, D, "Communication in Peace Operations: A Spokesperson's Perspective from UNAVEM III", in Malan, M (ed), Conflict Management, Peacekeeping and Peace Building: Lessons

for Africa from a Seminar Past, *ISS Monograph Series*, No 10, April 1997, p 55.
89. Berdal, M R, *op cit*, p 41.
90. Anyidoho, H, *op cit*, p 44.
91. Henk, D, *op cit*, p 27.
92. UN (Department of Public Information), Internet site http://www.un.org/ Depts/dpko/lessons/rwandles.htm, 1998.
93. Cilliers, J and Malan, M, *op cit*, p 339.
94. Henk, D, *op cit*, p 28.
95. *Ibid*, p 27.
96. Olonisakin, F, *op cit*, pp 362-363.
97. *Ibid*, pp 366-367.
98. *The Citizen* (Johannesburg), 27 May 1997.
99. Evans, G, "Responding to Crises in the African Great Lakes", *Adelphi Paper 311*, IISS, 1997, p 85.
100. Steyn, P, *op cit*, p 12.

Chapter 8

ARMED CONFLICT AND DEFENCE CO-OPERATION IN SUB-SAHARAN AFRICA

Michael Hough

1 INTRODUCTION

Although defence co-operation has increasingly become part of broader security co-operation, the emphasis in this chapter will fall on the development of initiatives aimed at continental defence co-operation and regional defence co-operation in sub-Saharan Africa. Peace support operations are discussed in a separate chapter, although the distinction between military intervention and peace enforcement specifically has, on occasion, become blurred. An overview of recent armed conflict in sub-Saharan Africa is also given with specific reference to sources and manifestations. Approaches to military security in sub-Saharan Africa, as *inter alia* embodied in regional and bilateral defence agreements, are then analysed.

A number of arguments for the establishment of an African High Command (AHC) were advanced in the 1970s and the 1980s. These included what was termed "effective defence against South Africa"; the savings that could be effected if overlapping and unnecessary military expenditures could be avoided; cooperation that could reduce the incentive to individual states to use force to resolve internal or external conflict; continental defence forces that could safeguard minorities until solutions regarding their accommodation could be found and hence help to manage or prevent the refugee problem in Africa; and cooperation in the prevention of nuclear proliferation in Africa.[1]

Some of these arguments have in the meantime become irrelevant or less relevant. Since 1994, South Africa has not been viewed as a military threat to other African countries; and Africa was declared a nuclear-weapon-free-zone in 1996.

South Africa also signed the *Non-Proliferation Treaty* in 1991, and abandoned its nuclear weapons programme. On the other hand, however, Libya is sometimes alleged still to have nuclear weapon aspirations; the refugee problem in Africa has increased; internal armed conflict in various African countries continues; and the increasing cost of national defence could be partially offset by some form of continental military co-operation.

The rationale for an AHC has also weakened following the increased emphasis on regional security co-operation and peace support operations, although the latter was also envisaged as a function of the proposed AHC.

2 PROPOSALS FOR AN AFRICAN HIGH COMMAND

2.1 Origin and development of the concept

Kwame Nkrumah reportedly first mooted the idea of an AHC during the Congo crisis of 1960.[2]

After the establishment of the Organisation of African Unity (OAU) in 1963, a Defence Commission was created as one of the five specialised OAU commissions. Under Article II of the *OAU Charter*, an important objective of the OAU was formulated as "co-operation for defence and security", and this formed the frame of reference for the Defence Commission. A Liberation Committee was also established to support nationalist movements in Rhodesia, South Africa, Angola and Mozambique.[3]

A proposal for a continental defence arrangement was presented by a delegate from Ghana at the first meeting of the Defence Commission in November 1963. The proposal provided for a defence and a peace-keeping capability, and the proposed arrangement would incorporate the OAU Defence Commission.[4]

During the Cairo Summit of the OAU in 1964 the idea of an AHC was rejected as premature. At the Accra Summit in 1965 the resolution adopted in this regard provided only for member states voluntarily to place units of their armed forces at the disposal of the OAU within the framework of an African Defence Organisation should the need for a specific operation arise.[5]

In 1971 the OAU Defence Commission again considered the issue of an AHC, following an attempted invasion of Guinea by Portuguese-led mercenaries. The proposal was that regional defence systems should be established instead of an AHC, with the OAU Defence Commission acting as co-ordinator. No agreement on the proposal could be reached at the 1972 OAU Summit in Morocco.[6]

At the OAU Summit in 1978 (Khartoum), a call was made for the reactivation of the OAU Defence Commission, anticipating the establishment of an African military force under OAU supervision. Nigeria emerged as a strong supporter of the idea.[7]

Similar appeals were made during the 1979 Monrovia Summit, and a resolution was adopted reiterating the need for such a force. By the mid-eighties, however, nothing had been done in this regard. The Chad crisis in 1981 and 1982 furnished the first occasion for the OAU to mount a peace-keeping operation, with Nigeria, Senegal and Zaire providing troops.[8]

The *Kampala Document* of 1991 attempted to revive the concept of an AHC. Although not an official OAU document (it was based on a conference sponsored by the African Leadership Forum, the OAU and the UN Economic Commission for Africa), it nevertheless carried considerable weight. The document also called for the establishment of a continental peace-keeping body:[9]

Peace-keeping operations

Building on the limited experiences of Africa and cumulative lessons of the United Nations' operations, and taking measures that would avoid the mistakes which have been committed in such instances, Africa under CSSDCA should institute a continental peace-keeping machinery as an important instrument for the preservation of peace in instances which potentially or actually threaten the security of African state(s) or the continent as a whole.

In order to realize the establishment of the continental peace-keeping body, each participating member state should implement special training measures in peace-keeping operations for a contingent of its armed forces. A continental peace-keeping operation will be an ad hoc operation through rapid mobilization of pre-agreed manpower and financial contributions from participating member states. In consideration of sub-regional and regional disparities in Africa in terms of resources and capabilities, the peace-keeping operations should be based and operated on a continental basis and subscribed to by all participating states in CSSDCA on the basis of an agreed formula.

Non-aggression pacts

A more enhanced policy measure for continental security requires a non-aggression treaty among all African countries under the CSSDCA process, along the model of a similar treaty that already exists between the member states of ECOWAS. The non-aggression treaty among African countries should also incorporate commitment to defend each other in the event of external military aggression.

Establishment of an African High Command

To forestall or ward off external military aggression against the continent or any member or group of members participating in CSSDCA, an African High Command should be established. Like the peace-keeping operations, the African High Command should rely on a small coordinating unit within the OAU structure and based on pre-agreed human and material contributions by participating member states when and if the need arises. The Command must be structured for rapid reaction to situations of aggression against participating member states. The High Command should undertake occasional joint military maneuvers to ensure its readiness for the defense of Africa's security.

The *OAU Mechanism for Conflict Prevention, Management and Resolution*, established in 1993, is less ambitious, focusing primarily on conflict prevention. No specific provision for a continental peace-keeping force is made, although peace support operations are referred to:[10]

15. The Mechanism will have as a primary objective, the anticipation and prevention of conflicts. In circumstances where conflicts have occurred, it will be its responsibility to undertake peace-making and peace-building functions in order to facilitate the resolution of these conflicts. In this respect, civilian and military missions of observation and monitoring of limited scope and duration may be mounted and deployed. In setting these objectives, we are fully convinced that prompt and decisive action in these spheres will, in the first instance, prevent the emergence of conflicts, and where they do inevitably occur, stop them from degenerating into intense or generalized conflicts. Emphasis on anticipatory and preventive measures, and concerted action in peace-making and peace-building will obviate the need to resort to the complex and resource-demanding peacekeeping operations, which our countries will find difficult to finance.

16. However, in the event that conflicts degenerate to the extent of requiring collective international intervention and policing, the assistance or where appropriate the services of the United Nations will be sought under the general terms of its Charter. In this instance, our respective countries will examine ways and modalities through which they can make practical contribution to such a United Nations undertaking and participate effectively in the peace-keeping operations in Africa.

The concept of an AHC has apparently been superseded by the emphasis on the role of the OAU and regional organisations in Africa in peace support operations. Simultaneously, as will be discussed, a number of regional agreements provide for mutual defence pacts in addition to peace support operations, although the dividing line may not always be clear. More recently, the concept of an African Crisis Reaction Force to fulfil the peace support role of the OAU has increasingly been mentioned, and also linked to United States, French and British initiatives in this regard.[11]

2.2 Scope and implications of an African High Command

It has been said that the concept of an AHC could not gain sufficient support because of its presumed supranational character and the high cost of maintaining such a military structure. The alternative to a standing force, namely the voluntary agreement of member states to be at the disposal of the OAU in specific operations, was also not approved during the 1960s and the 1970s, as already referred to.[12]

Other problems associated with an AHC, whether in a standing or voluntary form, is the question of African diversity, including language, ideology, military traditions, types and sources of equipment; logistical problems compounded by the lack of good communication infrastructure in Africa, as well as the lack of a well-developed transport command within the various armed forces; Africa's lack of technical expertise and the consequent dependence on external military sources; and lack of confidence in one another.[13]

The following has been stated in this regard:

> The problems mentioned here are not peculiar to Africa. They are problems which any group of nations trying to organize a collective defence system is bound to face. So in whatever form an African defence system is organized, whether on regional, ideological or continental lines, these problems will crop up.[14]

It is argued that some of these problems can be overcome. The perception of a common threat is an important prerequisite for this. The threat should be real, and beyond the ability of individual African states to deal with. The argument continues that any African defence structure should concentrate on threats that affect most if not all the members of the OAU. This implies that border conflicts between African states and insurgency would be excluded from collective military action. OAU involvement in such cases should largely be of a diplomatic nature, and military responses limited to a peace-keeping role. A decentralised AHC was also suggested.[15]

The argument above was based largely on the earlier perceived threats to Africa from South Africa and the then Rhodesia. Much of the argument concerning a common (external) threat has therefore fallen away. On the contrary, the major threats to African countries are currently internal (crime, corruption, hunger, civil war, *coups d'etat*), but with implications for neighbouring countries, for instance in the form of refugee flows. The demarcation between domestic and external threat is, however, not always clear, for example the alleged involvement of Rwanda and Uganda in the current rebellion in the Democratic Republic of the Congo (DRC).

Before analysing regional defence co-operation in sub-Saharan Africa (with the emphasis on defence pacts), an overview of recent armed conflict in, and the sources of military threats to sub-Saharan African countries, will be given.

3 ARMED CONFLICT IN SUB-SAHARAN AFRICA

Three sources of threats to African security have been identified. Of these, internal threats were most prominent, followed by threats from other African states and lastly by external threats.

3.1 Internal threats

Threats involving violent conflict and war and the armed forces in one or other way, revolve largely around tribal, religious or ethnic conflicts and rivalry; the activities of dissidents, including secessionist attempts; and *coups d'etat*. Domestic military threats are linked to, and often form manifestations of underlying non-military conditions and threats.

While some of these threats are the result of the colonial inheritance, others are the result of policies followed by the ruling elite or are due to inherent societal factors such as ethnic rivalry.

Armed conflict in sub-Saharan Africa has been waged or continues to be waged in Somalia between various armed factions; in Sudan between the Sudanese People's Liberation Army and the government; in Uganda between the Lord's Resistance Army and the government; in Kenya between extremists known as the Army of the Coastal People and the government; in Congo Brazzaville between government forces and dissidents under the former ruler General Denis Sassou Nguesso who subsequently toppled the Lissouba government; in Angola the threat of a new civil war between UNITA rebels and the Angolan government has not yet been ruled out; in the DRC, following the overthrow of the Mobutu regime by rebels under the leadership of Laurent Kabila, there is a Tutsi-led rebellion allegedly supported by Rwanda and Uganda; in Sierra Leone, rebel activity continues after the overthrow of the military government and the reinstatement of the former government.[16]

In addition, a civil war raged in Liberia from 1989 to 1996; armed rebellion broke out once again in the Central African Republic at the end of 1996, although agreements to end hostilities have since been negotiated; in Senegal, there is growing military pressure from separatist rebels in the southern region; in Chad there is ongoing rebellion; in Rwanda fighting between the army and Hutu rebel militiamen has erupted again; and in Burundi, Hutu rebels continue their campaign against the Tutsi-led military government.[17]

Included in the above conflicts, have been what are termed "major armed conflicts", which are defined as "prolonged combat between the military forces of two or more governments, or of one government and at least one organized armed group, incurring the battle-related deaths of at least 1 000 people during the entire conflict ...". During 1997 the conflicts in Sierra Leone, Burundi, Congo-Brazzaville, Senegal, Sudan, Uganda and the DRC were, for instance, placed in this category.[18]

Some of the internal armed conflict in sub-Saharan Africa has escalated into conventional or semi-conventional warfare, for example in Angola and Sudan. In the majority of instances, armed rebellion has taken the form of low-intensity warfare.

> The prospect for conflict in Africa is greatly worsened by the ease with which arms can be smuggled in to guerillas and dissident groups ... to create a conflict and destabilize a government, it needs only quite a small force of guerillas to attack strategic points periodically and then melt into the bush.[19]

In some cases, such as previously in Sierra Leone, dissident soldiers joined the rebel factions and mercenaries assisted the rebels and/or government forces.[20]

3.2 Intracontinental threats

As far as intracontinental threats are concerned, the series of "boundary disputes, territorial claims and counterclaims, ideological differences, opposing external affiliations and counter-affiliations involved" are evidence that some countries in sub-Saharan Africa are potential sources of threat to one another due to a conflict of interests.[21]

The movement of refugees across national boundaries and competition for influence within the region further contribute to interstate conflict, which at times involves direct or indirect military conflict. In some instances, domestic conflict in individual African countries had been fanned and even partially instigated by neighbouring countries (such as the involvement of Rwanda and Uganda in the overthrow of Mobutu in the former Zaire, as well as in the current rebellion in the DRC, and Uganda's support of the rebellion in Sudan). In other instances, direct military involvement in domestic conflict by a neighbouring country, and which is not part of UN-sanctioned peace support operations, has also occurred — for instance the ECOWAS Monitoring Group (ECOMOG) military involvement to oust the *coup* leaders in Sierra Leone and Angolan involvement in Brazzaville to oust President Lissouba.[22]

The war between Ethiopia and Somalia from 1976 onwards, the overthrow of Idi Amin's regime in Uganda in 1979, and the war between Eritrea and Ethiopia which erupted in 1997, are other examples of interstate armed conflict in sub-Saharan Africa. In this regard, it has been said:

> In general, these African wars were not directed at the redistribution of territory and population, through the

aggression of one state on another. The Somali occupation of the Ogaden in 1977, which was to end disastrously in the following year, is one of very few exceptions. Commonly, states intervened militarily in the affairs of other states in order to support a government against insurgency, or to support insurgents against the government. The usual purpose, in other words, was to defend or to subvert a government, to conserve or to change the location of power in the state subject to intervention.[23]

The current conflict between Eritrea and Ethiopia is a further example of a conflict over territory.[24] It is also said that African wars have largely been a reflection of internal power struggles, and that external powers (both African and non-African) have intervened in these situations and even at times fomented them.[25]

3.3 Extracontinental threats

The last category of security threats to sub-Saharan Africa are extracontinental threats. These include subversive penetration, economic squeeze, war by proxy and limited direct military intervention. Mercenaries, local dissidents and the arming and use of neighbouring states against target regimes or movements have been some of the methods involved here. Cases of external military intervention include France's use of troops to overthrow Bokassa in the Central African Republic.[26]

The use of Cuban soldiers by the Soviet Union in Angola; United States assistance to UNITA in Angola; and the involvement of French mercenaries in a *coup* attempt in Benin in 1977, are other examples of extracontinental intervention.[27]

The threat of direct full-scale external military invasion of sub-Saharan African countries is most unlikely. Rivalry between the major powers and competition for influence in Africa are more likely to be non-ideological in the post-Cold War period — i.e. sociocultural and economic rivalry. However, the main direct threats most African countries are currently facing are domestic (*coups*, secession, tribalism, ethnic and religious rivalry). This complicated state of affairs could make non-intervention more attractive to external powers than military intervention in Africa.[28]

4 APPROACHES TO MILITARY SECURITY IN SUB-SAHARAN AFRICA

Three options seem available to countries in sub-Saharan Africa for managing their security problems. The first is reliance on individual efforts; the second is intraregional collective security; and the third is reliance on protection from extracontinental sources. Reliance on the Organisation of African Unity (OAU) and United Nations (UN) initiatives, for example through peace support operations, could be added to this list.[29]

As far as self-reliance in the military sphere is concerned, it has been stated:

> A country operating on the basis of self-reliance would like to safeguard its security through unilateral military build-up in the form of mass armament, mass recruitment into and intensified training of its armed forces and the maximization of its defence production.[30]

In sub-Saharan Africa, military self-reliance faces major problems. No country except for South Africa has any real arms-manufacturing industry. Poverty, and industrial and technological underdevelopment are severe inhibiting factors.

Examples of the intraregional collective approach to security, with specific reference to mutual defence pacts, are discussed in a subsequent section. The following has been said about this approach to security:

> It follows that in addition to whatever individual self-help efforts they might undertake to safeguard their security, Sub-Saharan African states need deliberately to encourage

intra-African joint security arrangements at both the bilateral and multilateral levels in order to foster a climate of harmonious relationships within the region, build mutual confidence, promote the peaceful resolution of conflicts between one another and, in the process, minimize the possibility of foreign intervention in the region.[31]

From a military point of view, the limitations of this approach are that the multilateral defence agreements in sub-Saharan Africa exist largely on paper only, while the bilateral defence agreements have been relatively ineffective and invoked only in certain instances, for example the defence agreement between Senegal and Gambia and that between Guinea and Sierra Leone.[32]

Other issues here are that external threats to the security of specific regions in sub-Saharan Africa are largely non-military, requiring regional collective security co-operation in the broader sense rather than defence co-operation in the narrow sense only. In the Southern African Development Community (SADC) approach, as discussed earlier, security is defined in the broader context.

As far as mutual defence specifically is concerned, lack of confidence in the ability (and willingness) of regional partners to assist individual members of a collective security arrangement, should the need arise, constitutes a further problem. Intra-regional tensions also tend to undermine confidence. In Southern Africa, the expansion of Botswana's armed forces have for instance been viewed with suspicion by Namibia. This is linked to a territorial dispute between the two countries.[33]

The principle of non-interference in the internal affairs of other African states further impedes the functioning of intra-African collective security. The high level of internal armed conflict in Africa, and the relative absence of common external military threats, highlights the need for assistance in internal rather than external security. Defence agreements with foreign powers have the advantage that they can be invoked against external as well as internal security threats.[34] However, recent interventions by the Economic Community of West African States (ECOWAS) in Sierra Leone and SADC in Lesotho, as well as certain pronouncements by the OAU, which will be discussed later, seem to indicate that in practice the non-interference principle is being increasingly ignored.

The benefits of intra-African security arrangements are that they create the opportunity for joint planning; the sharing of intelligence; joint training; and some degree of policy co-ordination. Suspicion caused by increases in the level of arms in a member country of a regional security bloc, may also be reduced if the individual security efforts are seen as serving common interests.[35]

As far as reliance on extracontinental military support is concerned as a third approach to security, the point has been made that except for the obvious political cost, this is one of the most economical ways of dealing with national security problems. Extracontinental agreements can also be more readily invoked against external threats and internal disruptions.

At the beginning of the 1990s, 30 of the 44 sub-Saharan African countries were involved in some type of defence or security agreement with extracontinental powers. These agreements ranged from assistance and co-operation agreements to the provision of facilities for military bases. France has been the major role-player in this regard: in 1997 France for instance still had 1 300 troops based in the Central African Republic; 800 troops in Chad; 500 troops in the Ivory Coast; 3 900 troops in Djibouti; 600 troops in Gabon; and 1 500 troops in Senegal.[36]

In 1996 some 1 300 French troops intervened in the Central African Republic to prevent a group of rebel soldiers from destabilising the government. This was the seventeenth French military intervention in the region since 1991.[37] As noted previously, France has also assisted militarily in overthrowing various governments in Africa:

> What is clear from the pattern of foreign, especially French, intervention in Sub-Saharan Africa is that their subtle penetration or troop deployment are invariably meant to protect or install favoured regimes in power and to dethrone detested ones. In other words, they are useful for regime security rather than for national defence. Certainly the utility of these defence agreements to the affected African states is quite limited. Neutralizing dissenting opinions and perpetuating favoured, though unpopular, regimes in power could not be regarded as serving the best interests of the countries concerned. They merely promote a neo-colonial situation in which the regimes in power exist mainly to fulfil the wishes of their foreign protectors instead of aspiring to minister to the needs of their people.[38]

Recently President Chirac declared that there would be no further French political or military intervention in Africa. This has been interpreted as implying that France will gradually withdraw its troops from African countries and will intervene in internal conflicts only under the auspices of the United Nations or the OAU.[39]

Britain was less successful than France in its attempts to arrange post-independence defence co-operation. Some training agreements have however been concluded, such as those with Zimbabwe and South Africa.[40]

Following the end of the Cold War, previous direct Soviet and Cuban military intervention in Africa, including sub-Saharan Africa, for example in support of the MPLA government in Angola, now seems highly unlikely. Africa will, however, remain a recipient for Russian arms exports.

In addition to some of the problems already referred to in regard to reliance on extracontinental security protection, the loss of freedom of diplomatic manoeuvre and strategic deployment; the possibility of blackmail by the protecting power; and the possibility that popular aspirations may be ignored if they do not coincide with the aspirations of the protecting power, are included in the risks linked to extracontinental security arrangements. As mentioned earlier, these agreements have not deterred mercenary activities in the region, and mercenaries have in fact in certain instances been seen as convenient instruments for extracontinental interventionist policies in sub-Saharan Africa. The question is also whether an extracontinental power will protect one African state against aggression by another if the latter is also a protégé of that power. Military agreements with extracontinental powers could also have implications for the policy of non-alignment in Africa, especially where there is a need for the provision of military bases, although there are differences of opinion on how exactly non-alignment should be interpreted in this case.[41]

Reliance on extracontinental sources for weapons, training and technology will continue for sub-Saharan countries. Extracontinental defence pacts, however, seem to have been replaced by an increasing emphasis on peace support operations in Africa, although it is by no means certain that such operations will include the deployment of extracontinental soldiers.

5 REGIONAL DEFENCE CO-OPERATION

Regional defence co-operation is currently specifically provided for in the Southern African Development Community (SADC) Organ for Politics, Defence and Security, established in 1996, and in the West African region. The *Organization Africaine et Malagache de Cooperation Economique* (OAMCE), established in 1961, also provided for a Higher Defence Council although it was essentially an economic union. A number of other multilateral security agreements also existed previously, such as that between Burundi, Rwanda and the former Zaire, concluded in 1966. While reference has been made to L'ANAD (the Treaty of

Non-Aggression, Assistance and Mutual Defence signed by seven West African Francophone states in 1997), scant information about this agreement is available.[42]

5.1 Southern Africa

The SADC Organ had its origins in the Frontline States (FLS). For a period of more than 20 years starting in 1974, the FLS (comprising initially only Tanzania and Zambia), in consultation with the national liberation movements in Southern Africa, supported the independence struggle in countries such as Namibia and South Africa. Subsequently Angola, Botswana, Mozambique, Namibia and Zimbabwe also became part of the grouping. The FLS was a heads of state summit. Its functions were performed through a ministerial committee, the Inter-State Defence and Security Committee (ISDSC). The ISDSC in turn functioned through subcommittees on defence, state security and public security, composed of defence force chiefs, security chiefs and other officials.[43]

South Africa, Lesotho, Malawi and Swaziland became part of the ISDSC in November 1994, while Mauritius joined the SADC in 1995 and the ISDSC in October 1996.[44]

In July 1994 a proposal was adopted at a meeting of foreign ministers of Southern African states to create an Association of Southern African States (ASAS), while the SADC Council of Ministers recommended the creation of a sector on political co-operation, democracy and security. During the 1995 SADC Heads of State and Government Summit it was decided that ministers responsible for foreign affairs, defence and security and SADC matters, would be given more time to consult on the terms of reference, an appropriate institutional framework and operational procedures for co-operation in the area of politics, peace and security.[45]

At their meeting in Gaborone (Botswana) on 18 January 1996, the ministers agreed to recommend to the next summit the establishment of a SADC Organ on Politics, Defence and Security. The Summit of Heads of State and Government of the SADC later met (also in Gaborone) on 28 June 1996 under the chairmanship of Sir Kotumile Masire, President of the Republic of Botswana, to launch the proposed SADC Organ. The summit recalled that the heads of state and government had in May 1996 endorsed the recommendations of SADC ministers responsible for foreign affairs, defence and security concerning the establishment of the organ. The summit reaffirmed that the SADC Organ constituted an appropriate institutional framework through which SADC countries would co-ordinate their policies and activities in the areas of politics, defence and security. The ISDSC would be incorporated in the organisational structure of the SADC Organ.[46]

The objectives of the SADC Organ are set out as follows:[47]

THE OBJECTIVES OF THE ORGAN

The SADC Organ on Politics, Defence and Security shall work to the following objectives:

(a) to protect the people and safeguard the development of the region, against instability arising from the breakdown of law and order, inter-state conflict and external aggression;

(b) to promote political co-operation among member States and the evolution of common political value systems and institutions;

(c) to develop a common foreign policy in areas of mutual concern and interest, and to lobby as a region, on issues of common interest at international fora;

(d) to cooperate fully in regional security and defence through conflict prevention management and resolution;

(e) to mediate in inter-state and intra-state disputes and conflicts;

(f) to use preventative diplomacy to pre-empt conflict in the region, both within and between states, through an early warning system;

(g) where conflict does occur, to seek to end this as quickly as possible through diplomatic means. Only where such means fail would the Organ recommend that the Summit should consider punitive measures. These responses would be agreed in a Protocol on Peace, Security and Conflict Resolution;

(h) to promote and enhance the development of democratic institutions and practices within member states, and to encourage the observance of universal human rights as provided for in the Charters and Conventions of the OAU and the United Nations;

(i) to promote peace-making and peace-keeping in order to achieve sustainable peace and security;

(j) to give political support to the organs and institutions of SADC;

(k) to promote the political, economic, social and environmental dimensions of security;

(l) to develop a collective security capacity and conclude a Mutual Defence Pact for responding to external threats, and a regional peacekeeping capacity within national armies that could be called upon within the region, or elsewhere on the continent;

(m) to develop close cooperation between the police and security services of the region, with a view to addressing cross border crime, as well as promoting a community-based approach on matters of security;

(n) to encourage and monitor the ratification of United Nations, Organisation of African Unity, and other international conventions and treaties on arms control and disarmament, human rights and peaceful relations between states;

(o) to coordinate the participation of member states in international and regional peacekeeping operations; and

(p) to address extra-regional conflicts which impact on peace and security in Southern Africa.

5.2 West Africa

The treaty establishing ECOWAS includes the objective of the maintenance of regional peace, stability and security through the promotion and strengthening of good neighbourliness. Provision is also made for the setting up of a regional peace and security observation system and peace-keeping forces where appropriate. As far as defence issues are concerned, the *Protocol on Mutual Assistance on Defence* contains the following salient provisions:[48]

Article 2

Member States declare and accept that any armed threat or aggression directed against any Member State shall constitute a threat or aggression against the entire Community.

Article 3

Member States resolve to give mutual aid and assistance for defence against any armed threat or aggression.

Article 4

Member States shall also take appropriate measures such as specified in Articles 17 and 18 of the present Protocol in the following circumstances:

(a) In case of armed conflict between two or several Member States if the settlement procedure by peaceful means as indicated in Article 5 of the Non-Aggression Protocol mentioned in the Preamble proves ineffective;

(b) In case of internal armed conflict within any Member State engineered and supported actively from outside likely to endanger the security and peace in the entire Community. In this case the Authority shall appreciate and decide on this situation in full collaboration with the Authority of the Member State or States concerned.

Article 6

1. The Authority on the occasion of the annual ordinary meeting of ECOWAS shall examine general problems concerning peace and security of the Community;

2. The Authority may also hold extraordinary sessions on defence matters where circumstances so require;

3. The Authority shall decide on the expediency of military action and entrust its execution to the Force Commander of the Allied Forces of the Community (AAFC):

4. Decisions taken by the Authority shall be immediately enforceable on Member States.

Article 9

In case of armed intervention, the Defence Council assisted by the Defence Commission shall supervise with the authority of the State or States concerned, all measures to be taken by the Force Commander and ensure that all necessary means for the intervention are made available to him. The actions of the Force Commander shall be subject to competent political authority of the Member State or States concerned.

Article 13

1. All Member States agree to place at the disposal of the Community, earmarked units from the existing National Armed Forces in case of any armed intervention.

2. These Units shall be referred to as the Allied Armed Forces of the Community (AAFC).

3. In order to better realise the objectives set forth in this Protocol, the Member States may organise, from time to time, as may be approved by the Authority, joint military exercises among two or more earmarked Units of the AAFC.

Article 16

When an external armed threat or aggression is directed against a Member State of the Community, the Head of State of that country shall send a written request for assistance to the current Chairman of the Authority of ECOWAS, with copies to other Members. This request shall mean that the Authority is duly notified and that the AAFC are placed under a state of emergency. The Authority shall decide in accordance with the emergency procedure as stipulated in Article 6 above.

Article 17

1. When there is a conflict between two Member States of the Community, the Authority shall meet urgently and take appropriate action for mediation. If need be, the Authority shall decide only to interpose the AAFC between the troops engaged in the conflict.

Article 18

1. In the case where an internal conflict in a Member State of the Community is actively maintained and sustained from outside, the provisions of Articles 6, 9 and 16 of this Protocol shall apply.

2. Community forces shall not intervene if the conflict remains purely internal.

5.3 Assessment

As far as the practical manifestations of recent military intervention by ECOWAS and the SADC Organ are concerned, the following observations can be made.

5.3.1 ECOWAS

In the mid-1990s the ECOWAS Defence Pact was still not operational, and in what was described as an impromptu emergency measure the ECOWAS Standing Mediation Committee decided during August 1990, largely at the instigation of Nigeria, to create an ECOWAS Monitoring Group (ECOMOG) to keep the peace and restore law and order in Liberia.[49] This was followed by Nigerian and subsequently ECOMOG military intervention in Sierra Leone in 1998. Only the latter will be discussed, as the intervention in Liberia was primarily viewed as a peace support operation. In this regard, it has been claimed that "the Sierra Leone situation deviated from peace creation in many respects. It was more of an attempt by Nigeria to restore President Kabbah to power under a bilateral arrangement, than an attempt to bring about the peaceful resolution of conflict between warring parties."[50]

The agreement between Nigeria and Sierra Leone, concluded in 1997, referred to the "provision of military assistance for sustenance of the sovereignty and territorial integrity of the Republic of Sierra Leone".[51] At this stage, Sierra Leone was also a member of the ECOWAS Defence Pact. No explicit reference was, however, made to this pact or the bilateral agreement in the decision to intervene in Sierra Leone. The fact that the situation in Sierra Leone could largely be viewed as an internal issue (although Liberia allegedly supported their Revolutionary United Front – RUF rebels who were allies of the military junta led by major John Paul Koroma following a *coup* in May 1997), and therefore not meeting the requirements for military intervention in accordance with the ECOWAS Defence Pact, could be one explanation for this. Another possible explanation is that the commander of the ECOMOG force in Sierra Leone apparently based the initial intervention on a statement by the OAU Summit following the *coup* in Sierra Leone asking the member states of ECOWAS to do everything possible to restore President Kabbah to power.[52]

The OAU Council of Ministers subsequently paid a special tribute to Nigeria for the role ECOMOG played in removing the military junta from power in Sierra Leone, thus in fact condoning the military intervention. Emphasis was, however, placed on the need for a peaceful resolution of the conflict and national reconciliation, in view of the continued fighting following the overthrow of the military regime. The OAU had previously also referred to the possibility of adopting a declaration condemning unconstitutional changes of government in Africa, including military *coups*.[53)] This should not be interpreted as implying that military intervention to reverse a *coup*, would in all instances be condoned by the OAU, or that such intervention would necessarily comply with the requirements of international law.

It has been alleged that when the member states of ECOWAS took steps to address external security issues, internal security threats were not sufficiently considered. To a large extent, the same problem appears to be facing the SADC.

5.3.2 SADC

The decision by Angola, Zimbabwe and Namibia in August 1998 to prop up the Kabila government in the DRC was taken in the absence of a SADC mutual defence pact (or bilateral pacts). It was apparently based on requests from Kabila for military assistance (the DRC is a member of the SADC); allegations of foreign support (Rwanda and Uganda) for the rebels; and, of course, especially in the case of Angola, to prevent UNITA obtaining a renewed foothold in the DRC should Kabila's regime fall, and in the case of Zimbabwe, protection of financial investments in the DRC, as well as Mugabe's perception of his regional role. Some differences of opinion exist as to whether the decision to support Kabila was a unanimous SADC decision (nine members are reported to have supported the decision) as South Africa, specifically, stressed the need for a peaceful solution and declined to send troops. This led to criticism by Mugabe, who seems to have led the military mission.[54]

Subsequently it was reported that Mandela and other SADC leaders had praised the assistance given to Kabila, but South African Foreign Minister, Alfred Nzo, indicated that South Africa would consider providing logistic support only, if a peace-keeping force (presumably in accordance with a UN resolution), were deployed in the DRC.[55]

President Nujoma of Namibia maintained that the presence of troops of certain SADC countries was in accordance with agreements reached in the SADC, and that those agreements compelled regional members to go to the assistance of another member state if requested. He also referred to the need to oppose attempts to overthrow "legitimate" governments by force.[56]

Nujoma's views are contentious. Firstly, although the objectives of the SADC Organ include collective security and a mutual defence pact, this is linked to external aggression specifically, and no mutual defence pact is currently in place. Secondly, the formal status and interpretation of the "agreements" to which Nujoma refers (as well as their international legal standing), are debatable, and they do not constitute a separate protocol. These "agreements" are understood to refer to countering *coups* in SADC member countries, but it is uncertain whether they apply equally to elected and non-elected governments. Also, there are no clear guidelines in the SADC objectives regarding military responses to internal conflicts. Of course, in line with the provisions of the ECOWAS Defence Protocol, had a mutual defence pact existed between SADC members, it could possibly have been invoked by Kabila on the grounds of foreign assistance (Rwanda and Uganda) to the rebels in the DRC.

The issue is that a mutual defence pact (depending on its provisions) could place certain obligations on member states, and had such a pact been in force in the SADC, it could for instance have obligated South Africa to send troops. Also, it is highly probable that SADC member states will invariably attempt to "prove" external assistance to rebel movements if this is required to invoke a mutual defence pact in the case of internal conflicts.

Nujoma's reference to the "legitimacy" of Kabila's regime is also problematic. In view of accusations of corruption, authoritarianism and nepotism against Kabila, and taking into account his ascent to power through force, the question arises as to whether legitimacy is not in this case in the eye of the beholder.

President Mugabe elaborated on the military assistance to the DRC by stating that no SADC member had been forced to participate in the military intervention. Any military attack that undermines a sovereign government was, according to him, viewed by the SADC and the Organisation of African Unity (OAU) as a "rebellion", and this required immediate attention.[57]

Obviously again, legitimacy seems to be in the eye of the beholder. Mobuto's rule in Zaire was seen to be illegitimate, while Kabila's rule is seen to be legitimate. The question arises whether Mobuto's position would have been different had Zaire been a member of SADC at the time of the rebellion which eventually toppled him.

Criticism of Zimbabwe's military involvement in the DRC, *inter alia* specifically emphasised that "by no stretch of the imagination can it be said to be necessary for the defence of Zimbabwe that our forces should be used to support a foreign leader with whom Zimbabwe has no treaty or other obligations". It was added that the Zimbabwean Constitution did not allow Zimbabwean forces to be deployed except in defence of the country. Fears had in fact been expressed even prior to Zimbabwe's decision to intervene that Mugabe might use the SADC Organ, of which he is chairperson, to prop up unpopular governments.[58] The current distinction between chairing the SADC and chairing the SADC Organ, also remains a contentious issue.

Unlike the conflict in the DRC, the situation in Lesotho was essentially an internal crisis. Military intervention by South Africa and Botswana, during September 1998, under the auspices of the SADC, was justified by referring to a request for help received from the Prime Minister of Lesotho; that a military *coup* was imminent or had partially occurred and that military *coups* in SADC member countries would not be tolerated; that all attempts to resolve the dispute peacefully had failed; and that South Africa, specifically, had intervened to protect certain interests in Lesotho such as the Katse Dam. Mention was also made of the OAU statement regarding *coups* referred to above.[59]

President Mandela stated that the Lesotho government had been democratically elected (despite certain irregularities in the previous election), and that it was increasingly expected of South Africa to play a role in peace support operations as a whole in Southern Africa.[60]

Obviously, though, the intervention in Lesotho was not in the form of a peace support operation (including peace enforcement), but was primarily military intervention in support of the Lesotho government. The view was for instance expressed that opposition parties in Lesotho could take the issue to the UN Security Council, as South Africa had not obtained Security Council permission for its military intervention.[61] Other criticism of the intervention focused on the *modus operandi* and not the principle.

That the justification for the intervention was dubious under international law (except for the protection of interests argument), seems clear in the absence of a UN mandate or of the principle of self-defence, even though the intervention was by invitation. The broad objective of the Lesotho intervention went beyond "protection of interests", namely "to assist the Lesotho government to restore stability to the country".[62]

In addition to military intervention to prevent or reverse *coups*, human rights abuses as justification for SADC intervention have also been raised. During the SADC annual summit in Malawi in September 1997, President Chiluba of Zambia admonished African leaders intending to intervene militarily in other states on the pretext of sustaining human rights.[63] This was interpreted as an apparent reference to the statement by President Nelson Mandela that the SADC would in future intervene militarily where human rights were perceived to be grossly violated by their governments. Mandela's statement could, however, possibly also be seen in terms of UN mandated peace support operations, although the recent intervention in Lesotho without this mandate, could of course be repeated in other instances.

In all of the above examples of military intervention, certain objectives seem to have been reached. However, in the case of Sierra Leone, rebel activity in support of the previous military junta has not yet been eliminated and the country faces massive socio-economic problems. In the case of the DRC, although Kabila has retained power, the spectre of continued and prolonged conflict, drawing in more sub-Saharan states, looms; and in Lesotho, although some agreement regarding a new general election seems to have been reached, there is still no time-table for the withdrawal of troops from South Africa and Botswana, and uncertainty over who will eventually pay for the intervention (according to the Status of Forces Agreement between South Africa and Lesotho, Lesotho is liable for payment, although opposition party members have disputed this), as well as for the rebuilding of businesses destroyed in Maseru and elsewhere as a result of arson and looting by those opposed to the intervention force.

5.3.3 Bilateral agreements

As far as bilateral defence agreements in sub-Saharan Africa are concerned, Imobighe notes:

The conclusion that can be drawn is that these security arrangements exist more as non-aggression pacts than as mutual defence mechanisms for combating aggression. For instance, Ethiopia has fought intermittent border wars with Somalia, against whom her treaty with Kenya was contracted without the latter sending any meaningful help.[64]

As previously mentioned, Nigeria had concluded a defence agreement with Sierra Leone prior to the military *coup* in Sierra Leone, and Nigerian intervention to reinstate the government could *inter alia* be linked to this agreement, although it was never stated so explicitly.

In the case of the DRC, a defence pact was signed with the Central African Republic in May 1998, but has so far not been invoked in the current crisis in the DRC. A bilateral defence agreement between the DRC and Uganda, creating some legal basis for the presence of Ugandan troops in the DRC, was later terminated by the DRC.[65]

Bilateral (or multilateral) defence co-operation can take on forms other than defence pacts. South Africa and Togo, for instance, signed a memorandum of understanding during September 1997, which formed the basis for military co-operation, training, joint peace support exercises and technical assistance.[66]

6 CONCLUSION

At the level of the OAU, it is clear that peace support operations (and in a broader sense conflict prevention, management and resolution) have become the main focus, and that the concept of an African High Command seems to have receded. Also, no provision for a standing OAU peace-keeping force is made in the *Declaration* of 1993, which established the Conflict Resolution Mechanism.

On the regional level, the SADC Organ (in its objectives) and the ECOWAS Protocol of 1981 provide for mutual defence pacts, but not for any standing army. The ECOWAS Protocol specifically prohibits intervention in purely internal conflicts, and in cases of conflicts between two member states of ECOWAS, any troops deployed in accordance with the protocol will if necessary only be interposed between the parties engaged in the conflict.

The SADC Organ provides for "punitive measures" where conflict within and between states in the region occurs: the details have still to be spelt out in a Protocol on Peace, Security and Conflict Resolution. ECOWAS adopted a Protocol on Non-Aggression in 1978.

Regional defence pacts or collective security under the UN Charter should not be confused with peace enforcement or with the military personnel governments may agree to keep on stand-by for possible contribution to peace-keeping operations. However, the ready availability of armed forces on call to the UN or preventive deployment as part of UN peace support operations could supplement the deterrence provided for by regional defence pacts. The UN Secretary-General formulated this as follows:

> In cases where a nation fears a cross-border attack, if the Security Council concludes that a United Nations presence on one side of the border, with the consent only of the requesting country, would serve to deter conflict, I recommend that preventive deployment take place.[67]

The opinion has been expressed that mutual defence pacts on a regional level and specifically in the SADC are not necessary and that non-aggression pacts on an intraregional and interregional basis will suffice, although the one is not really a substitute for the other. The *Kampala Document* already referred to, recommends that non-aggression treaties should also incorporate common defence against external aggression.

The major issue as far as regional defence pacts (against extraregional aggression) are concerned, is that the vast majority of armed conflicts in Africa are internal (although there may be some external involvement). Regional defence pacts such as that of ECOWAS specifically exclude involvement in domestic conflict in the region. In this context, peace support operations under UN supervision would seem to be the appropriate instrument, or UN military intervention under Article 42 of the *UN Charter*. The consent of the parties involved in such a conflict can be forfeited should circumstances require certain types of UN-supervised peace support operations. The recent interventions of ECOWAS in Sierra Leone and the SADC in Lesotho are, however, neither examples of peace support nor, especially in the case of Lesotho, of collective defence against external military aggression. It could perhaps be argued that alleged Liberian assistance to the RUF in Sierra Leone constituted some form of external aggression.

Whether for purposes of individual national defence against internal revolt or external aggression; providing troops for peace support operations; or providing military assistance in terms of a bilateral or mutual defence pact, it is ultimately the military potential of individual African countries that has to be assessed in the absence of any standing continental or regional force. Where regional defence pacts or security communities do exist, they could augment national capabilities.

Intrastate and interstate armed conflict continues to be waged in sub-Saharan Africa. Peace support operations and military intervention in these conflicts are of course only part of the larger issues of national and regional security, which would include addressing the root causes of insecurity and conflict. Yet, a number of important issues regarding norms and principles have arisen as a result of recent military interventions in sub-Saharan African countries, and greater clarity on for instance the link (if any) between peace support operations and these types of military intervention is essential.

REFERENCES

1. Ostheimer, J M, "Peacekeeping and Warmaking", in Arlinghaus, B E (ed), *African Armies: Evolution and Capabilities*, Westview Press, Colorado, 1986, pp 46-48.

2. Imobighe, T A, "An African High Command: The Search for a Feasible Strategy for Continental Defence", *African Affairs*, Vol 79, No 314, January 1980, pp 241-242.

3. Woronoff, J, "The Case for an African Defense Organization", *Africa Report*, June 1971, p 23.

4. Imobighe, T A, "An African High Command...", *op cit*, p 242.

5. *Ibid*, pp 245-246.

6. *Ibid*, p 246.

7. Foltz, W J and H S Bienen, *Arms and the African: Military Influences on Africa's International Relations*, Yale University Press, New Haven, 1985, pp 184-185.

8. *Ibid*, p 185.

9. *Kampala Document for a Proposed Conference on Security, Stability, Development and Cooperation in Africa (CSSDCA)*, Kampala, Uganda, 23 May 1991.

10. OAU, *Declaration of the Assembly of Heads of State and Government on the Establishment Within the OAU of a Mechanism for Conflict Prevention, Management and Resolution*, Cairo, June 30, 1993.

11. OAU, Central Organ, *OAU's Position Towards the Various Initiatives on Conflict Management*, Min/3(iv), undated; and *The Star* (Johannesburg), 23 July 1997.

12. OAU, *Resolving Conflicts in Africa: Implementation Options*, OAU Information Services, Series II, 1993, p 29.

13. Imobighe, T A, "An African High Command...", *op cit*, p 249; Seegers, A M, "South African Liberation", in Arlinghaus, B E (ed), *African Security Issues*, Westview Press, Colorado, 1984, p 191; and Foltz, W J and H S Bienen, *op cit*, p 185.

14. Imobighe, T A, "An African High Command ...", *op cit*, pp 249-250.

15. *Ibid*, pp 250-252.

16. *The Star* (Johannesburg), 16 September 1997, 18 September 1997, 17 September 1997, 9 October 1997 and 10 March 1998; *Die Republikein* (Windhoek), 10 September 1997; *Pan-African News Agency*, 2 September 1997; *Business Day* (Johannesburg), 28 November 1997; International Institute for Strategic Studies, *The Military Balance, 1996/97*, Oxford University Press, London, p 236; *Africa Confidential*, 18 July 1997; and *The Star* (Johannesburg), 15 October 1998.

17. *The Star*, 24 September 1997 and 9 October 1997; *Global Newsbank*, 20 July 1997; *Africa Confidential*, 11 April 1997 and 9 May 1997; and *Die Republikein* (Windhoek), 11 November 1997.

18. SIPRI Yearbook, *Armaments, Disarmament and International Security*, Oxford University Press, New Jersey, 1998, pp 17-30.

19. Furley, O, "Introduction", in Furley, O (ed), *Conflict in Africa*, I B Travis Publishers, London, 1995, p 10.

20. IISS, *The Military Balance, 1996/97*, Oxford University Press, London, 1997, p 237.

21. Imobighe, T A, *op cit*, p 92.

22. *Africa Confidential*, 9 May 1997; *Pan-African News Agency*, 2 September 1997; and *Business Day.*, 14 October 1997.

23. Rimmer, D, "The Effects of Conflict, II: Economic Effects", in Furley, O, *op cit*, p 303.

24. *Africa Research Bulletin*, Vol 35, No 5, May 1998, pp 13102-13101.

25. Rimmer, D, "The Effects of Conflict, II: Economic Effects", in Furley, O, *op cit*, p 304.

26. Imobighe, T A, "Security in Sub-Saharan Africa", in Singh, J and T Bernauer (eds), *Security of Third World Countries*, UNIDR, 1993, p 95.

27. Moose, G E, "French Military Policy in Africa", in Foltz, W J and H S Bienen, *Arms and the African*, Council on Foreign Relations, New York, 1985, p 84; Imobighe, T A, "Security in Sub-Saharan Africa", *op cit*, p 96; and O'Neill, K and B Munslow, "Angola: Ending the Cold War in Southern Africa", in Furley, O, *op cit*, pp 184-195.

28. Lyon, P, "The Ending of the Cold War in Africa", in Furley, O, *op cit*, p 180.

29. Imobighe, T A, "Security in Sub-Saharan Africa", *op cit*, p 97.

30. *Ibid*, p 98.
31. *Ibid*, p 107.
32. *Ibid*, p 105.
33. Republic of Namibia, *Debates of the National Assembly*, 1-9 March 1995, Vol 46, pp 283-284.
34. Imobighe, T A, "Security in Sub-Saharan Africa", *op cit*, pp 99 and 102.
35. *Ibid*, p 103.
36. IISS, *The Military Balance, 1997/98*, Oxford University Press, London, 1997, pp 236-263; and Imobighe, T A, "Security in Sub-Saharan Africa", *op cit*, p 99.
37. IISS, *The Military Balance, 1996/97*, *op cit*, p 236.
38. Imobighe, T A, "Security in Sub-Saharan Africa", *op cit*, pp 100-101.
39. *Beeld* (Johannesburg), 29 August 1997; and *The Star* (Johannesburg), 9 October 1997.
40. Imobighe, T A, "Security in Sub-Saharan Africa", *op cit*, p 100.
41. *Ibid*, pp 100-101.
42. *Ibid*, pp 103-104; and Malan, M (*et al*), *African Capabilities for Training for Peace Operations*, IISS Monograph Series No 17, November 1997, p 77.
43. Hough, M and A du Plessis (eds), *Africa: Selected Documents on Political, Security, Humanitarian and Economic Issues*, Institute for Strategic Studies,, University of Pretoria, 1996, p 32.
44. *Ibid*.
45. *Ibid*.
46. *Ibid*, pp 32-33.
47. SADC, *Organ for Politics, Defence and Security*, Gaborone, Botswana, 28 June 1996.
48. ECOWAS, *Protocol Relating to Mutual Assistance on Defence*, A/SP3/5/81.
49. Baah-Duado, K, *ECOWAS*, Occasional Paper — Africa Group, No 2, 25 August 1995, p 13; and Imobighe, T A, "Security in Sub-Saharan Africa", *op cit*.

50. Olonisakin, O, "The role of Nigeria in ECOWAS peace support operations and some lessons for South Africa", *ISSUP Bulletin*, No 6/98, October 1998, p 12.

51. *Status of Forces Agreement (SOFA) between the Government of the Federal Republic of Nigeria and the Government of the Republic of Sierra Leone Concerning the Provision of Military and Security Assistance to the Republic of Sierra Leone*, 7 March 1997.

52. Khabe, M M (Brig-Gen), *Anatomy of the Sierra Leone Conflict and its Resolution by ECOWAS*, Paper presented to the ECOWAS Regional Forum, Burkina Faso, date unknown.

53. OAU, *Conflict Management Bulletin*, Vol 2, No 2, 1997, p 10; and OAU, *Resolving Conflicts*, Vol 2, No 4, 1998, p 11.

54. *Business Day* (Johannesburg), 18, 19 and 21 August 1998; and *Beeld* (Johannesburg), 20 August 1998. This section is also partially based on an article published by the author in *Strategic Review for Southern Africa*, Vol XX, No 2, November 1998.

55. *The Star* (Johannesburg), 7 September 1998; and *Beeld* (Johannesburg), 9 November 1998.

56. *The Star* (Johannesburg), 3 September 1998.

57. *Beeld* (Johannesburg), 25 September 1998.

58. *Business Day* (Johannesburg), 4 September 1998; *Mail and Guardian* (Johannesburg), 17 July 1998; and *The Star* (Johannesburg), 5 August 1998.

59. RSA, Department of Defence, *Bulletin*, No 57/98, 22 September 1998; *The Star* (Johannesburg), 28 September 1998; *Beeld* (Johannesburg), 12 October 1998; OAU, *Conflict Management Bulletin*, Vol 2, No 2, 1997, p 10; and OAU, *Resolving Conflicts*, Vol 2, No 4, 1998, p 11.

60. *Beeld* (Johannesburg), 25 September 1998.

61. *Beeld* (Johannesburg), 28 September 1998.

62. Shearer, I A, *Starke's International Law*, Eleventh Edition, Butterworths, London, 1994, pp 94-98. It is, however, stated that "co-operation in peace-enforcement, peace-keeping and humanitarian relief is not always either prompt or adequate". Also see, *Bulletin*, No 57/98, *op cit.*

63. *Pretoria News* (Pretoria), 17 September 1997.

64. Imobighe, T A, "Security in Sub-Saharan Africa", *op cit*, pp 104-105.
65. Radio Kinshasa, 12 May 1998: BBC Monitor; and *Business Day* (Johannesburg), 28 September 1998.
66. *Beeld* (Johannesburg), 23 September 1997.
67. UN, Secretary-General, *An Agenda for Peace*, S/2411, 17 June 1992, pp 17 and 24.

Chapter 9

PROSPECTS FOR SUB-SAHARAN ARMED FORCES IN THE TWENTY-FIRST CENTURY

Louis du Plessis

1 INTRODUCTION

Images of sub-Saharan Africa are usually painted in the darkest colours. At the end of the twentieth century, readers and television audiences are repeatedly reminded: Africa is a nightmarish world where chaos reigns. Nothing works. Illiteracy, poverty, war and corruption rule.[1] Constantly confronted by these images, the question in the mind of students of security is thus inevitably: What are the prospects for sub-Saharan armed forces at the beginning of the twenty-first century? Although valid deductions on this issue may be made from the previous chapters, a brief but separate chapter is necessary to provide an independent perspective.

The model that is used to analyse probabilities contains four related perspectives. These may be applied to military and non-military fields of study, as well as to collective and individual endeavours (see figure on p 262). The first perspective, called constraints, focuses on the most severe future limitations that are inherent in existing obstacles; while the second perspective, called opportunities, concentrates on the vision and motivation required to transform these constraints into challenges. The third level of analysis, called operations, examines the present roles and patterns of behaviour to determine what is being done and can be done; while the last level, called capabilities, investigates the basic abilities, expertise and tools available for action.

FIGURE
FRAMEWORK FOR PROSPECTS ANALYSIS

| CONSTRAINTS |
| OPPORTUNITIES |
| OPERATIONS |
| CAPABILITIES |

To elaborate on this model, a few comments on the four related fields: first, some elements that limit the freedom of movement of the societies in general, and the armed forces specifically, will be outlined, followed by an optimistic vision of a possible growth in African self-reliance in which the constraints may be viewed as opportunities. Flowing from this, prospects for probable future operations will be outlined, and basic abilities defined.

It should be emphasised that the relationship between present and future trends is complicated and, moreover, clouded by several issues surrounding the nature of conceptualisation. No attempt is being made here to uncover the underlying scientific presuppositions for determining long-term developments. It is stated clearly that references to probable future developments are definitely not predictions. Such references merely provide a broad framework for the analysis of a few trends. Furthermore, since the framework is based on the investigations in the preceding chapters, it should be viewed in that context. Since some suggestions on enhancing the defence capability of sub-Saharan states will be made, a few comments to avoid confusion between information, on the one hand, and suggestions, proposals and values, on the other hand, are appropriate.

The prospects will be discussed as objectively as possible and may be tested at some future date. However, in addition to the informative statements on prospects, a few normative remarks will be made. They will point to some of the main requirements for sub-Saharan states to protect themselves and their region. Although these remarks may also be evaluated in future, they are, like other normative statements, determined not by the study of facts alone but also by value preferences.

The normative point of departure is that it will serve the long-term interests of sub-Saharan societies to develop in a certain direction. This direction will promote profitable economic systems, democratic political processes and professional armed forces. Professional armed forces consist of well-trained and disciplined units, they support the principle of civilian supremacy, and are prepared to protect their societies individually and regionally against threats. The emphasis of effective strategy falls on national and regional self-defence and not on military expansion or occupation. From a subjective point of view, one of the central problems of sub-Saharan Africa is that some prominent political and military leaders do not share these values. However, the factual analysis of future prospects is independent of normative considerations and proposals.

Before exploring the growing need for self-reliance, the restrictive nature of a few current limitations will be examined.

2 CONSTRAINTS

The world of sub-Saharan Africa is characterised by constraints imposed by the historical environment. The influence of geographic obstacles, economic deficiencies and historical conflict is exceptionally severe.

2.1 Geographic obstacles

Some of the most fundamental limitations to which African countries are subjected arise from their geographical location in the tropics. Tropical climates affect all parts of sub-Saharan Africa except the Republic of South Africa. They undermine long-term planning, as unpredictability is one of their principal characteristics.[2]

Moreover, in many sub-regions of Sub-Sahara the soil is inadequate to sustain permanent agriculture, and pests and diseases proliferate. The ecological constraints faced by sub-Saharan Africans are far more severe than those in most Western countries.[3]

A specific aspect of geography that overlaps with politics is that of the boundaries of states. At the Congress of Berlin in 1885, European colonial powers partitioned Africa into territorial units. Kingdoms, states and communities were arbitrarily divided; unrelated areas and peoples were just as arbitrarily joined together.[4] Since the Congress of Berlin delineated spheres of influence and laid down the ground rules for imperial expansion, the political frontiers of Africa have undergone only minor adjustments. In the 1960s, the newly independent states inherited these boundaries.

Consequently, a profound characteristic of sub-Saharan Africa became the artificiality of its political boundaries: they do not reflect sub-Saharan geographical or ethnic realities.[5]

The wars between neighbouring countries, often inhabited by the same peoples, were referred to as a "pernicious threat as they are a sequel of colonialism", because the conflicts were often about the drawing of these borders.[6]

None of these geographic obstructions will change at the beginning of the twenty-first century. Sub-Saharan Africa will maintain its tropical climate, agricultural impediments and, in all probability, most of its political borders.

2.2 Economic deficiencies

The ability of states to protect their societies is related to available material assets, on the one hand, and to the ability to finance socio-economic development and security services on the other. The capacity to govern is directly linked to the capacity to budget.[7]

In sub-Saharan Africa, financial constraints were one of the main factors limiting modernisation, and are likely to be so for the foreseeable future. According to an analyst at the University of Botswana, one reason is that, with a few notable exceptions, sub-Saharan governments have tended to ignore budget constraints, and have been unable to increase state extractive capacity or reduce dependence on foreign aid. The fact is: "Three decades after independence, most sub-Saharan African nations are still not able to finance public expenditure out of their own resources". Official development assistance from donor countries continues to play a major role in public investment and government budgets.[8]

Consequently, sub-Saharan states are becoming more and more dependent on foreign powers and international economic agencies. The International Monetary Fund (IMF) and the World Bank have been involved in extensive operations to bail African economies out of their economic morass. However, the price for this support has been the forfeiture of control over certain facets of economic decision making, as well as increasing foreign debts and mounting social inequalities.[9]

Poor economic performance, which will continue into the next century, will be aggravated by the impact of a population explosion. Although the continent's total population is relatively low, the population growth is the highest in the world. The average African woman will bear seven children.[10] This has serious negative implications, first for *per capita* income and second, for the provision of public services. Without economic progress and financial expertise, states inevitably find it difficult to develop or maintain military capabilities.[11]

When looking at the future, it is highly probable that the severe economic difficulties experienced by most sub-Saharan societies during the last years of the twentieth century, will not soon disappear. Moreover these difficulties, and the reaction of the IMF and the World Bank, have influenced the stabilisation or reduction of military expenditure by several sub-Saharan countries during the 1990s. Based on these considerations, it may be safely assumed that financial resources will continue to be a severe constraint in the development of military manpower, weapons systems and logistics.[12]

2.3 Historical conflicts

Some of the harshest constraints on the development of sub-Saharan armed forces are related to the legacy of armed conflict.

As was pointed out in previous chapters, internal and cross-border conflicts erupted in every region during the first decades of independence. The reasons for them were often linked to ethnic divisions,[13] and several governments were confronted by wars of secession.

The lack of political stability had grave effects on human and animal life and on the standard of living.[14] Moreover, the internal and cross-border battles caused massive disturbances in the settlement of whole communities, often displacing them into vast squatter settlements on the edges of towns. This gave rise to international refugee problems.

According to Chazan and others, conflicts related to ethnic self-determination, political violence and civil dissension, have not subsided but have unquestionably proliferated.[15] At the end of the twentieth century, many sub-Saharan states are unable to maintain authority outside the capital; and in some countries, like Nigeria, highway robbery has become commonplace.[16]

According to the United Nations Secretary-General, more than 30 wars have been fought in Africa since 1970, the vast majority of them intrastate in origin. In 1996 alone, 14 of the 53 countries of Africa were afflicted by armed conflicts, accounting for more than half of all war-related deaths worldwide and resulting in more than 8 million refugees, returnees and displaced persons.[17]

Many sub-Saharan sub-regions will necessarily enter the next century under some of these brutal conditions. Such circumstances, which might not disappear soon, are detrimental not only to the existence of stable societies but also to the development of well-organised and self-disciplined military forces.

3 OPPORTUNITIES

Although geographic obstructions, economic scarcity, historical conflicts and related characteristics, such as fragile state institutions and gross civilian inequalities, have severely circumscribed the range of manoeuvrability within the political domain,[18] a new faith in progress has evolved in sub-Saharan Africa at the end of the twentieth century. This faith is associated with both external marginalisation and an internal spirit of self-reliance.

3.1 Marginalisation by non-Africans

After the Cold War competition, sub-Saharan states are now less able to rely on outside assistance to end local wars, rivalries and antagonisms that are no direct threat to vital foreign interests.[19] In fact, in the 1990s a common thread running throughout most relationships of sub-Saharan countries is fading international attention. This marginalisation is found in the attitudes of the most developed societies and "the outstanding feature of Western policy in Africa is its absence".[20]

Consequently, many sub-Saharan intellectuals, economists and politicians are gradually realising that security problems in their subcontinent will not be solved from outside. The ball is in their court.

3.2 Renaissance by Africans

This realisation is linked to what is called "an African renaissance". The South African president and deputy president refer to a revival and re-awakening in Africa.[21] The deputy president, Mr Thabo Mbeki, is credited with coining the phrase, as well as with being the driving force behind it. Mbeki regards the African renaissance as Africa's revival across all spheres of public and private life, and even as Africa's salvation, despite all historical constraints.

With reference to several sub-Saharan sub-regions, academics, bankers and security analysts are talking seriously about this African renaissance. The phrase is used to describe slow, fragile, difficult changes that are giving the continent a second chance.[22]

Mbeki sees this revival as having two main dimensions — a democratic one and an economic one. The conditions for the renaissance are the establishment of democratic systems and sustainable economic development. It implies a growing entrepreneurial class.[23]

According to Mbeki: "The key to the vision of a renaissance is that Africans should take charge of their own destiny. Africa will succeed or fail in the long term due to its own efforts and should not attempt to place any future blame on anyone else".[24]

Although the support of the major powers is regarded as necessary, it is argued that their involvement must be limited to a truly authentic African agenda.

3.3 Spirit of self-reliance

In his analysis of sub-Saharan conflict-resolution, Brooks notes that Africa has a history of disunity and instability for which there is "no end in view". However, "there is an increasing willingness among Africans to solve their own problems".[25] Norms of social interaction have been formulated in many countries and a modicum of civic order has been established.[26] There is a growing concern for achievement and democratic values.

Connell and Smyth argue that sub-Saharan Africa is experiencing its "most profound changes since the early years of independence". A new generation of leaders are increasingly taking matters into their own hands.[27] In a recent investigation under the title *Africa Rising*, McGeary and Michaels maintain that a "new spirit of self-reliance is taking root among many Africans as they seize control of their destiny".[28]

Several countries have already achieved a dose of national economic success, with higher growth rates, lower inflation and more stable currencies that flow from obedience to stringent International Monetary Fund reform programmes.[29] In fact, several sub-Saharan societies have recently grown economically at more than five per cent annually.

The United Nations Secretary-General stated in April 1998 that, despite the fact that in many parts of Africa progress remains threatened or impeded by conflict, Africa as a whole has begun to make significant economic and political progress in recent years.[30]

This growing faith in the ability to overcome constraints also has a pertinent security dimension.

3.4 Implications for defence

In the mind of the South African Minister of Defence, a renaissance implies the burgeoning of new ideas, the flowering of culture, the progress of science and the growth of prosperity. He is convinced that defence reinforces such a renaissance by guaranteeing peace and security. In addition, historically, defence has always acted as a driver in developing technology.[31]

According to the United Nations Secretary-General, "all states have the right and responsibility to provide for their own defence".[32] In concrete terms, this also applies to African capabilities. The South African Minister of Defence is adamant and determined: "In an unpredictable world African states must be able to protect the people, resources, and the sovereignty of the countries on the continent. This security has to be ensured by the capacity of Africa's own defence forces, which need to be developed and strengthened".[33]

4 OPERATIONS

When attempting to define the type of operations sub-Saharan armed forces are at present capable of conducting and will be able to conduct in the near future, internal and external roles should not be confused. These roles are related, but different.

4.1 Internal probabilities

The main activities of post-independence sub-Saharan armed forces were related to the unconstitutional changing of governments in power. Authoritarian politics dominated the domestic scene in the first post-colonial phase. The military became an important mechanism for bringing about political change, which often took place by way of *coups d'état*. Virtually every African state has been subjected to an attempted *coup*. In fact, the move from civilian to military rule and back again became an essential part of the rhythm of sub-Saharan politics.[34]

The underlying causes of military intervention were and are related to the absence of genuinely democratic means for changing the government, but also to the characteristics of sub-Saharan military institutions which have enjoyed a virtual monopoly of organised state violence. Crucial factors are the nature of the sub-Saharan state, with its overwhelming concentration of resources in political leadership, together with the non-existence of a viable civil society. In many countries these factors still exert a dominant influence and will continue into the twenty-first century. The implication is that several armed forces will still be prone to intervening in the political process.

On the other hand, many states remained free of military domination owing to the existence of a series of mechanisms for maintaining civilian authority. Among these were maximising the material service conditions for officers, the creation of competing security formations, and the establishment of representative structures. The number of societies in which mechanisms for civilian control of the armed forces are developing is increasing, and will probably continue to increase into the twenty-first century. The implication is that military professionalism will probably also increase and that military *coup* attempts will continue to decrease.

The development of professional forces, which fulfil the military line function, depends not only on the nature of the armed forces but also on the nature of society. Enhanced military professionalism, measured by increased technical capabilities and an ethic of national service, may alter the style of the political involvement of armed forces. It implies that an area of professional autonomy will develop, the bounds of which will be recognised by government and military leaders alike.[35]

In addition, the political culture of civilian society is as important as the military subculture. Despite serious efforts to democratise, most sub-Saharan countries lack a strong civil society to contain authoritarian leaders.[36] The domestic role of the armed forces is and will be related not only to the development of professionalism in the armed forces, but also to the development of a culture of political participation and independent interest groups in broader civilian society.

In addition to military intervention in domestic politics, sub-Saharan armed forces often perform functions related to serving the national societies. They are relatively disciplined compared with other parts of the civil service; and it can thus be safely foreseen that, during the present phase of societal change and modernisation, they will continue to strengthen civilian state departments. The armed forces will also continue to support the other branch of the security forces, namely the police, in maintaining law and order and the rule of law. In many countries, including Botswana, Kenya, Namibia, Nigeria, South Africa and Zimbabwe, this function will probably be more prominent than external military activities. All over sub-Saharan Africa armed forces will continue to play a major role in combating internal disorder and in countering insurgencies of all kinds, thus ensuring the sovereignty of the state.

Sub-Saharan armed forces will also still be utilised as powerful socialisation agents for inculcating modern behavioural patterns. These patterns are related to the classless nature of military training and conditions, which fosters a broader, more tolerant attitude towards all social groups; emphasis on achievement and diligence; and the politically stabilising effect of a clearly delineated hierarchical structure.[37] In addition to being training institutions inculcating the belief in national unity, sub-Saharan armed forces will also continue their roles as developmental agents who construct parts of the infrastructure and promote health and literacy. In this way the military will further contribute to economic progress and nation building.

The international involvement of the armed forces will also follow a similar pattern of divergent and even opposite kinds of operation.

4.2 External probabilities

International military relations will continue to express themselves in contrasting ways. Several states will become involved in cross-border excursions and in destabilising neighbours. From a perspective of peace, the picture is pessimistic. The more an African country acquires the military capability to take effective action against a neighbour, the more likely it is to use that capability. As military balances become more pronounced, political pressures may be less effective in preventing the eruption of armed clashes. Thom says that although the image of widespread, uncontrolled future warfare sweeping the continent should not be created, it is necessary to point out that the potential for armed conflict will be significantly enhanced.[38]

As sub-Saharan states improve the capabilities of their armed forces, the more competent ones may be tempted to solve disputes by threats or use of force if their neighbours are weak. Barrows[39] correctly maintains that unless the drive toward enhanced military strength is carefully balanced among potentially antagonistic neighbours, the likelihood of armed conflict will increase.

Low-intensity conventional wars may not become the most characteristic African wars by number, but they will probably be more common than in the past. Nevertheless, it can be argued convincingly that counterinsurgent warfare will remain the most difficult task for African armies to perform effectively (as compared to conventional warfare or assisting in guerrilla operations). Consequently, this will ensure that insurgencies will continue to be mounted against African states and that they will remain the most common form of warfare in Africa for some time to come.[40]

As African warfare becomes more sophisticated, it will pose an even greater threat to the often delicate infrastructure of African states. At the same time, multilateral co-operation will probably increase. Actions may include the development of joint security structures, the signing of defence agreements and military assistance to protect endangered neighbours. One of the first visible results of defence co-operation will be the increase in regional training courses for land, air and maritime forces, especially at military institutions in countries such as Kenya, South Africa and Zimbabwe.

Regional structures that promote defence co-operation, such as the Economic Community of West African States (ECOWAS) and the Southern African Inter-State Defence and Security Committee (ISDSC) will expand in due time. Likewise, the Organisation for African Unity (OAU) will respond faster and more effectively to sub-Saharan conflicts, through bodies such as the OAU Mechanism for Conflict Prevention, Management and Resolution.

These conflicts may often be related to support for democratically elected governments against armed rebellions or planned military *coups*. At the end of the twentieth century examples included the role of Zimbabwe, Namibia and Angola in the Democratic Republic of the Congo (DRC) and that of South Africa and Botswana in Lesotho.

The United Nations Secretary-General underscores the financial dimension of defence co-operation. Africa's compelling developmental interests require that a minimum of resources be diverted for military purposes. African states can help to diminish the need for large military expenditures by implementing transparency and confidence-building measures in the military and security fields. According to the United Nations such measures could include the harmonisation of policies against illicit arms trafficking; the signing of non-aggression pacts and security co-operation agreements; and participation in joint military training exercises and patrols.[41] In a rich continent full of poor countries, unity and co-operation appear to be the only means of resolving regional conflict short of armed force.[42]

At the beginning of the next century, regional powers will necessarily play a more prominent role than other countries. This may happen within or without regional structures. These powers may include Nigeria, Ethiopia, Kenya, South Africa and Zimbabwe.

Sub-Saharan armed forces will continue to participate in peace support operations in other parts of the world, but also in United Nations peace support operations in sub-Saharan countries. In the twenty-first century these forces will probably gradually acquire the ability to conduct effectively such operations without non-African assistance.

The trends of increased civilian control of the military and growing interstate co-operation for well-being and common security are also implied by endeavours emanating from the faith in an African renaissance referred to earlier.[43]

5 CAPABILITIES

The nature of probable internal and external operations is directly related to, and depends on, the underlying capabilities of armed forces. Less than two years before the dawn of the twenty-first century, the armed forces in sub-Saharan Africa are almost as diverse as its geography and languages. Despite these differences, a general evaluation of ability is possible. Unfortunately for sub-Saharan forces, such a judgement is not very positive. As a result of slow growth or outright decline of forces during the 1980s and 1990s, with some exceptions here and there, sub-Saharan states are hardly capable of defending themselves either individually or regionally. Furthermore, owing to the internal divisions in many countries and the role of dissident forces, sub-Sahara will enter the twenty-first century with more armies than states!

The first five years of the twenty-first century will not see a change in the fundamental processes of military proficiency, namely: financing defence; recruiting adequate human resources; utilising competent human resources; providing armament and logistics, and ensuring operational mobility.

Forces will continue to expand. The incremental growth in the quantitative size of armies, determined by factors such as the demographic composition of the different societies and their threat perceptions, seems to be a long-term trend that will continue. At the beginning of the new century, the numerically strongest forces will be those of (alphabetically) Congo Kinshasa, Ethiopia, Kenya, Nigeria, South Africa, Sudan, Tanzania and Zimbabwe.[44]

The generally low-level intellectual, scientific and technological development in most societies may change only gradually and will continue to make it difficult to recruit quality human resources, especially specialists, for military organisations. However, the more prominent sub-Saharan powers will promote military professionalism through more goal-directed training at their military colleges and military academies, and through training at foreign military institutions.

The economic deficits referred to as main constraints (at the beginning of this chapter) will inevitably impact negatively on arming and supplying sub-Saharan forces. Although light military industries will be developed in some countries such as Nigeria and Zimbabwe, sub-Saharan states, with the exception of South Africa, will have to import practically all military systems. The implication is that, by the turn of the century, most sub-Saharan states will still lack modern equipment and weapons systems.[45]

Despite these restrictions, most states will acquire the important ability to airlift sub-units over short distances. But only a few will be able to airlift battalion-size units, and very few will have sealifting capabilities. The availability of sophisticated weapons and training will accelerate the progression from the hit-and-run tactics of irregular operations to the fire-and-movement tactics of mobile operations. However, at the beginning of the twenty-first century only a few sub-Saharan countries will be capable of conducting mobile combat operations in which armoured vehicles, self-propelled artillery and combat aircraft are deployed.

The high technological and electronic requirements for air and maritime defence have a particularly negative influence on sub-Saharan air forces and navies. From a policy viewpoint, a mix of helicopters; fixed-wing aircraft for reconnaissance, search and rescue, and counterinsurgency, and light fighters would be the most appropriate for most sub-Saharan countries. In reality, many sub-Saharan air forces have lapsed into disrepair, with more derelict than operational systems. The growth of air forces will probably not be steady and well planned but fragmented and erratic.

The same trend is visible in maritime defence. Sub-Saharan states are vulnerable to the foreign exploitation of marine and mineral resources such as fish, oil and gas, and to the threats of pollution and the dumping of toxic waste. In addition to the availability of fish resources, the potential for exploitation is underlined by the huge assets of gas around Africa, and by oil resources at the coast of West Africa that are comparable to those of Latin-America and bigger than those of the United States.[46] The main maritime threats to sub-Sahara, emanating from virtually uncontrolled shipping, also include electronic surveillance, the smuggling of arms and narcotics, the landing of dissidents, and terrorism at sea.

Despite these threats, most navies face such serious problems of ageing that they may degenerate into offshore coast guards. At the end of the twentieth century their operational state, with the possible exception of Kenya, Nigeria and South Africa, is in serious decline and will probably continue to decline in the short- to medium-term.

However, many of these problems can be transformed into opportunities. This will happen if, in the functional dimension, sub-Saharan states concentrate on a series of policing tasks for ensuring safety in their territorial waters and for keeping the sea lines of communication open; and, in the material dimension, if they focus on procuring robust craft and squadrons of dedicated maritime patrol aircraft for quick reconnaissance missions and patrols. Activities and structures for closer regional co-operation will improve maritime expansion substantially.

6 CONCLUSION

To a large degree the future of sub-Saharan armed forces at the beginning of the twenty-first century will be determined by the tension between severe geographic, economic and conflict-related constraints on the one hand, and enticing opportunities, motivated by a new spirit of self-reliance and a concern for achievement, on the other hand.

Internal military operations may still be associated with intervention in the political process, but will also focus on countering insurgencies and serving national societies in a variety of ways. Increasing military professionalism and growing civil societies may enhance the civilian control of armed forces.

Ironically, both interstate armed conflict and interstate defence co-operation will probably increase simultaneously. Although insurgencies will remain the most common form of warfare, combined peace support operations will become more popular and regional structures for defence co-operation will expand.

From the point of view of self-defence, the prognosis is not too optimistic. At the beginning of the twenty-first century, many sub-Saharan states will be hardly capable of defending themselves. Although most armed forces will expand slowly, main challenges will be to recruit quality human resources and to arm and supply them. Especially air and maritime capabilities will be negatively influenced by financial and technological restrictions. However, a few states will be able to conduct mobile combat operations.

In an attempt to ensure adequate self-defence in the twenty-first century, a growing number of sub-Saharan leaders will share the principle formulated by the United Nations Secretary-General: "All states have the right and responsibility to provide for their own defence".[47] They will be convinced of the validity of the (previously quoted) viewpoint of the South African Minister of Defence: "In an unpredictable world African states must be able to protect the people, resources and the sovereignty of the countries on the continent. This security has to be ensured by the capacity of Africa's own defence forces, which need to be developed and strengthened".[48]

REFERENCES

1. McGeary, J, and Michaels, M, "Africa Rising", *Time*, 30 March 1998, p 39-40.

2. Chazan, N; Mortimer, R; Ravenhill, J; and Rotchchild, D, "The diversity of African politics: Trends and approaches", in *Politics and Society in Contemporary Africa*, Lynne Rienner Publishers, Boulder, Colorado, 1992, pp 23-24.

3. Chazan, N, *et al, op cit*, pp 24-25.

4. United Nations Secretary-General, *The Causes of Conflict and the Promotion of Durable Peace and Sustainable Development in Africa*, Report of the Secretary-General, New York, 23 April 1998, p 3-4.

5. Chazan, N, *et al, op cit*, pp 25-26.

6. Ngari, I, "African military perspectives", *African Armed Forces*, December/January 1995, p 13.

7. Maipose, G S, "State capacity and development in Africa", *Politeia*, Vol 16-3, 1997, p 11.

8. *Ibid*, p 11.

9. Chazan, N, *et al, op cit*, p 13.

10. *Ibid*, p 25.

11. See MacDonald, B S, *Military spending in developing countries: How much is too much?*, Carleton University Press, Canada, 1997.

12. See Roux, A, "Defence expenditure and development in South Africa", *Development in Southern Africa*, Vol 14-4, December 1997, for an analysis of the military as moderniser (pp 532-535) and the military as an absorber of scarce resources (pp 535-537).

13. Thom, W G, "Sub-Saharan Africa's Changing Military Capabilities", in Arlinghaus, B E and Baker, P H, *African Armies: Evolution and Capabilities*, London, Westview Press, 1986, p 104; and Williams, G, "Africa in retrospect and prospect", *Africa South of the Sahara 1997*, Europa Publications, London, 1997, p 3.

14. Cornwall, R, "Democratisation and security in Africa", *African Security Review*, Vol 6(5), 1997, p 17.

15. Chazan, N, *et al, op cit*, p 7.

16. *Ibid*, p 12.

17. United Nations Secretary-General, *op cit*, p 3.

18. Chazan, N, *et al, op cit*, p 31.

19. Cornwall, R, *op cit*, p 16.

20. International Institute for Strategic Studies, *Strategic Survey 1996/97*, Oxford University Press, London, 1997, p 223.

21. Modise, J, "The SA Navy and an African renaissance", *ISS Papers*, 27, November 1997, p 1.

22. McGeary, J, and Michaels, M, *op cit*, p 40.

23. Williams, M, and Robertson, H, "Thabo Mbeki: Destiny's man at the dawn of a new Africa", *Sunday Independent* (Johannesburg), 13 July 1997.

24. *Ibid*, p 4.

25. Brooks, J P J, "A military model for conflict resolution in sub-Saharan Africa", *Journal of the US Army War College*, Vol 27-4, Winter 1997-98, pp 108-120.

26. Chazan, N, *et al, op cit*, p 12.

27. Connell, D, and Smyth, F, "Africa's new bloc", *Foreign Affairs*, Vol 77-2, March-April 1998, pp 80-94.

28. McGeary, J, and Michaels, M, *op cit*, p 39.

29. *Ibid*, p 40.

30. United Nations Secretary-General, *op cit*, p 2.

31. Modise, J, *op cit*, p 1.

32. United Nations Secretary-General, *op cit*, p 9.

33. Modise, J, *op cit*, p 1. Modise originally made this statement at a security conference on 23 October 1997.

34. Chazan, N, *et al, op cit*, p 12-13.

35. Compare the distinctions made by Welch, C E jr (ed), *Civilian Control of the Military: Theory and Cases from Developing Countries*, State University of New York Press, Albany, 1976, pp 319-322.

36. Cornwall, R, *op cit*, pp 16-17.

37. Roux, A, *op cit*, p 533.

38. Thom, W G, *op cit*, p 106. Thom's prospects and arguments are valid for the mid 1990s and will probably still be valid in the beginning of the twenty-first century.

39. Barrows, W L, "Changing military capabilities in Black Africa", in Foltz, W J, and Bienen, H S (eds), *Arms and the African - Military Influences on Africa's International Relations*, Yale University Press, New Haven, 1985, p 118.

40. Thom, *op cit*, pp 109-110.

41. United Nations Secretary-General, *op cit*, p 9.

42. Arlinghaus, B E, "African Armies - An Analytical Approach", in: Arlinghaus, B E and Baker, P H, *op cit*, p 7.

43. Modise, J, *op cit*, p 2.

44. Compare International Institute for Strategic Studies, *The Military Balance 1997/98*, Oxford University Press, London, 1997: Sub-Saharan Africa, pp 230-263.
45. "Defence", *Africa Research Bulletin*, Vol 35-2, 20 March 1998, pp 13021-13022. Also compare the arguments of Barrows, W L, *op cit*.
46. Van der Kooy, R, "Afrika begin koers kry", *Finansies en Tegniek*, 27 June 1997, pp 9-10.
47. United Nations Secretary-General, *op cit*, p 9.
48. Modise, J, *op cit*, p 1.